# Jesus *Being* Jesus

# Jesus *Being* Jesus

## A Theological Interpretation of the Acts of the Apostles

VOLUME 1 · CHAPTERS 1–14

Thomas G. Weinandy, OFM, Cap.

The Catholic University of America Press
Washington, D.C.

The paper used in this publication meets the minimum requirements of
American National Standards for Information Science—Permanence of Paper
for Printed Library Materials, ANSI Z39.48-1992

∞

Cataloging-in-Publication Data is available from the Library of Congress

ISBN: 978-0-8132-4021-3
eISBN: 978-0-8132-4022-0

*Dedicated to*
*the Apostles*
*Peter and John*
*Stephen and Philip*
*Barnabas and Paul*

## CONTENTS

# PREFACE

This first volume (a second volume will ensue) of *Jesus Being Jesus: A Theological Interpretation of the Acts of the Apostles: Chapters 1–14* has a unique personal academic history. Ten years ago, back in November of 2014, while I was in Jerusalem on a sabbatical, I began to write what I thought would be a one-volume systematic theology. After about six weeks of writing, I found myself immersed in Scripture, though I had thought I would swiftly proceed to the patristic, medieval, and contemporary treatments of various Christian doctrines. Although I was enthused by what I was finding in my examination of the Gospels, I became somewhat confused as to how to continue, so I prayed, asking for guidance. I thought the Lord said to me—"Just stay with the Scriptures." After almost seven years, in attempting to be faithful to the task that I thought the Lord had given me, I completed a three-volume work on the Gospels—*Jesus Becoming Jesus*. In 2018, the first volume, a theological interpretation of the Synoptic Gospels, was published. In 2021, a second volume followed on the theological interpretation of the Gospel of John, the prologue and the Book of Signs. In 2022, the second volume (the third of the set) on the theological interpretation of the Book of Glory and the passion and resurrection narratives within John's Gospel was published. Having completed three volumes of *Jesus Becoming Jesus*, the thought came to me that I should now do a theological interpretation of the Acts of the Apostles where we find the risen and glorious Jesus *being* Jesus.

In the remainder of this preface, I will repeat some of what I have written in introducing the previous three volumes on the Gospels, that is, I will provide some of the theological and scriptural presuppositions that have governed my theological interpretations of the Acts of the Apostles.

## Scripture and Theology

I have not attempted to write a "normal" scriptural commentary. I have written a theological interpretation. As a systematic or doctrinal theologian, I intended to discern the theological and doctrinal content of Acts. This means that I do not treat many of the issues that Scripture scholars normally address when writing their scriptural commentaries, such as, textual and form criticism, nor do I employ what is known as the historical-critical method. Such would be outside my competence and, more importantly, these methods of scriptural interpretation would not advance what I am attempting to achieve theologically. I believe that the strength of my theological interpretation lies in the fact that I am doing it as a systematic theologian, searching out the doctrinal content as found in Luke's historical narrative of the nascent church. This does not make this present book any less scriptural. My aim is to help the reader find in the Acts of the Apostles what is fruitful to know, and so to cherish more deeply the doctrinal truth that Acts contains.

As with my previous volumes on the Gospels, I am again attempting to apply the teaching of the Second Vatican Council as found in its *Dogmatic Constitution on Divine Revelation* (*Dei Verbum*). There, the council rightly perceives a close unity between the written word that is the New Testament and the oral kerygmatic preaching that gave rise to it, as well as the living magisterial and theological tradition that flows from it (see *DV* 9 and 11). Scripture, then, must be read within the ever-living apostolic tradition and it must also continually be interpreted within the light of later magisterial conciliar teaching—the doctrine that flowed from it. Moreover, the living apostolic and magisterial tradition continues to be nurtured on the life-giving source of Scripture itself. Together, Scripture and tradition ever more clearly proclaim, protect, and enhance the church's understanding of what the Father has revealed through his Word/Son in communion with the Holy Spirit. Per *Dei Verbum*, "sacred Tradition and sacred Scripture make up a single sacred deposit of the Word of God, which is entrusted to the Church" (*DV* 10). Because Scripture and the church's magisterial and theological tradition flourish together, I have attempted, throughout my theological interpretation of the Acts of the Apostles, to follow *Dei Verbum*'s significant interpretive principle:

> Sacred theology relies on the written Word of God, taken together with sacred Tradition, as on a permanent foundation. By this Word it is most firmly strengthened and constantly rejuvenated, as it searches out, under the light of the faith, the full truth stored up in the mystery of Christ. Therefore, the "study of the sacred page" should be the very soul of sacred theology. (*DV* 24)

I have presently, then, endeavored to allow the Acts of the Apostles to be the soul of my theological interpretation, while simultaneously employing the church's sacred theological tradition to enhance my examination of it. Thus, my goal is to provide an interpretation of the Acts of the Apostles that would be genuinely faithful to it, as well as an interpretation that would authentically enrich and accurately illuminate its theological content.

As noted in my previous volumes on the Gospels, I have not read or consulted any biblical commentaries on the Acts of the Apostles. I avoided such commentaries because I did not want to engage in arbitrating various scholarly debates. Thus, in this volume, there are no footnotes to any secondary literature other than to some of my own previous work that may be relevant to the topic at hand. I simply desired to offer, in an unencumbered manner, my theological reading of the Acts of the Apostles. There are three components that make up my present study: (1) the text of the Bible itself as canonically given, (2) my own theological and academic background, and, hopefully, (3) the light of the Spirit of truth.

## Jesus Being Jesus: His Saving Acts

As I stated in previous prefaces to *Jesus Becoming Jesus*, since my student seminary days when studying Thomistic philosophy, I have been fascinated by the notion of "act." God is pure act, being itself, and in the act of creation, creatures come to be in act, and so further become who they are through their subsequent actions. Later, I came to realize that the persons of the Trinity are persons-fully-in-act. The Father is the act of fatherhood-fully-in-act; the Son is the act of sonship-fully-in-act; and the Holy Spirit is the act of love-fully-in-act. This threefold perichoretic act is the one God-fully-in-act.

In writing my theological interpretation of the Synoptic Gospels, I came to see that, although the angel Gabriel told Mary (Luke's Gospel), and later Joseph (Matthew's Gospel), to name their child, Jesus, that is, YHWH-Saves, Jesus was only Jesus in embryo. While the Son of God had assumed his saving ministry in becoming man, he had yet to complete his saving work. He was "Jesus" in potency and not yet Jesus-fully-in-act. Thus, in my interpretation of the Synoptics, I primarily focused on Jesus's saving actions as they are narrated within Matthew, Mark, and Luke, for it was through these actions that Jesus was enacting his name and so becoming who he is—the divine Savior. Jesus becoming Jesus became, then, the overarching theological theme throughout the whole of the volume on the Synoptic Gospels.

In writing the volumes on John's Gospel, I also perceived Jesus becoming Jesus. The act of becoming man is the primordial act by which Jesus becomes Jesus—that God's Word commences, in coming to exist as man, his work of salvation. Thus, for John, as the Father brought all into existence through the creating action of his Word, so now, through that same Word, the Father is re-creating the sin-fallen world. He is doing so through the saving acts, the re-creating acts, of his now incarnate Word, Jesus, YHWH-Saves. Moreover, as testified by John the Baptist, Jesus will perform his saving acts as the sacrificial Lamb of God, and so become Jesus, through the power, the divine vitality, of the Holy Spirit, the Spirit that ever remains upon him. Jesus is and will become the Savior, for he is the Father's Messianic Son, the Lord's anointed. All the intertwining themes within John's Gospel are the interweaving of Jesus's salvific acts, acts in and through which he enacts his saving-name, and so becomes Jesus.

If in the Gospel narratives we come to know the acts in and through which Jesus becomes Jesus, ultimately through his salvific acts of his death and resurrection, so in the Acts of the Apostles we observe how Jesus, having become Jesus, now acts as Jesus. In Acts, we find Jesus *being* Jesus. As we will see, having ascended into heaven as the risen Lord and Savior, Jesus's inaugural act is found in the pouring out of his Holy Spirit on Pentecost. In this act, Jesus enacts the consummate act of being Jesus, for this Pentecostal act of sending forth the Holy Spirit is the supreme fruit of Jesus's saving work—of Jesus becoming Jesus. In bestowing his Spirit, Jesus is being Jesus, for he, in that act, gives birth to the apostolic church, an ecclesial assembly that would ever act in communion with the Spirit. Moreover, within every Spirit-filled act of the church, the risen Jesus is acting as Savior and Lord, for all that the church enacts is enacted in, with, and through Jesus. Thus, by means of the church, Jesus is ever being Jesus—YHWH-Saves.

## ACKNOWLEDGMENTS

As with the previous volumes, many friends have generously helped in writing this volume. First, I am indebted to my provincial, Fr. Robert Marva, for allowing me and encouraging me to pursue my academic writing. I am also grateful to my Capuchin brothers here at Capuchin College. They have also been encouraging and have ever shown interest in the book's progress, even when I repeatedly had to say that I still have a long way to go.

Then, there are many of my academic colleagues and friends who read draft chapters. They offered insightful scriptural and theological suggestions, as well as assisting me in clarifying and developing my theological interpretations. In this regard, there is Fr. William Ryan, who ministers in the African country of Togo. Bill did yeoman's work in correcting and improving, by way of revision, the grammatical structure of many of my overly complex sentences. Two other priests also have been most encouraging. Fr. James Thermos, of the Archdiocese of Denver, was a formator of seminarians for many years and is presently a pastor of a parish. His spiritual insights into the Acts of the Apostles were always most welcome. The other is Msgr. James Overton, of the Archdiocese of Westminster, London. James, a friend of many years, always had something heartening to say upon reading my draft chapters. Moreover, I must not forget my close friend, Mrs. Kathleen Jones, who not only prayed for the success of my undertaking, but also read all the draft chapters. I asked her to do so for two reasons—to find all the typos, of which she found many, and to ensure that non-academic lay readers could understand what I was attempting to communicate. I am also grateful for the encouragement, support, and prayers of other family and friends—particularly my brother, Robert, my cousins, John Pohlman and Louise Pohlman, Mrs. Doris Ferlman, Mrs. Elizabeth Connor, and the Poor Clare Nuns in Alexandria, Virginia. For me, it was a joy to have them along on this academic journey. As I have stuck with the task, so they have persevered with me.

The Catholic University of America Press has published not only three volumes of *Jesus Becoming Jesus,* but also has now published the first volume of *Jesus Being Jesus: A Theological Interpretation of the Acts of the Apostles.* I have always been grateful that its acquisitions editor, Mr. John Martino, eagerly urged me to pursue writing these volumes. I am also indebted to Louise Mitchell for her patient and meticulous work as copy editor. Furthermore, I gratefully acknowledge, again, Mr. Matthew Alderman as the artist who illustrated the front covers of all three volumes of *Jesus Becoming Jesus* and for the present volume of *Jesus Being Jesus.*

Lastly, I would be amiss not to acknowledge all the saints whose intercession I daily sought. Here I will only salute by name, St. Luke, who wrote the Acts of the Apostles and St. Thomas Aquinas, my patron saint. Also, there are Mary and Joseph, who, at God's command, named their son "Jesus," YHWH-Saves, not fully comprehending, when they did so, what it would entail for him to become Jesus, and what he would do in being Jesus.

*Thomas G. Weinandy, OFM, Cap.*
*The Feast of the Presentation of the Lord, 2024*

# Jesus *Being* Jesus

# INTRODUCTION

Before beginning a theological interpretation of the Acts of the Apostles, it would be helpful to provide the necessary contextual background.

## Luke and the Acts of the Apostles

Luke was a Gentile and physician. One several occasions, Luke provides some detail of sick persons' ailments prior to their being healed.[1] He was observant, an important quality for a historian.[2]

Though not one of Jesus's initial Jewish disciples, Luke was a traveling companion of Paul. Paul laments that most of his comrades had abandoned him. "Luke alone is with me" (2 Tm 4:11).[3] Paul conveys to Philemon the greetings of those who are with him, one of whom is Luke (see Philemon 24). Significantly, beginning with Acts 16:10, the narrative speaks in terms of "we," that is, Paul and Luke.[4] The "we" gives more veracity to Luke's historical account, though he may place such a historical narrative within a theological context. As with the Old Testament and the Gospels, Luke provides the theological and

1. See Acts 9:18, 28:6 and 8; and Lk 4:38 and 8:43-44.

2. There is an ancient tradition, first documented in the sixth century, though the tradition must have been earlier, that Luke painted icons of Mary while she was still alive. See Anastasia Parkhomchik's 2021 article, "St. Luke the Apostle as an Icon Painter: Did He Really Paint Icons?" January 21, 2021, *The Catalogue of Good Deeds*, https://catalog.obitel-minsk.com/blog/2021/01/st-luke-the-apostle-as-an-icon-painter-did-he-really-paint-icons.

At the onset of his Gospel, Luke informs the reader that he historically researched the initial gospel proclamation, "having followed all things closely," in preparation for writing his own account (Lk 1:1-4). The question arises as to the manner in which Luke obtained his information concerning the conception and birth of John the Baptist and Jesus. I would argue that two of Luke's sources are Mary and John the Evangelist. I believe that Luke traveled to Ephesus to "interview" them. Thus, if Luke did paint an icon of Mary, it would been while he was in Ephesus.

3. Unless otherwise noted, all biblical quotations in this book are taken from *The Holy Bible*, Revised Standard Version, Catholic Edition (1957; San Francisco: Ignatius Press, 1966).

4. See also Acts 16:10-17, 20:5-15, 21:1-18, 27:1-28:16.

ecclesial significance of the historical events he is narrating. In so doing, he accentuates what the risen and ascended Jesus is doing through the Holy Spirit by means of the nascent church, primarily through Peter and Paul. Although the book is titled the Acts of the Apostles, the Holy Spirit is the primary actor throughout its entirety. The acts of Peter and Paul are inspired by and empowered by the Holy Spirit.[5] Moreover, through the Spirit-imbued preaching of the Gospel, the church grew in great numbers and at an amazing rate.[6]

Luke also recounts the type of life that the early Christians lived as a community of believers—their moral and liturgical life (see Acts 2:43–47). This exemplary ecclesial lifestyle often was lived, as was Jesus's own life, in the midst of suffering and persecution, and thus was a model of encouragement and fortitude to future Christian generations.[7]

As implied in the above, Luke is traditionally believed to be the author of both the third Gospel as well as the Acts of the Apostles. Irenaeus (AD 180), Clement of Rome (AD 200), and Eusebius (AD 325) designated Luke as the author of this twofold work. The opening verses of Acts state, "In the first book, O Theophilus, I dealt with all that Jesus began to do and teach, until the day he was taken up, after he had given commandment through the Holy Spirit to apostles whom he had chosen." As Luke, in his Gospel, first wrote "an orderly account for you, most excellent Theophilus, concerning the truth of the gospel," so he now writes what has taken place after Jesus's departure. Thus, the Acts of the Apostles is a continuation of a historical narrative. The Gospel contains what Jesus historically said and did until his Ascension into Heaven. Acts is the historical narrative of what followed upon Jesus's ascension and the pouring out of the Holy Spirit at Pentecost that gave birth to the Church, and the first preaching of the Good News.

## Jesus Being Jesus

If in Luke's gospel account one finds Jesus *becoming* Jesus through his saving actions which culminate in his death and resurrection, in the Acts of the Apostles, one finds the risen Jesus *being* Jesus through the preaching and actions of the apostolic church. Jesus continues to enact his name, YHWH-Saves. Such saving words and actions are particularly within the evangelistic ministry of Peter and Paul. The chart below illustrates the parallels between Luke's Gospel and the Acts of the Apostles.

5. See Acts 4:3, 10:44–48, 13:2, 15:8 and 28, 16:6–10, and 20:22–23.
6. See, for example, Acts 2:41, 4:4, and 6:7.
7. See, for example, Acts 5:17–42, 7:54–60, and 12:1–19.

| *The Apostles in Acts* | *Jesus in Luke's Gospel* |
|---|---|
| The Holy Spirit descends on the apostles at Pentecost (2:1-4) | The Holy Spirit descends on Jesus at his baptism (3:21-22) |
| Peter preaches, quoting from the prophet Joel (2:16-36; quoting Jl 2:28-32) | Jesus preaches, after reading from the prophet Isaiah (4:14-30; quoting Is 61:1-2) |
| The apostles call people to join them (2:37-41, 47b) | Jesus calls his first followers (5:1-11, 27-32) |
| Peter and John heal a lame beggar (3:1-10) | Jesus heals a blind beggar (18:35-43) |
| The high priest arrests several apostles and questions them before the council (4:1-22) | Jesus is arrested and interrogated by the council (22:47-71) |
| The narrator summarizes the "signs and wonders" of the apostles, especially their healings and exorcisms (5:12-16; 8:6-7, 13) | The narrator summarizes the miraculous activity of Jesus, esp. his healings and exorcisms (4:40-41; 6:17-19) |
| The sick are healed through Peter's shadow (5:15) and Paul's handkerchiefs (19:11-12) | A woman is healed when she touches the fringes of Jesus's clothing (8:43-48) |
| The Jewish leaders want to kill the apostles because of their teachings (5:17-42) | Jewish leaders plot to kill Jesus, partly due to his teachings (19:45-48) |
| Peter raises Tabitha (aka Dorcas) from the dead at Joppa (9:36-42) | Jesus raises a widow's son from the dead at Nain (7:11-17) |
| The apostles encounter a pious Roman centurion (10:1-48) | Jesus heals the slave of a faithful Roman centurion (7:1-10) |
| Paul feels compelled by the Spirit to go to Jerusalem despite the dangers that await him there (19:21; 21:8-17) | Jesus is determined to go to Jerusalem, despite the dangers that await him there (9:51; 13:33; 19:11-28) |
| Paul is welcomed in Jerusalem by the believers and soon goes to the temple (21:17-26) | Jesus is welcomed in Jerusalem by large crowds and soon goes to the temple (19:28-48) |
| Paul is seized by a Jewish mob that wants him killed, but later stands trial before Roman governors (21:30-36; 23:23-26:32) | Jesus is arrested by a Jewish mob, but is later turned over to the Roman procurator for trial (22:47-54; 23:1-25) |
| Paul argues against the Sadducees, who do not believe in the resurrection (23:6-9) | Jesus is questioned by some Sadducees, who deny the concept of resurrection (20:29-38) |
| Paul takes bread, gives thanks, breaks it, and eats (27:35; cf. 20:7-11) | Jesus takes bread, blesses it, breaks it, and gives it to his disciples to eat (22:19; cf. 24:30) |
| As he is being stoned to death, Stephen hands his spirit over to the Lord Jesus and forgives his executioners (7:59-60) | As he is dying on the cross, Jesus forgives his executioners and hands his spirit over to God (23:34, 46) |

TABLE 1. (*Table courtesy of Fr. Felix Just, SJ. See https://catholic-resources.org/Bible/Acts.htm.*)

## The Date of Composition

The Acts of the Apostles was written either in the 60s or 80s. The early 60s would be the likelier date, sometime after Paul's arrival in Rome as contained in the final chapter of Acts. Moreover, Luke does not mention Emperor Nero's persecution of the Christians in AD 64. This would have been the year of both Peter's and Paul's martyrdom, both of whom figure prominently in Acts. Thus, Luke, most likely, composed Acts around AD 63 just prior to Paul's death.

## The Parallel Ministries of Peter and Paul

There are various ways of structuring the Acts of the Apostles. One way of dividing Acts is in relationship to Peter and Paul. Chapters 1-12 focus on Peter and his ministry in Jerusalem and the founding of the early church. Chapters 13-28 center on Paul and his missionary activity. Another manner of reading Acts is geographically. Jesus commands that his disciples be his witnesses "in Jerusalem and in Judea and Samaria and to the end of the earth" (Acts 1:8). This being the case, chapters 1 to 7 narrate the Jerusalem ministry, then the preaching of the gospel in Judea and Samaria (chapters 8-12), followed by Paul's missionary journeys throughout the whole of the Roman empire, concluding at Rome, the capital of the empire (chapters 13-28). What is notable is that Luke traces the ministry of Peter and Paul, and in so doing does not narrate the early missionary activity of the other apostles and first Christian converts in Africa or the Far East, such as the traditional legend that Thomas went to India. Nonetheless, Luke does provide a historical narrative of an arc that begins at Jerusalem, curves around the Mediterranean Sea, and reaches its end point at Rome. Thus, Luke authenticates that Jerusalem is the mother city where the good news was born and from which it proceeds, and confirms that Rome is the premier ecclesial seat wherein Holy Mother Church, under the apostleship of Peter, as the prince of the apostles, and Paul, as the exemplar evangelist, now resides. What conjoins Jerusalem and Rome, and binds together the ends of the earth, is Peter's and Paul's one, holy, catholic, and apostolic faith.

Within Luke's historical narrative of the growth of the apostolic church through the working of the Holy Spirit, some scholars also perceive a "subnarrative." No one would doubt the apostolic nature of Peter's ministry, for he was clearly head of the apostles. On Pentecost, he was the first to preach the good news of Jesus's saving death and resurrection. However, what about Paul? He was not one of the original twelve apostles. He was an ardent persecutor of the church, and so a person to be feared. He burst upon the ecclesial scene unknown and unexpected. Who was this perplexing fellow, and where did he obtain the authority to claim that he too was an apostle, equal to Peter and all the other apostles? As seen in some of his epistles, Paul's ministry was often questioned, as if it were not authentically apostolic. In the light of his dubious apostolic credentials, Paul declares that he is not inferior to the "superlative apostles," for "the signs of a true apostle were performed in all patience, with signs and wonders and mighty works."[8] Founded upon the risen Jesus's appearance to him, Paul is fully confident of his status as an apostle, because he knows it is founded upon the risen Jesus's appearance to him, even as he goes on to say that "he is the least of the apostles, unfit to be called an apostle, because I persecuted the church. But by the grace of God I am what I am, and his grace toward me was not in vain. On the contrary, I worked harder than any of them, though it was not I, but the grace of God which is with me" (1 Cor 15:8-10).

In this light, the Acts of the Apostles can be interpreted as Luke's attempt, as Paul's companion, to validate Paul's apostolic ministry by affirming that Paul too was an authentic apostle. Significantly, Luke gives not just one but three accounts of Paul's conversion. In each account, Paul himself tells how the risen Lord Jesus revealed himself.[9] Jesus's glorious appearance to him substantiates that Paul is indeed an apostle. He received his apostolic authority not from some earthly man, nor even from another apostle, but from the very source of all apostolicity—the risen Savior and Lord Jesus Christ himself. Therefore, his subsequent ministry to the Gentiles is apostolic in nature, and its astounding success bears unimpeachable proof that such is the case.

Thus, Luke provides a series of parallels between Peter and Paul. They were both filled with the Holy Spirit (see Acts 4:8 and 13:9). They were both miraculously freed from prison (see Acts 12:6-11 and 16:25-34). They both preach their first sermons to "the men of Israel" (see Acts 2:22-36 and 13:26-41). They both quote Psalm 16 in relation to Jesus's resurrection—God will not let his "Holy One see corruption" (see Acts 2:25-28 and 13:35). They both heal paralytics, and work other miracles, including raising the dead.[10] Peter rebuked Simon for offering him money so as to obtain the power of the Holy Spirit (see Acts 8:14-24), and Paul did the same in Cyprus to Elymus the magician (see Acts 13:4-12). Lastly, both refused to be worshiped as if they were divine

8. 2 Cor 12:11-12; see also 11:4-6.

9. See Acts 9:1-19, 22:3-16, and 26:2-18.

10. See Acts 3:1-10, 5:15-16, 9:36-41, 14:8-10, 19:11-12, and 20:9-12.

(Acts 10:25-26 and 14:11-15). By demonstrating that Peter and Paul share equally in the power of the Holy Spirit, these parallels authenticate Paul's apostolic ministry as equal to that of Peter's. See the chart below which clearly shows the parallels between Peter and Paul.

With this biographical, historical, literary, and theological background, we can now proceed to our theological interpretation of the Acts of the Apostles.

| *Parallel Action* | *Peter* [*In Acts 2-12*] | *Paul* [*In Acts 13-28*] |
|---|---|---|
| They both function as witnesses to the risen Christ | 1:21-22 | 23:11; 26:16 |
| The Holy Spirit initiates and guides their actions | 2:1-40 | 13:1-40 |
| Both heal people who are lame or unable to speak | 3:12-26 | 13:1-40 |
| Both are defended by Pharisees in the Sanhedrin | 5:34-39 | 23:9 |
| Both appoint other leaders with prayer and laying on hands | 6:1-6 | 14:23 |
| Their persecution (stoning) leads to broadening the mission | [6:8-8:4, Stephen] | 14:19-23 |
| Both are accused of acting against Moses | [6:13-14, Stephen] | 21:20-21; 25:8 |
| Both encounter and confront a magician | 8:9-24 | 13:6-12 |
| Both bestow the Spirit through the laying on of hands | 8:14-17 | 19:1-6 |
| Both raise a dead person back to life | 9:36-43 | 20:9-12 |
| Some Gentiles try to worship them | 10:25-26 | 14:13-15 |
| In Jerusalem, they defend the mission to the Gentiles | 11:1-18 | 21:15-40 |
| Both are imprisoned at a Jewish feast | 12:4-7 | 21:16-28 |
| Both are delivered from prison | 12:6-11 | 16:24-26 |
| Conclusion: The word of God continues to spread | 12:24 | 28:30-31 |

TABLE 2. (*Table courtesy of Fr. Felix Just, SJ. See https://catholic-resources.org/Bible/Acts.htm.*)

*Chapter 1*

# THE ASCENSION OF JESUS

## Introduction to the Acts of the Apostles (Acts 1:1–5)

> In the first book, O Theophilus, I dealt with all that Jesus began to do and teach, until the day when he was taken up, after he had given commandment through the Holy Spirit to the apostles whom he had chosen. To them he presented himself alive after his passion by many proofs, appearing to them during forty days, and speaking to them of the kingdom of God. And while staying with them he charged them not to depart from Jerusalem, but to wait for the promise of the Father, which, he said, "you heard from me, for John baptized with water, but before many days you shall be baptized with the Holy Spirit."[1]

As we saw from our previous introductory remarks, in his first volume Luke informs Theophilus that, after careful examination of the eyewitness sources and ministers of the word, he narrated Jesus's salvific work up until the day of his ascension. This present second volume will now continue that historical narrative—what the ascended Jesus is now doing in founding the church through the outpouring of the Holy Spirit.

Luke's introduction to Acts must, therefore, be read and interpreted in the light of the conclusion of his Gospel, for he is meticulously intertwining the two books together. Luke concludes his Gospel with Jesus's last words to his apostles.

> "These are my last words which I spoke to you, while I was still with you, that everything written about me in the law of Moses and the prophets and psalms must be fulfilled." Then he opened their minds to understand the

1. Unless otherwise noted, all Scripture passages in this section are taken from Acts 1:1–5.

> Scriptures, and said to them, "Thus it is written, that the Christ should suffer and on the third day rise from the dead, and that repentance and forgiveness of sins should be preached to all nations, beginning in Jerusalem. You are my witnesses to these things. And behold, I send the promise of my Father upon you; but stay in the city, until you are clothed with power from on high." (Lk 24:44–49)

After opening the true prophetic meaning of the Scriptures, and commissioning them to preach the gospel beginning in Jerusalem, he commanded them to remain in the city until he sends the Holy Spirit upon them. In Acts the above is the "commandment," given "through the Holy Spirit," that Jesus gave to "the apostles whom he had chosen."

Following the recounting of Jesus's last risen appearance to his apostles, Luke concludes his Gospel with Jesus leading his apostles "as far as Bethany," where, "lifting up his hands he blessed them." Then, "he parted from them, and was carried up into heaven." The apostles "worshiped him and returned to Jerusalem with great joy, and were continually in the temple blessing God" (Lk 24:50–53). However, in Acts, Luke now informs the reader that Jesus "presented himself alive after his passion by many proofs, appearing to them during forty days, and speaking of the kingdom of God." We perceive here a discrepancy. In his Gospel, Luke has Jesus appearing to his apostles on the evening of his resurrection, followed immediately by his ascension. In Acts, Jesus's ascension takes place forty days after his resurrection.

Theologically Jesus's resurrection, ascension, and the outpouring of his Spirit are all one sequential event—the totality of the one paschal mystery. Being gloriously raised from the dead entails, by necessity, Jesus's ascension into heaven. Sitting at the Father's right hand as the glorious Lord, Jesus is empowered to send forth the Holy Spirit upon his apostles, thus giving birth to his church.[2] In Acts, the paschal mystery is enacted and so revealed over a forty-day period. While Luke could have fabricated this forty-day period for theological reasons—accentuating each aspect of the paschal mystery individually, I would argue the difference between Luke's Gospel account and his Acts historical narrative are both true and can be reconciled.

2. Similar to Luke, the Gospel of John tells of Jesus's first risen appearance to his disciples on the evening of Easter Sunday. In both instances, Jesus proclaims, "Peace to you" (Luke's account) or "Peace be with you" (John's account). In both accounts, Jesus then displayed his wounded hands, feet, side. Moreover, in John's Gospel, Jesus, as the risen Lord, proceeds to breath the Holy Spirit upon his disciples. John's Gospel, unlike Luke's, does not include an ascension account. The reason is that Jesus's glorious resurrection inherently entails his ascension. They are one and the same mode of existence—to be gloriously risen is to abide in heaven.

Yes, the entire paschal mystery of Jesus's resurrection, ascension, and sending forth of the Spirit are one consecutive act as found in Luke's Gospel. Yet, Jesus himself, as a good teacher, also separated them in a historical, chronological time-sequence in order to accentuate the distinct truth contained in each aspect of the one paschal mystery—first his resurrection and then his glorious ascension forty days later, both of which manifested why Jesus, as Lord, could subsequently send forth the Holy Spirit ten days later on Pentecost.

Now, is there any biblical or theological significance in Jesus appearing to his apostles over a forty-day period? Within Scripture, forty days is a revered number. Because of humankind's sinfulness, God commanded that it rain forty days and forty nights, thus cleansing the world of all sinfulness.[3] With Noah, his family, and the animals, God was attempting to make a "new creation." However, he failed in his attempt. Sin continued to abound upon the earth. Moses went up the mountain to receive the covenantal commandments, and "he was with the Lord forty days and forty nights; he neither ate bread nor drank water" (Ex 34:28). The Israelite spies reconnoitered the land of Canaan for forty days, finding it to be prosperous. However, because the people refused to enter it, God declared, "According to the number of the days in which you spied out the land, forty days, for every day a year, you shall bear your iniquity, forty years" (Nm 14:34). Thus, the Israelites wandered in the desert for forty years, so that God could test their humility and their faithfulness to him—the keeping of his commandments.[4] Because of Israel's sinfulness, "the Lord gave them over into the hand of the Philistines for forty years" (Jgs 13:1). Having eaten the cake and drunk from the jug, Elijah was able to walk "forty days and forty nights to Horeb the mount of God" (1 Kgs 19:8). Jonah declared that unless the Ninevites repented of their sin, God would destroy their city in forty days (Jon 3:4). After being baptized by John, "Jesus was led by the Spirit into the wilderness to be tempted by the devil. And he fasted for forty days and forty nights, and afterwards was hungry" (Mt 4:1–2). Within Scripture, then, forty days is seen as a sacred time of fasting, testing, obedience, faithfulness, and trust. Ultimately, it was a time of preparing, learning, and waiting upon the Lord. Thus, the forty days between Jesus's resurrection and ascension was, for the apostles, a period of patiently and humbly being taught by the risen Jesus in preparation for the descent of the Holy Spirit at Pentecost. Upon receiving the Holy Spirit, they would be freed from the slavery of sin and the curse of death. They would be equipped to undertake their

3. See Gn 7:4 and 7.

4. See Dt 8:2.

ecclesial and evangelistic mission, a commission that would bring hardship, suffering, and even death. Above all, by the transforming indwelling of the Spirit, they would abide in the risen Jesus, he who embodies the real Promised Land—the kingdom of God and the heavenly Jerusalem.

Acts mentions that Jesus appeared to his apostles many times as proof of his resurrection. This observation refers back to Luke's Gospel, chapter 24, verses 1-43. However, in the Gospel, all of the appearances took place on Easter Sunday. Since the many proof-appearances were over the course of forty days, it would seem that there were more appearances than those recounted in Luke's Gospel. Also, that the risen Jesus remained with his apostles for forty days implies that he gave them multiple teachings concerning the meaning of the kingdom of God, and, as in the Gospel, opened their minds to a full understanding of the Scriptures. The issue of God's kingdom, as we will shortly see, arises again just prior to Jesus's ascension as narrated in Acts.

Likewise, in both his Gospel and Acts, Luke speaks of Jesus commanding his apostles to remain in Jerusalem until the coming of the Holy Spirit. In the Gospel, Jesus tells them that he will "send the promise of my Father upon you; but stay in the city, until you are clothed with power from on high" (Lk 24:49). In Acts, "while staying with them he charged them not to depart Jerusalem, but wait for the promise of the Father, which he said, 'you heard from me, for John baptized with water, but before many days you shall be baptized with the Holy Spirit.'"[5] In both the Gospel and Acts, Jesus speaks of "the promise of the Father." The goal toward which the whole history of salvation pointed, from Moses and the prophets and the psalms, and which is now about to be fulfilled because of Jesus's saving death and resurrection, is the sending of the Father's promised Holy Spirit. This outpouring of the Holy Spirit will bring into being God's kingdom, for one will be baptized with the Holy Spirit, and thus be assumed into the kingdom of God, a kingdom that the risen Jesus himself embodies. To abide in the risen Jesus is to abide in God's Kingdom.

Nonetheless, when and where did Jesus say that John baptized in water with the implication that in a few days he himself would baptize with the Holy Spirit? In Luke's Gospel, John the Baptist declared, "I baptize with water;

5. The phrase, "while speaking with them," can also be translated "while eating with them." This later translation would be in keeping with Jesus's last resurrection appearance in Luke's Gospel. Because the apostles were startled in joyful and wonderous disbelief at his bodily resurrection, Jesus said to them, "Have you anything to eat?" In response, "they gave him a piece of broiled fish, and he took it and ate it before them" (Lk 24:41-42). Right before their very eyes, the bodily-risen Jesus consumed a piece of fish, thus manifesting his authentic resurrection as a complete human being.

but he who is mightier than I is coming ... he will baptize you with the Holy Spirit and with fire."[6] However, Luke's Gospel never gives an account of Jesus saying that he would do so. I noted previously that there are similarities between Luke's and John's accounts of Jesus's first risen appearance on Easter evening. Because of this similarity and others, I believe Luke went to Ephesus to consult John concerning the accuracy and reliability of the apostolic kerygma. In that light, the closest to what Jesus implies in Acts, that regarding his baptizing with the Holy Spirit, is found in John's Gospel. In keeping with Acts, that the Holy Spirit is the promise of the Father, Jesus tells his disciples that he "will ask the Father, and he will give you another Counselor, to be with you forever, even the Spirit of truth."[7] Subsequently, Jesus states that the Counselor will come, "whom I shall send to you from the Father, even the Spirit of truth, who proceeds from the Father, he will bear witness to me; and you also are witnesses, because you have been with me from the beginning."[8] Jesus further tells his disciples that it is to their advantage that he leaves, "for if I do not go away, the Counselor will not come to you; but if I go, I will send him to you" (Jn 16:7). With Jesus's ascension imminent, so too is his impending sending forth of the promise of the Father—the Holy Spirit. Only as the risen Savior and ascended Lord is Jesus empowered to baptize with the Father's Holy Spirit.

As remarked at the onset, what we perceive in Luke's introduction to the Acts of the Apostles is the sewing together of the conclusion of his Gospel with Acts. In so doing he is also weaving together the whole of salvation history—the interlacing of what was written in the law of Moses and the prophets and the psalms, and what was enacted by Jesus while he was still on earth, prior to his being taken up. This inherent conjoining allows Luke to proceed with his continuing narrative—the birth of the church at Pentecost and the subsequent Spirit-filled growth of the nascent apostolic community.

6. Lk 3:16. That John the Baptist speaks both of Jesus baptizing with the Holy Spirit and with fire prophetically anticipates Luke's account of Pentecost in Acts. "And there appeared to them tongues as of fire, distributed and resting on each one of them. And they were all filled with the Holy Spirit and began speaking in tongues, as the Spirit gave them utterance" (Acts 2:3–4).

7. Jn 14:16–17. See also Jn 14:26.

8. Jn 15:26–27. Interestingly, as we will see shortly, when Peter discerns that someone must take the place of Judas, the requirement for apostolic succession is the following: "So one of the men who have accompanied us during all the time that the Lord Jesus went in and out among us, beginning from the baptism of John until the day when he was taken up from us—one of these men must become with us a witness to the resurrection" (Acts 1:21–22). To be an apostolic witness, in accord with Jesus's words in John's Gospel, demands that one had to be Jesus's follower from the beginning of his ministry, as well as a witness to his resurrection.

Significantly, for Luke, salvation history is the authentic history of the world. History is not comprised of the rise and fall of earthly kings and empires, but of God's action within time and history, actions that preceded and anticipated the incarnation of the Father's Messianic Son, the Spirit-filled Jesus, and now continues in and through Jesus's Spirit-imbued church. All of human history leads to Jerusalem, and to the coming of the Messiah, and, after the saving work of the Father's messianic incarnate Son, all history flows from Jerusalem. Although the church has only just come to be, it will continue to be the saving, Spirit-empowered instrument through and in which the risen Jesus continues to act until the end of time. Then, when he returns in glory, salvation history will reach its divine, preordained goal and will find its completion: the establishing of the heavenly eschatological Jerusalem.

## The Ascension of Jesus (Acts 1:6–11)

> So when they had come together, they asked him, "Lord, will you at this time restore the kingdom of Israel?" He said to them, "It is not for you to know times or seasons which the Father has fixed by his own authority. But you shall receive power when the Holy Spirit has come upon you; and you shall be my witnesses in Jerusalem and in all of Judea and Samaria and to the end of the earth." And when he had said this, as they were looking on, he was lifted up, and a cloud took him out of their sight. And when they were gazing into heaven as he went, behold, two men stood by them in white robes, and said, "Men of Galilee, why do you stand looking into heaven? This Jesus, who was taken up from you into heaven, will come in the same way as you saw him go into heaven."[9]

Having conjoined the present book with his Gospel, and having spoken of the apostles' forty-day wait in Jerusalem, Luke now proceeds to initiate his historical narrative by recounting Jesus's ascension. His Acts account contains much more detail than that found in his Gospel accounts. Nonetheless, his Gospel rendering does provide particulars not found in Acts. Jesus himself "led them as far as Bethany," and it is from here that he gave the apostles his final "blessing," and "parted from them," having been "carried up into heaven" (Lk 24:50–51).

Acts simply states that "they," Jesus and his apostles, "had come together"—the location is not specified.[10] However, unlike in the Gospel, the apostles and

9. Unless otherwise noted, all Scripture passages in this section are taken from Acts 1:6–11.

10. However, after Jesus's ascension, Acts will inform the reader that the apostles "returned to Jerusalem from the mount called Olivet, which was near Jerusalem, a sabbath day's

Jesus engage in a brief conversation immediately prior to Jesus's ascending. The apostles ask, "Lord, will you at this time restore the kingdom of Israel?" For forty days Jesus spoke to them concerning "the kingdom of God" (Acts 1:3) We do know that the disciples on the road to Emmaus were hoping that Jesus "was the one to redeem Israel," but with his death that hope appeared to be shattered. In response Jesus explained to them that the Christ had to suffer and die so as to "enter into his glory." He also explained to them as well as to the apostles all that pertained to him in the law of Moses, the prophets and the psalms.[11] Moreover, the apostles knew that they were to remain in Jerusalem until they were "baptized in the Holy Spirit" (Acts 1:5). Thus, there is some relationship, yet to be fully revealed, between the coming of God's kingdom and the imminent outpouring of the Holy Spirit. Other than that, we do not know what else Jesus may have taught the apostles concerning God's kingdom and its coming.

Nonetheless, it would appear that the apostles were themselves still unsure about the nature of God's kingdom and confused about its coming. They give the impression that, with Jesus's departure, the kingdom of Israel would certainly now be restored. However, the apostles' question itself raises questions about their expectations and their mental disposition. Why did they raise the issue? Why does the kingdom of Israel need to be restored and in what form is this restoration expected to take? Here we must examine the history of Israel. What were the expectations pertaining to the coming of God's kingdom within ancient Israel and at the time of Jesus?

There were various expectations at the time of Jesus. Most Jews were hoping for and expecting a Messiah who would free them from the tyranny of Roman rule—a military and political savior. The men on the road to Emmaus probably were of this mind—though they thought their hopes were dashed by Jesus's death. Others, though not as numerous, would have hoped for an eschatological messiah—one who would usher in a new and glorious heavenly age—an age freed from not only earthly tyranny but also sin and evil. In either case, what would be restored would be the ancient divinely promised kingdom of David. This is seen in what is proclaimed upon Jesus's triumphal entry into Jerusalem. "Blessed is the King who comes in the name of the Lord! Peace in heaven and glory in the highest!"[12] Significantly, in Luke's infancy

journey away" (1:12). As noted earlier, Luke's Gospel states that Jesus led his apostles "as far as Bethany" where he ascended (Lk 24:50). Bethany is just over the crest of Mount Olivet.

11. Lk 24:21-25 and 44-46.

12. Lk 19:38. The designation of Jesus as "King" contains within it a Davidic meaning. The proclamations found in Matthew and Mark are more explicit. "Hosanna to the Son of David!

narrative, when the angel Gabriel appears to Mary, we are told that she was "betrothed to a man whose name was Joseph, of the house of David." Thus, Jesus's foster-father was of the royal lineage of King David. Not surprisingly, then, Gabriel proclaims to Mary that the son to be born of her "will be great, and will be called the Son of the Most High, and the Lord God will give to him the throne of his father David, and he will reign over the house of Jacob forever; and of his kingdom there will be no end" (Lk 1:26, 23–24). Thus, the son that Mary will conceive by the overshadowing of the Holy Spirit, the messianic incarnate Son of God, will fulfill the ancient divine promises. Moreover, when John the Baptist was born, his father, Zechariah, proclaimed that the Lord God should be blessed, "for he has visited his people, and has raised up a horn of salvation for us in the house of his servant David, as he spoke by the mouth of his holy prophets from of old, that he should save us from our enemies, and from the hand of all who hate us" (Lk 1:68–71). God has visited his people by raising up, as he promised, a descendant of David, a king who would free God's people from their enemies. Zechariah may have had in mind the Romans who presently ruled Israel, but ultimately Israel's enemies are the sin that enslaves them and sin's resultant curse of death. By being freed from these, they would be able "to serve him [God] without fear, in holiness and righteousness before him all the days of our life" (Lk 1:74–75).

The promises to which the angel Gabriel and Zechariah refer are those the Lord made to David: "When your days are fulfilled and you lie down with your fathers, I will raise up your offspring after you, who shall come forth from your body, and I will establish his kingdom. He shall build a house for my name, and I will establish the throne of his kingdom forever" (2 Sm 7:12–13). Psalm 132:11 professes, "The Lord swore to David a sure oath / from which he will not turn back: / 'One of the sons of your body / I will set on your throne.'"[13] Lastly, Isaiah prophesied that

> to us a child is born, to us a son is given; and the government will be upon his shoulder, and his name will be called "Wonder Counselor, Mighty God, Everlasting Father, Prince of Peace." Of the increase of his government and of peace there will be no end, upon the throne of David, and over his kingdom, to establish it and to uphold it with justice and with righteousness from this time forth and forevermore. (Is 9:6–7)

---

Blessed is he who comes in the name of the Lord! Hosanna in the highest!" (Mt 21:9). "Hosanna! Blessed is he who comes in the name of the Lord! Blessed is the kingdom of our father David that is coming! Hosanna in the highest" (Mk 11:9–10).

13. Psalm 89:25–29 contains a similar pledge to David.

Although the above conveys God's promises concerning one of David's future sons inheriting his everlasting kingdom, the history of Israel, following the death of King Solomon, is a travesty. Two warring kingdoms were established, the kingdom of Israel and the kingdom of Judah. David's kingdom was in tatters. Beginning with the demise of both kingdoms, the Jews were exiled to Babylonia and to Egypt, though God promised that he would bring them out of Assyria and Egypt and "return them to their homes," and that he would "restore the tribes of Jacob."[14] Nonetheless, various foreign powers and empires continued to govern the Jews, the Roman Empire being the most recent. Within this historical, biblical background, and within the contemporary expectations of which they shared, the apostles asked Jesus if this is the time, the "now," when he will restore, finally, the everlasting Davidic kingdom to Israel. Jesus does not address their question directly, for it is not the proper manner in which the issue should be considered. His response attends to the real issue by informing the apostles what they are to do subsequent to his ascension. Moreover, the attending angels at Jesus's ascension will reveal to them the manner in which God's kingdom will be fully restored. In this light, we can examine Jesus's response.

He said to his apostles, "It is not for you to know times or seasons which the Father has fixed by his own authority. But you shall receive power when the Holy Spirit has come upon you; and you shall be my witnesses in Jerusalem and in all Judea and Samaria and to the end of the earth" (Acts 1:7–8). First, Jesus reprimands the apostles' inappropriate curiosity. It is not for them to know when the kingdom of Israel will be restored. The times and the seasons that compose the world's history are known to the Father in his providence, specifically concerning the restoration of the kingdom, a kingdom that will not only embrace Israel, but also all the Gentile nations.[15]

14. Hos 11:11 and Sir 48:10.

15. In Mark's Gospel, Jesus tells his disciples that, while his words will never pass away, heaven and earth will pass away. "But of that day or that hour no one knows, not even the angels in heaven, nor the Son, but only the Father" (Mk 13:31–32). Since the Son is as divine as the Father is divine, the Son, as God, would know when this world will pass away. However, Jesus, as the Father's incarnate Son, would not know, as man, when the last day will arrive. I think this continues to be the case even though Jesus is now gloriously risen. Interestingly as man, the risen Jesus does not know when the end will come even though the last day will be the day when Jesus returns in glory and the whole of creation will be made new. The just will rise glorious from the dead and the unjust will be condemned. Then God's kingdom will be fully made manifest. This, as we will see shortly, is made evident at the conclusion of Jesus's ascension in Acts.

Echoing Jesus's words in Acts, Paul declares to the Thessalonians, "But as to the times and the seasons, brethren, you have no need to have anything written to you. For you yourselves

Second, what is of immediate importance is not when the kingdom of Israel will be restored, but what the apostles are to do in the here and now. Upon receiving power "when the Holy Spirit has come upon" them, the apostles will become Jesus's witnesses. Significantly, Luke employs the same Greek word for the Holy Spirit coming upon Mary when she conceives Jesus (*epeleusetai*) as he does for the Holy Spirit coming upon the apostles (*epelthontos*). As Mary conceived Jesus by the Holy Spirit, so the Holy Spirit, by coming upon the apostles, will bring to birth the church.[16] Moreover, the Greek word for "witnesses" is *maptupes* (martyrs). The apostles by bearing witness to Jesus will, except for John, become martyrs, that is, they will lay down their lives on behalf of Jesus and the gospel. In Acts, Steven and James become the first witnesses who become full martyrs.[17] Likewise, as the primary witnesses in Acts, Peter and Paul suffer greatly for the sake of the gospel, though Acts concludes just prior to their being martyred during Nero's persecution of the church.

With the coming of the Holy Spirit upon the apostles, they will become Jesus's witnesses, but to what will they bear witness? Their witness is found primarily in the lengthy sermons of Peter and Paul, which we will examine more fully at the appropriate time. Nonetheless, two examples are the following. Although he died and was buried, "this Jesus God raised up, and of that we are all witnesses" (Acts 2:32). Or again, "And we are witnesses to all that he did both in the country of the Jews and in Jerusalem. They put him to death by hanging him on a tree; but God raised him on the third day and made him manifest; not to all the people but to us who were chosen by God as witnesses, who ate and drank with him after he rose from the dead."[18]

---

know well that the day of the Lord will come like a thief in the night. When people say, 'There is peace and security,' then sudden destruction will come upon them as travail comes upon a woman with child, and there will be no escape" (1 Thes 5:1–3).

16. Luke does not explicitly employ this imagery, but Mary, by being the mother of Jesus, brings salvation into the world, so the church is the instrument through which salvation continues to be made present in the world. Thus, Mary is an icon of the church, for both are bearers of salvation. The Gospel of John clearly contains this imagery when Mary stands beneath the cross of Jesus, her son. From the cross Jesus breathes forth his spirit not only unto his Father, but also upon Mary—the now Spirit-filled icon of the church. Moreover, the water and blood that comes forth from the side of Christ falls upon Mary and John. The water and blood are signs of baptism and the Eucharist. Through baptism, the believer is initiated into Christ and his church, and in the Eucharist the baptized come into full communion with Christ and his church. For a fuller exposition of this understanding, see T. G. Weinandy, *Jesus Becoming Jesus: A Theological Interpretation of the Gospel of St. John*, vol. 3, *The Book of Glory and the Passion and Resurrection Narratives* (Washington, DC: The Catholic University of America Press, 2022), 242–65.

17. See Acts 7:58–60 and 12:1–2.

18. Acts 10:39–41. See also Acts 1:21, 3:15, and 5:32.

Third, the apostles will be witnesses "in Jerusalem and in Judea and Samaria and to the end of the earth" (Acts 1:8). As was already observed in our introductory remarks, the Acts of the Apostles can be divided in accordance with Jesus's words. Chapters 1-7 pertain to the preaching of the gospel in Jerusalem. The gospel is proclaimed in Judea and Samaria in chapters 8-12, and chapters 13-28 tell of Paul bearing witness to the gospel all of the way to Rome, which, as the capital of the Roman Empire, is seen as the symbolic end of the world. Nonetheless, "the end of the earth" is also a way of declaring that the gospel has no limits within the entire world. It is to be proclaimed to the whole of humankind.[19]

Luke next informs the reader that after "he had said this, as they were looking on, he was lifted up, and a cloud took him out of their sight." As the apostles look upon Jesus, who had just told them what they are to do upon his departure, Jesus was lifted up. This beholding of Jesus being lifted up ceased when a cloud took him out of their sight. Now, Jesus did not actively enter a cloud that concealed him. Rather, "a cloud" actively took Jesus out of the sight of the apostles. Within the Bible, "a cloud" manifests God's presence. In Exodus, "the Lord went before them [the Israelites] by day in a pillar of cloud to lead them along the way, and by night in a pillar of fire to give them light that they might travel by day and night: the pillar of cloud by day and the pillar of fire by night did not depart from before the people."[20] The Lord's guiding presence was made visible in the pillar of cloud and in the pillar of fire. God, through the prophet Isaiah, speaks of this divine guiding light as "his holy Spirit" (Is 63:11).

19. That the good news is to be declared throughout the whole world is in keeping with what God prophesies in Isaiah. There he proclaims that God's salvation will reach the ends of the world (see Is 45:22, 48:20, 49:6, and 62:11). Also, Psalm 98 declares, "All the ends of the earth have seen / the victory of our God" (Ps 98:3).

Moreover, what Jesus tells the apostles in Acts is in conformity with the "great commission" given to them at his ascension in Matthew's Gospel. "Go therefore and make disciples of all nations, baptizing them in the name of the Father and of the Son and of the Holy Spirit, teaching them to observe all that I have commanded you; and behold, I am with you always, to the close of the age" (Mt 28:19-20). To make disciples of all nations is to preach the gospel to the ends of the earth. In agreement with Acts and Matthew, the Gospel of Mark says that, after Jesus ascended into heaven, his disciples "went forth and preached everywhere, while the Lord worked with them and confirmed the message by signs that attended to it" (Mk 16:19-20). To preach the gospel to all nations, to the ends of the earth, is, simply, to make it known "everywhere." That Mark says that such preaching was confirmed by signs is also in keeping with Acts, for Luke narrates the miracles that accompanied the apostles' proclamation.

20. Ex 13:21-22. The glory of the Lord also appeared to Aaron and Moses in a cloud in Ex 16:10. See also Ex 19:9, 34:5, and 40:34-38.

Moreover, when Moses went up the mountain to obtain the covenantal commandments,

> [a] cloud covered the mountain. The glory of the Lord settled on Mount Sinai, and covered it six days; and on the seventh day he called to Moses out of the midst of the cloud. Now the appearance of the glory of the Lord was like a devouring fire on the top of the mountain in the sight of the people of Israel. And Moses entered the cloud, and went up on the mountain. (Ex 24:15–18)

The cloud, therefore, that *took* Jesus up and out of the apostles' sight on Mount Olivet, the new and everlasting Mount Sinai, was the Father *actively taking* Jesus up into his glorious presence so that he could sit at his right hand.[21] As the incarnate Son who conquered sin and death, Jesus merited to abide with his Father as the risen divine Lord of heaven and earth. The cloud, then, not only manifested Jesus's entrance into his Father's divine presence, but also bore witness to his own risen glory as the Father's divine Son. Moreover, as God led his people out of Egypt by the pillar of cloud by day and the pillar of fire by night, and so guided them to the Promised Land, so the cloud-ascended Jesus will lead and guide his apostles and his church into the true promised land of heaven. From his heavenly throne, Jesus would send forth his Father's Spirit-filled fire upon his apostles, and so give birth to his church, the renewed and restored Israel that would be the saving light to all nations.

What the apostles witnessed in Jesus's ascension is the fulfillment of a vision that the prophet Daniel experienced.

> I saw in the night visions, and behold, with the clouds of heaven there came one like a son of man, and he came to the Ancient of Days and was presented before him. And to him was given dominion and glory and kingdom, and all peoples, nations, and languages should serve him; his dominion is an everlasting dominion, which shall not pass away, and his kingdom one that shall not be destroyed. (Dn 7:13–14)

In his ascension, the incarnate Son of God, Jesus, the now glorious son of man, was taken up upon the heavenly clouds to the Ancient of Days, his eternal Father. There, the Father conferred upon him an everlasting Davidic kingly dominion, one that will never end or be destroyed.[22]

21. The Gospel of Mark states, "So then the Lord Jesus, after he had spoken to them, was taken up into heaven, and sat down at the right hand of God" (Mk 16:19).

22. Later in Acts, as Stephen was being stoned, "he, full of the Holy Spirit, gazed into heaven and saw the glory of God, and Jesus standing at the right hand of God; and he said, 'Behold, I see the heavens opened, and the Son of man standing at the right hand of God'" (Acts 7:55–56).

In Luke's account of Jesus's transfiguration, Moses and Elijah appeared in glory and spoke with Jesus. They "spoke of his exodus, which he was to accomplish at Jerusalem." In Jerusalem, Jesus was to pass over, through his sacrificial death, into the transfigured glory of his resurrection, and so ascend into his Father's heavenly presence. Moreover, as Peter was speaking about making three tents for Jesus, Moses, and Elijah, "a cloud came and overshadowed them; and they were afraid as they entered the cloud. And a voice came out of the cloud, saying, 'This is my Son, my Chosen [or my Beloved]; listen to him!'" By means of the overshadowing cloud, the frightened Peter, James, and John were taken up into the glorious presence of Jesus's Father. Thus, the three apostles came to partake of Jesus's transfigured glory, his passing over into his Father's heavenly glory. From within that divinely imbued cloud, the Father commanded them to listen to his chosen beloved Son. But what were they to hear from Jesus? Summarily, they were to pay close attention to all that Jesus would reveal, particularly through his death and resurrection in Jerusalem.

In Acts, the last thing that Jesus tells his apostles, just prior to the cloud taking him up into the heavenly presence of his Father, the abode where he will be transfigured forever, is that they are to be his witnesses. That final command from the Father's beloved Son is what the apostles are to heed and obey. This is the final, definitive commission to the church. By witnessing to Jesus, the church not only obeys Jesus, but it also obeys the Father's command—"Listen to him." To bear witness to Jesus, the universal Savior and definitive Lord, is to glorify God the Father.

While the apostles "were gazing into heaven as he went, behold, two men stood by them in white robes, and said, 'Men of Galilee, why do you stand looking into heaven? This Jesus, who was taken up from you into heaven, will come in the same way as you saw him go into heaven.'" Even though they could no longer see the cloud-ascended Jesus, the apostles continued to gaze into heaven, as if they hoped to glimpse him one last time. However, "behold," two men, dressed in white, stood by them. Although they have the appearance of men, it would seem that they are really angels, since they appeared all of a sudden, out of nowhere. Moreover, these two "men" must be the same two men who appeared at Jesus's empty tomb in Luke's Gospel. On the day after the sabbath, women came to the tomb and found it empty. "While they were perplexed about this, behold, two men stood by them in dazzling apparel" and told them that Jesus has arisen (Lk 24:1–5). Here the "two men" also suddenly appear, but now they are described as wearing, not simply white robes, but dazzling garments. Again, the suddenness of their appearance and the manner of their dress betokens that they are angels. While they were heavenly angels, they truly "stood by" the apostles here on earth. That they are angels denotes that what they have to proclaim on earth is of divine heavenly origin. At the empty tomb they revealed that Jesus is risen. Similarly, with Jesus now having been taken up into heaven, the two suddenly arrived angelic men have another divine message to proclaim to the heaven-gazing men of Galilee.

Before examining their message, we must examine why the angelic men called the apostles "men of Galilee."[23] Obviously, they were from Galilee, but significantly so was Jesus, who began his ministry in Galilee. "And Jesus returned in the power of the Spirit into Galilee, and a report concerning him went out through all the surrounding country.... And he was preaching in the synagogues of Galilee" (Lk 4:14 and 44). Moreover, at Jesus's trial the chief priest complained to Pilate that "he stirs up the people, teaching throughout all Judea, from Galilee even to this place" (Lk 23:5). Importantly, the two angelic men reminded the women at the empty tomb what Jesus had previously said: "Remember how he told you, while he was still in Galilee, that the Son of man must be delivered into the hands of men, and be crucified, and on the third day rise" (Lk 24:6).

Now, the "Galilean" geographical indicator is theologically significant. The angels assure the heaven-gazing men of Galilee that "this Jesus," who is from the same region and not some other man from a different place, will return. The Galilean designation accentuates the identity of Jesus and all that he has said and done. The Jesus whom the men of Galilee heard preach in Galilee and throughout the whole of Judea, and even in Jerusalem, the Jesus who was crucified, died and rose on the third day, the Jesus who himself was from Galilee, "[this] Jesus, who was taken up from you into heaven, will come in the same way as you saw him go into heaven."

Having accentuated who Jesus is, in what manner was the risen Jesus taken up into heaven? He was "lifted up, and a cloud took him out of their sight." The next time the men of Galilee will see him is when he comes down on the same cloud that took him up. The ascension cloud will become the eschatological cloud—the cloud upon which Jesus will return in glory at the end of time. In declaring the manner in which Jesus will return in glory, the two angelic men have now answered the apostles' initial question to Jesus: "Lord, will you at this time restore the kingdom to Israel?" It may be inappropriate for the apostles "to know times and seasons," for such knowledge is reserved to the

23. This is the only instance in the New Testament where Jesus's apostles are designated "men of Galilee."

Father. Nonetheless, the time of the restoration of the kingdom to Israel will not be an earthly renovation as they might have expected, but an all-embracing eschatological restoration, for it will usher in new heavenly Davidic kingdom that will never end and never be destroyed.

In keeping with the angelic men's prophetic word to the men of Galilee, that Jesus will return upon the same cloud upon which he ascended, Luke's Gospel narrates Jesus's own words concerning his glorious coming on the clouds of heaven at the end of time. Jesus foretells the destruction of the temple and of Jerusalem, and of wars and persecutions. There will also be signs in the heavens, and great fearful foreboding among the people. "And then they will see the Son of man coming in a cloud with power and great glory. Now when these things begin to take place, look up and raise your heads, because your redemption is drawing near."[24] The cloud of which Jesus speaks is the cloud which will take him up into heaven, and upon which he will descend from heaven upon his triumphant return.[25] Interestingly, while the angelic men ask why the men of Galilee keep looking up into heaven even though they can no longer see Jesus, Jesus encourages the faithful, upon seeing the signs of the end times, to "look up and raise their heads," for their redemption is near at hand. The men of Galilee, in looking up into heaven, thought they were seeing the last of Jesus, when they should have been raising their heads and looking up to heaven in anticipation of his return.[26]

24. Lk 21:27–28. See also Lk 21:5–26.

25. In Matthew's Gospel, Jesus similarly speaks of the coming of the end of the world. There will be persecutions with false prophets and apostasy, yet the gospel will continue to be preached throughout the world. The temple will be desecrated, with some men proclaiming to be the Christ. The sun and the moon will be darkened, and stars will fall from heaven. After these signs, the people "will see the Son of man coming on the clouds of heaven with power and great glory; and he will send out his angels with a loud trumpet call, and they will gather his elect from the four winds, from one end of heaven to the other" (Mt 24:29–31). Moreover, unlike in Luke's Gospel, Jesus prophesies at his trial before the high priest who asked if he was the Christ, the Son of the living God. "You have said so. But I tell you, hereafter you will see the Son of man seated at the right hand of Power, and coming on the clouds of heaven" (Mt 26:64).

Similarly, in Mark's Gospel, Jesus, having described all of the evil that will occur at the end of time, declares, "And then they will see the Son of man coming in the clouds with great power and glory. And then he will send out his angels, and gather his elect from the four winds, from the ends of the to earth to the ends of heaven" (Mk 13:24–27). In accordance with Luke's Gospel, in both Matthew's and Mark's Gospels, Jesus speaks of his glorious coming on the clouds of heaven at the end of time. Moreover, what Jesus declares is in keeping with what the angelic men tell the men of Galilee in Acts—that Jesus will return on the same cloud upon which he was taken up into heaven.

26. Paul, in his First Letter to the Thessalonians, also speaks of the hope of Jesus's glorious return. "For the Lord himself will descend from heaven with a cry of command, with the

## Returning to Jerusalem (Acts 1:12–14)

At the conclusion of Jesus's ascension, Luke narrates what the apostles did next.

> Then they returned to Jerusalem from the mount called Olivet, which is near Jerusalem, a sabbath day's journey away; and when they had entered, they went to the upper room, where they were staying, Peter and John and James and Andrew, Philip and Thomas, Bartholomew and Matthew, James the son of Alphaeus and Simon the Zealot and Judas the son of James. All these with one accord devoted themselves to prayer, together with the women and Mary the mother of Jesus, and with his brethren.[27]

In returning to Jerusalem from Mount Olivet, near Bethany, the apostles were obeying Jesus's command. They were not to depart from Jerusalem until they received the Father's promised Holy Spirit, the Spirit in whom they

---

archangel's call, and with the sound of the trumpet of God. And the dead in Christ will rise first; then we who are alive, who are left, shall be caught up together with them in the clouds to meet the Lord in the air; and so we shall always be with the Lord" (1 Thes 4:16–17).

Paul describes the drama of Jesus's descent from heaven, a descent accompanied by his loud command, and by angels and trumpet blasts. This angelic trumpeted command is the summoning of the dead from their tombs to be joined to the living and to enter into the heavenly cloud. In this manner all will be united with the risen Jesus, who hovers in the cloud-covered air. Thus, the eschatological goal will be achieved—the everlasting abiding with Jesus, the Lord.

The book of Revelation also speaks of Jesus coming again upon a cloud. "To him who loves us and has freed us from our sins by his blood and made us a kingdom, priests to his God and Father, to him be glory and dominion forever and ever. Amen. Behold, he is coming with the clouds, and every eye will see him, everyone who pierced him; and all the tribes of the earth will wail on account of him. Even so. Amen" (Rv 1:5–7).

Because Jesus, through his death and resurrection, made us part of his Father's priestly kingdom, he will return upon the clouds. All people, nations, and tribes will see him. Although only the one centurion pierced his side, yet all sinners have pierced his side, for his pierced side is for the forgiveness of all sin. Thus, everyone will cry in anguish that their sins have caused such suffering to their crucified Savior and risen Lord. Even so—Amen, so be it, for "behold" this Jesus will return upon the clouds so as to lift the faithful into heaven.

This last point is made evident later in the book of Revelation. When it is time to reap the final salvific harvest, John declares what will take place. "Then I looked, and behold, a white cloud, and seated upon the cloud one like a son of man, with a golden crown on his head, and a sharp sickle in his hand. And another angel came out of the temple, calling with a loud voice to him who sat upon the cloud, 'Put in your sickle, and reap, for the hour to reap has come, for the harvest of the earth is fully ripe.' So he who sat upon the cloud swung his sickle on the earth, and the earth was reaped" (Rv 14:14–16).

As in the Acts of the Apostles, when the royal and kingly risen Jesus returns upon the cloud, he will reap, at the eschatological hour, the fully ripe harvest, thus establishing the eschatological, eternal Davidic kingdom.

27. Unless otherwise noted, all scripture passages in this section are taken from Acts 1:12–14.

would be baptized.[28] Upon entering Jerusalem, Luke informs the reader that the apostles "went up to the upper room, where they had been staying."[29] Luke immediately provides the names of the men of Galilee.[30]

Acts continues by relating that all the apostles "devoted themselves to prayer, together with the women and Mary the mother of Jesus and with his brethren." That the entire group devoted themselves to prayer implies that their waiting in Jerusalem was watchful prayer in anticipation of the coming of the Holy Spirit. The unnamed women would be those who accompanied Jesus and who cared for his and the apostles' financial and physical needs. Not only were the Twelve with Jesus, but "also some women who had been healed of evil spirits and infirmities: Mary, called Magdalene, from whom seven demons had gone out, and Joanna, the wife of Chuza, Herod's steward, and Susanna, and many others, who provided for them out of their means."[31] Significantly, Jesus's mother, Mary, was also present with the apostles in the upper room, for she must have had a motherly care and concern for her son's closest associates and friends.[32] Jesus's "brethren" would have been his relatives.[33]

28. See Lk 24:50 and Acts 1:4-5. A "sabbath day's journey" is about three-quarters of a mile (see Ex 16:29 and Nm 35:5).

29. The upper room has traditionally been placed on Mount Zion, and thus, the apostles going "up" to the upper room. This, then, is the large "upper room" that Jesus requested for celebrating his last Passover meal with his apostles. It is, therefore, the room where Jesus instituted the Eucharist, and according to theological tradition, ordained the apostles as priests. See Lk 22:7-20.

30. Luke's order of naming of the apostles is slightly different from the order he gives in his Gospel. There he states that Jesus called twelve of his disciples "whom he named apostles; Simon whom he named Peter, and Andrew his brother, and James and John, and Philip, and Bartholomew, and Matthew and Thomas, and James the son of Alpheus, and Simon who is called the Zealot, and Judas the son of James, and Judas Iscariot, who became a traitor" (Lk 6:13-16). Obviously, Judas Iscariot is missing from the list in Acts. As will be seen shortly, the lack of a twelfth apostle needs to be addressed.

There are slight differences in the list of apostles in Matthew and Mark from that of Luke. Although John's Gospel does not have a list, yet Luke's Bartholomew is John's Nathanael (see Jn 1:45-49 and 21:2). Judas the son of James in Luke and Acts is Thaddaeus in Matthew and Mark. The difference may be due to the desire of not wanting to confuse Judas the son of James with Judas Iscariot. If this is so, James the son of James probably appreciated the change.

31. Lk 8:1-3. See also Mt 27:55-56, Mk 15:40-41, and Lk 23:55-56.

32. This is the final time Mary is mentioned in the New Testament. Since she was in the upper room with the apostles and relatives, one can presume she was present when the Holy Spirit descended upon them on Pentecost.

33. In Matthew's Gospel the people of Galilee were astounded and irate at Jesus's preaching and miracles. They asked, "Where did this man get this wisdom and these mighty works? Is not this the carpenter's son? Is not his mother called Mary? And are not his brethren James and Joseph and Simon and Judas? And are not his sisters with us? Where then did this man get

## Choosing a Twelfth Apostle (Acts 1:15-26)

Having named the now-eleven apostles and situated them with Mary and Jesus's brethren in the upper room in Jerusalem awaiting the outpouring of the Father's promised Spirit, Luke proceeds to narrate a pressing apostolic issue—that of choosing the replacement for Judas Iscariot.

> In those days Peter stood up among the brethren (the company of persons was in all about a hundred and twenty), and said, "Brethren, the Scripture had to be fulfilled, which the Holy Spirit spoke beforehand by the mouth of David, concerning Judas who was guide to those who arrested Jesus. For he was numbered among us, and was allotted his share in this ministry. (Now this man bought a field with the reward of his wickedness; and falling headlong, he burst open in the middle and all of his bowels gushed out. And it became known to the inhabitants of Jerusalem, so that the field was called in their language Akeldama, that is, Field of Blood.) For it is written in the book of Psalms, 'Let his habitation become desolate, and let there be no one to live in it;' and 'His office let another take.' So one of the men who have accompanied us during the time that the Lord Jesus went in and out among us, beginning from the baptism of John until the day when he was taken up from us—one of these men must become with us a witness to his resurrection." And they put forward two, Joseph called Barsabbas, who was surnamed Justus, and Matthias. And they prayed and said, "Lord, you know the hearts of all men, show which one of these two you have chosen to take the place in this ministry and apostleship from which Judas turned aside to go to his own place." And they cast lots for them, and the lot fell on Matthias; and he was enrolled with the eleven apostles.[34]

In the midst of approximately one hundred twenty people in the upper room, Peter broached a concern that was probably on the minds of those gathered. That it was Peter who raised the issue is of ecclesiological significance. For the first time after Jesus's ascension, Peter is now exercising his Christ-appointed primacy as the designated prince of the apostles, and thus the head of what will shortly become, on Pentecost, the apostolic church.[35] The question

all of this? And they took offense at him" (Mt 13:53-57). The above-named relatives could have been some of "his brethren" who were in the upper room with the apostles and Mary.

34. Unless otherwise noted, all Scripture passages in this section are taken from Acts 1:15-26.

35. Peter's primacy will also be seen on Pentecost when it is Peter who first addresses the crowd that gathered around the upper room upon the outpouring of the Holy Spirit (see Acts 2:14).

In Luke's Gospel, it is Peter who declares that Jesus is "the Christ of God" (Lk 9:20). In so doing, he manifests his primacy among the apostles. In Matthew's Gospel, Peter's primacy is also founded upon his profession of faith, and is more fully established by what Jesus declares

at hand is that of who will take Judas Iscariot's place as the twelfth apostle. Peter first provides the biblical context from which this problem needs to be addressed.

He informs the gathered brethren that Scripture had to be fulfilled, that is, the words of the Holy Spirit that the psalmist David spoke. These words prophetically pertained to Judas who betrayed Jesus. Peter reminds everyone present that Judas "was numbered among us, and was allotted his share in this ministry." Importantly, then, Judas was one of the twelve apostles, and as such, he shared in this apostolic ministry. By accentuating Judas's ecclesial apostolic significance, Peter is making evident the magnitude of what they are about to do, for whoever takes Judas's place will be numbered among the Twelve, and thus exercise an apostolic ministry with apostolic authority. The seriousness of the choice and the consequences that follow upon that choice are of everlasting historical significance, for the soon to be born church must be and will always be founded upon the apostles. Theologically what we perceive here is the singular nature of the apostles and their ministry. The apostles will appoint successors, and successors of the apostles will be appointed throughout the succeeding centuries. However, those who will be later designated as ordained bishops are not apostles. They may be rightly referred to as "successors of the apostles," but they are not themselves apostles. The "twelve apostles" possess a unique, distinct, irreplaceable ministry, for they are the ones, as we will see shortly, who bear eyewitness testimony to all that Jesus said and did. The church's "apostolic faith" is solely founded upon the Twelve. This understanding is verified later. While an "apostle" must take the place of Judas, when the apostle James later suffers martyrdom, he is not replaced, and he cannot be replaced, by another "apostle."[36]

There now appears in Luke's narrative what might be seen as a footnote, rather than the continuance of Peter's instruction concerning the choosing of a replacement for Judas. The narrative speaks of the manner in which Judas died. The man Judas purchased a field with the money he received for betraying Jesus. But he fell "headlong" and "burst open in the middle and all his

to him in response. "Blessed are you Simon Bar-Jonah! For flesh and blood has not revealed this to you, but my heavenly Father. And I tell you, you are Peter, and on this rock I will build my church, and the powers of death shall not prevail against it. I will give you the keys of the kingdom of heaven, and whatever you bind on earth shall be bound in heaven, and whatever you loose on earth shall be loosed in heaven" (Mt 16:15–20). Peter (Rock) is the rock upon which the church is founded because his profession of faith is the rock upon which the church's faith is built.

36. See Acts 12:2.

bowels gushed out." The disgusting and repulsive manner in which Judas died is seen as fitting and just, given the horrific deed of his betrayal.[37] Luke (or Peter) notes that the manner of Judas's death became known to the "inhabitants of Jerusalem, so that the field was called in their language Akeldamma, that is, Field of Blood."[38]

At the conclusion of this aside, the narrative continues with Peter referencing the Davidic psalms that foretell Judas's death and the need for his replacement. "For it is written in the book of Psalms, 'Let his habitation become desolate, and let there be no one to live in it;' and 'His office let another take.'" First, Peter quotes Psalm 69:25. The Psalmist entreats the Lord to save him from the one who persecutes and betrays him—may that man's "habitation become desolate," and may "there be no one to live in it." The Field of Blood, because of Judas's self-inflicted death, has now become abandoned and uninhabitable, thus fulfilling the Psalmist's pleading. Second, Peter quotes Psalm 109:9. Again, the Psalmist bemoans his wicked false accuser, and prays, "May his days be few; may another take his office." In the light of this scriptural confirmation, Peter proceeds to enumerate the qualifications needed for taking Judas's place among the Twelve.

Whoever is chosen must "have accompanied us during all of the time that the Lord went in and out among us, beginning from the baptism of John until the day when he was taken up from us—one of these men must become with us a witness to his resurrection." Peter emphasizes the totality of the man's presence with them and with Jesus—"all of the time."[39] He then specifies what this totality of time entails. The man chosen must have been with Jesus from the time he was baptized by John until the day that Jesus ascended into heaven, thus the entirety of his earthly salvific mission. Moreover, by accompanying

37. Matthew's Gospel provides the only other account of Judas's death. Having "repented," he returns the reward-money to the chief priest acknowledging that he had betrayed "innocent blood." He threw the money into the temple, and upon departing, "he went and hanged himself" (Mt 27:3–5). While there is a discrepancy between Matthew's and Luke's accounts, yet the difference could possibly be resolved. Judas did hang himself, but in so doing, he fell headlong to the ground, whereupon his bowels gushed forth.

As a historical aside, the heretic Arius (early fourth century) denied that Jesus was truly the Son of God, and so God as the Father is God. Traditionally he is said to have died in a like manner to Judas. His belly split open and his bowels gushed forth. To deny that Jesus is truly God is equivalent to being a traitor, and so deserving the same death.

38. The text, in specifying that "in their language" the Field of Blood is rendered in Aramaic, Akeldama, implies that the author of Acts is a Greek-speaking Gentile. This inference lends support to the tradition that Luke, a Greek-speaking Gentile, wrote the Acts of the Apostles.

39. The phrase "went in and out" appears to be a maxim, since Jesus did not literally appear and disappear while he was with them. Thus, again, it would emphasize the totality of the time that Jesus was with the apostles.

Jesus through the whole of his ministry, the candidate would become, with all of the other apostles, a witness to Jesus's resurrection. The ability to testify that Jesus is risen, by being specifically singled out, becomes a *sine qua non* for becoming the twelfth apostle. If one has not seen the risen Lord Jesus, and so is incapable of bearing witness to his being raised from the dead, one cannot provide the necessary apostolic testimony that is absolutely essential for being in apostolic communion with the other eleven apostles.

Theologically, Jesus's resurrection is essential for salvation. Without the resurrection, Jesus's entire earthly ministry, as well as his death on the cross would be meaningless. They would have no salvific value. If Jesus did not rise, it would confirm what the chief priests, Pharisees, and scribes claimed all along—Jesus is not the Father's messianic incarnate Son, but an impostor. Jesus's resurrection manifests the efficacious nature of his sacrificial death on the cross—that he had reconciled humankind to the Father through the forgiveness of its sins, and in rising from the dead vanquished the curse of death. The ultimate fruit of Jesus's death and resurrection is what the hundred twenty are now anxiously awaiting—the outpouring of the Holy Spirit in whom they will become new creations in Christ.

Having established the criteria that the replacement of Judas must possess, "they put forward two, Joseph called Barsabbas, who was surnamed Justus, and Matthias."[40] In prayer they said, "Lord, you know the hearts of all men, show which one of these two you have chosen to take the place in this ministry and apostleship from which Judas turned aside to his own place." Although the apostles and people in the upper room are performing the actions necessary for choosing Judas's replacement, yet it is the Lord Jesus himself who is making the choice. As he chose the original Twelve while on earth, so he is going to choose who will now take the place of Judas, for the enacting of "this ministry and apostleship."[41]

40. In the light of the fact that Matthias will be the one chosen, it is almost humorous that Luke goes into such detail concerning the name of the other candidate. Nonetheless, such detail does contribute to the historicity of the entire event.

41. Peter states that in setting aside his apostolic ministry in the betrayal of Jesus, Judas has done so "to go to his own place." To what place is Peter referring? I would offer that Peter may have had in mind what Jesus declared at the Last Supper. In Matthew's Gospel, Jesus informs the apostles that one of them was about to betray him. In response to the apostles each asking if it is him, Jesus responded, "He who has dipped his hand in the dish with me, will betray me. The Son of man goes as it is written of him, but woe to that man by whom the Son of man is betrayed! It would have been better for that man if he had not been born." Then Judas, the betrayer, said, "Is it I, Master?" To which Jesus replied, "You have said so" (Mt 26:2–25).

Although Jesus must suffer and die in accordance with the Scriptures, yet "woe" to the one who betrays him. The "woe" is so great that it would have been better for that man never to

Who Jesus chose is determined by casting lots, and "the lot fell on Matthias; and he was enrolled with the eleven apostles." To our contemporary ears, "casting lots" sounds like rolling dice at a casino—by mere chance Matthias won the throw. However, within a biblical context, the casting of lots was seen as a way of determining God's will. "The lot is cast into the lap, but the decision is wholly from the Lord."[42] In this instance, the lots were cast, but Jesus wholly made the decision. Because the lot fell to Matthias, "he was enrolled with the eleven apostles." Moreover, the casting of lots was also a priestly action. In his Gospel Luke states, "Now while he was serving as priest before God when his division was on duty, according to the custom of the priesthood, it fell by lot to enter the temple of the Lord and burn incense" (Lk 1:8–9). Thus, this enrollment by lot certified that Matthias was now officially and formally the twelfth priestly apostle along with the other eleven. This action also implies that the successors of the apostles also shared in their priestly ministry.

## Why Twelve?

The question that has yet to be addressed is why there is such an insistence on the number twelve. Why "twelve apostles?" Why not ten or fifteen? Jesus chose twelve apostles to replicate the twelve tribes of Israel. This replication is of immense theological significance, for it has to do with the restoration of the kingdom to Israel—the concern that the apostles expressed just prior to Jesus's ascension. In Luke's Gospel, Jesus declares to the apostles that "those who have continued with me in my trials," that is, from the beginning of his ministry in Galilee, from John's baptism to his ascension, a kingdom will be given to them. For "as my Father appointed a kingdom for me, so do I appoint for you that you may eat and drink at my table in my kingdom, and sit on thrones judging the twelve tribes of Israel."[43] Within Jesus's heavenly kingdom, wherein they will partake of the heavenly banquet, the apostles, as the eschatological successors of the twelve sons of Jacob, will judge the twelve tribes of Israel. While only the Father knows the times and seasons as to when this restoration will fully take place, the apostles, in the interim, will be Jesus's

---

have been born. But what could be so woeful that non-existence would have been better? Hell! I suggest that hell is Judas's "own place" to which Peter is now referring. We do not know if Judas went to hell, but the implication of what Jesus says, and the insinuation contained in what Peter declares leads in that direction.

42. Prv 16:33. See also Lv 16:7–10 and 1 Chr 24:31.

43. Lk 22:28–29. In the book of Revelation, the risen Jesus declares, "He who conquers, I will grant him to sit with me on my throne, as I myself conquered and sat down with my Father on his throne" (Rv 3:21).

witnesses to that restorative kingdom in Jerusalem, Judea, Samaria, and to the ends of the earth. Only when the ascended Jesus descends on the same cloud that took him up into heaven will Jesus's kingdom be fully established, and so the restoration of Israel's kingdom be fully restored. This complete restoration of Israel's kingdom entails the eschatological fulfillment of the apostles' apostolic ministry, for they will then judge the twelve tribes of Israel and the whole of humankind.

What is anticipated in Luke's Gospel finds its prophetic fulfillment in what is found in the book of Revelation. In a vision, an angel showed John the following.

> And in the Spirit he carried me away to a great high mountain and showed me the holy city Jerusalem coming down out of heaven from God, having the glory of God, its radiance like a most rare jewel, like a jasper, clear as crystal. It had a great high wall, with twelve gates, at the gates the names of the twelve tribes of the sons of Israel were inscribed; on the east three gates, on the north three gates, on the south three gates, and on the west three gates. And the wall of the city had twelve foundations, and on them the twelve names of the twelve apostles of the Lamb. (Rv 21:10–14)

The names of the twelve sons of Israel are written on the gates of each side of the heavenly Jerusalem, for one is only able to obtain eternal salvation through the prophetic and anticipatory Israelite ancestry.[44] Moreover, the foundations of the heavenly Jerusalem, the foundations upon which the fullness of everlasting salvation is achieved, are that of the apostolic foundation of the twelve apostles—the gospel that they first proclaimed to the ends of the earth, a gospel foundation that will never be destroyed or come to an end.[45]

44. This is in keeping with what the prophet Ezekiel proclaimed. "These shall be the exits of the city: On the north side, which is to be four thousand five hundred cubits by measure, three gates, the gate of Rueben, the gate of Judah, and the gate of Levi, the gates of the city being named after the tribes of Israel. On the east side, which is four thousand five hundred cubits, three gates, the gate of Joseph, the gate of Benjamin, and the gate of Dan. On the south side, which is four thousand five hundred cubits in measure, three gates, the gate of Simeon, the gate of Issachar, and the gate of Zebulun. On the west side, which is to be four thousand five hundred cubits, three gates, the gate of Gad, the gate of Asher, and the gate of Naphtali. The circumference of the city shall be eighteen thousand cubits. And the name of the city henceforth shall be, The Lord is there" (Ez 48:30–35).

In constructing the tabernacle, God commanded Moses, "There shall be twelve stones with their names according to the names of the sons of Israel; they shall be like signets, each engraved with its name, for the twelve tribes" (Ex 28:21). This earthly tabernacle prophetically prefigured the heavenly tabernacle in the new Jerusalem, upon whose gates were engraved the names of Israel's twelve tribes.

45. Paul reminds the Ephesians that they "are no longer strangers or sojourners, but fellow

## Conclusion

We have now reached the end of chapter one of Luke's Acts of the Apostles. Chapter one, as our theological interpretation has shown, is divided into four parts. In part one, Luke sows together his first book, his Gospel, with his second book, the Acts of the Apostles. Moreover, this intertwining is also the conjoining of salvation history. Jesus, as the Father's messianic Incarnate Son, fulfils what Moses, the prophets, and psalms prophetically anticipated. Salvation history leads to Jerusalem where Jesus enacted his salvific acts—his sacrificial death and his glorious resurrection. Presently, the apostles are remaining in Jerusalem, in obedience to Jesus, awaiting the Father's promised Holy Spirit.

In part two, Luke narrates Jesus's ascension into heaven. The apostles question whether this is the time for the kingdom of Israel to be restored. Jesus tells them that only the Father knows times and seasons. What they are to do, after being baptized in the Holy Spirit, is to be his witnesses, beginning in Jerusalem, Judea, Samaria, and even to the ends of the earth. In so doing they will be contributing to the restoration of Israel's kingdom—the kingdom of God. The two angelic men inform the men of Galilee that as Jesus was actively taken up into heaven upon a cloud, so upon that same cloud he will return. Upon this eschatological cloud, Jesus will restore the eschatological kingdom of Israel.

In part three, Luke speaks of the apostles' return to Jerusalem. There, in the upper room, with about one hundred twenty people, including Mary, they prayerfully awaited the coming of the Holy Spirit. This is, again, in accordance with Jesus's command.

In part four, Luke recounts the manner in which Judas's replacement was chosen. Peter, as the head of the apostles, orchestrates this event. He provides the biblical basis for the need of choosing a twelfth apostle, as well as the criteria required of the candidate. The man must have been with Jesus and the other apostles for the entirety of Jesus's earthly ministry, and, above all, he must be a witness to Jesus's resurrection. Through the casting of lots, Matthias was chosen. The full complement of the twelve apostles is now in place.

---

citizens with the saints and members of the household of God, built upon the foundation of the apostles and prophets, Christ Jesus himself being the cornerstone, in whom the whole structure is joined together and grows into a holy temple in the Lord; in whom you also are built into it for a dwelling place of God in the Spirit" (Eph 2:19–22).

Having narrated all of the above, Luke has set the stage for the next era within the history of salvation—the outpouring of the Holy Spirit upon the apostles and the birth and growth of the church. Pentecost will initiate the remainder of Acts—the preaching of the gospel and the bearing witness to Jesus to the ends of the earth. Thus, along with Luke, we now turn to chapter two of the Acts of the Apostles.

*Chapter 2*

# PENTECOST: THE BIRTH OF THE CHURCH

## Pentecost: Filled with the Holy Spirit (Acts 2:1–4)

With the one hundred twenty brethren prayerfully awaiting the coming of the Holy Spirit, and the assembly having obtained a full complement of twelve apostles, Luke, in the Acts of the Apostles, immediately proceeds to narrate what took place on the feast of Pentecost.

> When the day of Pentecost had come, they were all together in one place. And suddenly a sound came from heaven like the rush of a mighty wind, and it filled all the house where they were sitting. And there appeared to them tongues as of fire, distributed and resting on each of them. And they were all filled with the Holy Spirit and began to speak in other tongues, as the Spirit gave them utterance.[1]

Presumably the "one place" where the one hundred twenty were located on the feast of Pentecost was the upper room where they had been staying.[2] The feast of Pentecost (the Greek word *pentekoste* means fifty) or the feast of Weeks (*Ḥag Shavuot*) was celebrated fifty days after the Passover. It commemorated the spring harvest when the first loaves of bread were offered in thanksgiving to the Lord. "You shall count seven weeks; begin to count the seven weeks from the time you first put the sickle to the standing grain."[3]

1. Unless otherwise noted, all scripture passages in this section are taken from Acts 2:1–4.

2. See Acts 1:13.

3. Dt 16:9. See also Lv 23:15–17. Pentecost is the second of three yearly feasts that adult Jewish men were required to go to Jerusalem to celebrate. The other pilgrim festivals were the feast of Passover or Unleavened Bread (*Pesach*), which commemorated Israel's exodus from Egypt, and the feast of Booths or Tabernacles (*Sukkoth*), which recalled the forty years that the Israelites sheltered in booths as they journeyed in the wilderness. "Three times a year all your males

The Jewish feast of Pentecost (the feast of Fifty), then, is chronologically conjoined to the earlier feast of Passover. This chronology possesses theological significance. In the book of Exodus, after the angel of death had passed over their blood-sprinkled door posts, the Israelites proceeded to pass over from their Egyptian slavery into the freedom of the promised land. During their journey, God made a covenant with them on Mount Sinai. This covenant was ratified by sprinkling the blood of the lamb upon them and upon the altar, and by God giving them the Torah—the Law. The original agricultural significance of Pentecost later became more theological when it also came to recall God's covenantal giving of the Torah to Israel, wherein Exodus 19–20 was read. Thus, the feast of Passover is intrinsically conjoined to the subsequent feast of Pentecost fifty days later. Pentecost is, therefore, the dual intertwined commemoration of the abundant bread of the spring harvest and the divine conferral of the Law. Now, all the above prophetically anticipates its fulfillment in Jesus.

As the supreme high priest, Jesus, the Father's Spirit-filled incarnate Son, offered on the cross the definitive and everlasting Passover sacrifice of himself, the perfect lamb of sacrifice—the blood of the new covenant. In so doing he freed humankind from slavery to sin with its curse of death. By rising from the dead and ascending into heaven, Jesus was empowered to establish the new creation of everlasting life. Thus, having passed over from death to life, Jesus, fifty days later, on the feast of Pentecost, now sends forth the Holy Spirit. This outpouring of the Holy Spirit is the spring fruit of the new Passover covenant—the birth of the church. Jesus poured forth the Father's promised Holy Spirit, the first and everlasting Pentecostal fruit, and in so doing brings to life the new heavenly land of promise, God's kingdom. What was prophetically anticipated in the first Passover, with its ensuing commemorative Passover feasts, Jesus definitively enacted—the passing over from death to life. Likewise, what was prophetically anticipated in the previous feasts of Pentecost, Jesus definitively enacted on Pentecost—the giving of the definitive fruit of his passing over, the heavenly springtime gift of the Holy Spirit. Pentecost, then, is the Spirit-filled fruit of the Passover, the fruit of Jesus's death and resurrection; and the Holy Spirit will produce, until the end of time, an abundant harvest through the proclamation of the apostolic gospel unto the ends of the earth.

---

shall appear before the Lord your God at the place which he will choose: at the feast of unleavened bread, at the feast of weeks, and at the feast of booths" (Dt 16:16). See also Ex 23:14–17, Lv 23, and Nm 28–29.

Thus, having become Jesus, YHWH-Saves, through his death and resurrection, Jesus is now *being* Jesus. By pouring out his Spirit on Pentecost, Jesus enacts the inaugural enactment of his name—YHWH-Saves. Moreover, he will continue, until the end of time, to enact his name through the actions of his Holy Spirit. Moreover, he will specifically enact his name, YHWH-Saves, through his Spirit-born and Spirit-imbued apostolic church, a church that will do everything in his name—YHWH-Saves.

With the one hundred twenty in one place, "suddenly a sound came from heaven like the rush of a mighty wind, and it filled all the house where they were sitting." Now, close attention must be given to the imagery portrayed here. First, what was unexpectedly heard was a sound, but it was not an earthly noise that came from outside and entered the house. The sudden sound came from heaven, and thus it was a celestial sound that heralded a divine event. Second, the sudden sound was perceived as if it were that of a mighty wind. It was not that the room was filled with a violent, and, so, noisy, wind. Rather, the sound itself resonated throughout the house as though it were borne on a wind. The sound came sweeping through the room. That the heavenly sound was perceived as that of a powerful wind betokened the exceptional nature of this transcendent phenomenon. It was this heavenly sound that pervaded the entire house where the one hundred twenty were sitting. Interestingly, the powerful sound, as though carried on a powerful of wind, came upon those who were sitting. They were not standing. If they had been standing, it would imply that they were fretfully expecting something imminent to happen. Yes, they were anticipating the Father's promised Spirit to come down upon them, yet their waiting was a calm, prayerful watchfulness. They were not nervously pacing the floor. Thus, while they were serenely sitting in prayer, the heavenly sound, as of a mighty wind, took them by surprise.

Amid this sudden house-filling heavenly sound swooshing about the one hundred twenty, "there appeared to them tongues as of fire, distributed and resting on each of them. And they were all filled with the Holy Spirit."[4] In Luke's Gospel, John the Baptist prophesied that, while he was baptizing with

4. In the Gospel of John, Jesus tells Nicodemus that he should not marvel that he must be born anew. "The wind blows where it wills, and you hear the sound of it, but you do not know where it comes from or where it goes; so it is with everyone who is born of the Spirit" (Jn 3:7–8). On Pentecost, the Holy Spirit was borne on the sudden sound of the wind, and alighted upon those present as if tongues of fire. In so doing, all were born anew in the Holy Spirit.

Later, again in John's Gospel, Jesus proclaimed, "If anyone thirsts, let him come to me and drink. He who believes in me, as the Scripture has said, 'out of his heart shall flow rivers of living water.'" As an aside, the Evangelist notes, "Now this he said about the Spirit, which those who believed in him were to receive; for as yet the Spirit had not been given, because Jesus was

water, there is one greater than him who is coming after him, "he will baptize you with the Holy Spirit and with fire."[5] This prophetic word is presently being fulfilled. With the tongues of fire resting upon each of them, the risen and ascended Jesus is baptizing them with the Holy Spirit and with fire. Jesus can do so because he himself, at his baptism in the Jordan, was baptized in the Holy Spirit manifesting that he is the Father's beloved, incarnate Spirit-filled Messianic Son. Having achieved the forgiveness of sin through his death on the cross and having risen gloriously from the dead, the now-ascended Jesus, as Savior and Lord, is empowered to do what the Father intended from the foundation of the world—the sending forth of his Father's eternally promised Spirit. The reason for Jesus's command to remain in Jerusalem and to await the coming of the Holy Spirit has now been achieved.

The question arises as to why the filling with the Holy Spirit is accompanied by the resting of tongues of fire upon those so baptized? In Luke's Gospel,

---

not yet glorified" (Jn 7:37–39). Having been glorified, the Spirit-filled Jesus, on Pentecost, pours out the living waters of his Spirit upon all those who believe in him.

5. Lk 3:16. In Luke's Gospel this outpouring of the Holy Spirit is anticipated in the coming of John the Baptist. The angel that appeared to Zechariah told him that the son to be born of Elizabeth "will be filled with the Holy Spirit, even from his mother's womb" (Lk 1:15). Moreover, Elizabeth, upon hearing Mary's voice, was "filled with the Holy Spirit and exclaimed" that she was blessed by being visited by the mother of her Lord (Lk 1:41–43). Likewise, Zechariah "was filled with Spirit" as he professed his canticle concerning his son (Lk 1:67). The reason that John the Baptist, Zechariah, and Elizabeth are filled with the Holy Spirit is Jesus being present—he who would baptize in the Holy Spirit.

In Matthew's Gospel, John declares that the one coming after him "will baptize you with the Holy Spirit and fire" (Mt 3:11). In Mark, John says that the one coming after him "will baptize you with the Holy Spirit," and does not contain the word "fire" (Mk 1:8). John's Gospel is distinctly different. John the Baptist, upon seeing Jesus, declares, "Behold the Lamb of God, who takes away the sin of the world!" He points out that Jesus ranks ahead of him and that he baptizes in water, so that Jesus might be revealed to Israel. Then, John bears witness to Jesus. "I myself did not know him, but he who sent me to baptize with water said to me, 'He on whom you see the Spirit descend and remain, this is he who baptizes with the Holy Spirit.' And I have seen and have borne witness that this is the Son of God" (Jn 1:29–34). Jesus can baptize in the Holy Spirit because he is the Father's incarnate divine Son upon whom the Spirit abides. Although the Synoptics do not contain this declaration from the Baptist, yet within their narratives of Jesus's baptism, upon the descent of the Holy Spirit, the Father does declare that Jesus is his beloved Son in whom he is well pleased (see Mt 3:13–17, Mk 1:9–11, and Lk 3:21–22). Importantly, in all four gospel accounts, Jesus is declared to be the one who baptizes in the Holy Spirit.

In Luke's infancy narrative, the angel Gabriel, informs Mary that "The Holy Spirit will come upon you, and the power of the Most High will overshadow you; therefore the child to be born will be called holy, the Son of God" (Lk 1:35). Because he is conceived by the overshadowing power of the Holy Spirit, Jesus, as the Father's Son, possesses the Holy Spirit from his conception. The outpouring of the Holy Spirit that he will later receive at his baptism, is the Father's "commissioning-Spirit" whereby Jesus is sent forth to inaugurate his saving ministry.

Jesus prophetically declares, "I came to cast fire upon the earth; and would that it were already kindled! I have a baptism to be baptized with; and how I am constrained until it is accomplished!"[6] Jesus, the Son of God incarnate, came to cast a fire upon the earth. That fire was the fire of God's judgment against evil and for the purification of sin. However, it could not be kindled until Jesus underwent his baptism. This baptism is the baptism of Jesus's death and resurrection.[7] Until Jesus accomplishes his saving death and life-giving resurrection, he is constrained. He is incapable of setting the world ablaze. However, now that Jesus's baptismal death and resurrection has been accomplished, he is no longer constrained. Rather, he is empowered to send forth the fire of the Holy Spirit. Having accomplished his own baptism, he is able to baptize with the Holy Spirit for the purification from sin and for enlivening the apostolic community, the thus giving birth to the church, the church that will preach the gospel to the ends of the earth. In so doing the world will be set ablaze with the fire of the Holy Spirit until the end of time.[8]

In baptizing the apostles with the Holy Spirit and all who were with them, Jesus brought to life the apostolic church. Now, if the church was to preach the gospel even to the ends of the earth, it must speak all the languages spoken upon earth. Thus, Luke concludes his account of the coming of the Spirit by adding that all who had received the Spirit "began to speak in other tongues, as the Spirit gave them utterance." This closing remark anticipates what Luke immediately recounts next.

6. Lk 12:49–50. Interestingly, this saying is found only in Luke's Gospel, but it is theologically important for his narrative.

7. Paul's understanding of the nature of baptism is in keeping with that of Jesus's own baptism. "Do you not know that all of us who have been baptized into Christ Jesus were baptized into his death? We were buried therefore with him by baptism into death, so that as Christ was raised from the dead by the glory of the Father, we too might walk in newness of life" (Rom 6:3–4).

8. Within Scripture, fire often denotes the presence of God. In Deuteronomy, God "is a devouring fire" (Dt 4:24). See also Ex 19:16–19, Ps 18:12–13, and Ez 1:4. The prophet Malachi asks who will be able to endure the day of the Lord's coming. "For he is like a refiner's fire and the fuller's soap; he will sit as a refiner and purifier of silver, and he will purify the sons of Levi and refine them like gold and silver, till they present right offerings to the Lord. Then the offerings of Judah and Jerusalem will be pleasing to the Lord as in the days of old and as in former years" (Mal 3:2–4). Peter speaks of faith, which is more precious than gold, being refined and tested. Such purification will "redound to praise and glory and honor at the revelation of Jesus Christ" (1 Pt 1:7). See also Rv 3:18.

## The Gathering of All the Nations (Acts 2:5-13)

> Now there were dwelling in Jerusalem Jews, devout men from every nation under heaven. And at this sound the multitude came together, they were bewildered, because each one heard them speaking in his own language. And they were amazed and wondered, "Are not all these who are speaking Galileans? And how is it that we hear, each of us in his own native language? Parthians and Medes and Elamites and residents of Mesopotamia, Judea and Cappadocia, Pontus and Asia, Phrygia and Pamphylia, Egypt and the parts of Libya belonging to Cyrene, and visitors from Rome, both Jews and proselytes, Cretans and Arabians, we hear them telling in our own tongues the mighty works of God." And all were amazed and perplexed, saying to one another, "What does this mean?" But others mocking said, "They are filled with new wine."[9]

All one hundred twenty who were in the upper room and who were baptized in the Holy Spirit immediately began to speak in languages other than their own. The languages that they presently spoke were those of all who came to Jerusalem to celebrate Pentecost—"Jews, devout men from every nation under heaven." Jesus had commanded his apostles, upon receiving the Holy Spirit, to be his "witnesses in Judea, Samaria, and to the end of the earth" (Acts 1:8). Now, here on Pentecost, not only were Jews gathered in Jerusalem, but also "devout men from every nation under heaven." By identifying both "Jews" and "devout men from every nation," Luke is informing the reader that not only were there pious Jews, but that there were also devout Gentiles. As will be evident later in Acts, the issue of Gentiles becoming Christian becomes problematic. However, Luke, by enumerating men from various nations, is already alerting the reader that Gentiles can hear and receive the good news of Jesus Christ. Thus, this gathering of all nations is a prophetic anticipation of the future peaching of the gospel to the ends of the earth. Moreover, to preach the gospel to the ends of the earth is to preach the gospel to every nation under heaven, and so all earthly peoples and nations belong to the transcendent heavenly God.[10]

These Jews and devout men from all the nations came together because they heard "this sound," that is, the heavenly sound as of a wind that filled the whole house.[11] Moreover, having heard the sound, the gathered men from

9. Unless otherwise noted, all scripture passages in this section are taken from Acts 2:5-13.

10. Luke, being a Gentile himself, was probably happy to note that Gentiles can become Christian. Moreover, as Paul's future companion, Luke would be active in proclaiming the gospel to his fellow Gentiles—to the ends of the earth.

11. The gathering of all the nation and the hearing in one's own tongue is the reversal

every nation heard the one hundred twenty speaking their own languages. It is somewhat difficult to picture this event. Presumably the sound in the house was also heard outside the house. However, how was it possible for them to hear those inside the house speak their languages when they were outside the house? Shortly, Peter will address them, but it remains unclear as to whether he came out of the house to do so. A possible solution is that the upper room contained a multiplicity of open windows, thus allowing the sound and the speakers inside the house to be heard by those outside. Nonetheless, upon hearing their own languages being spoken, they were "bewildered," and "amazed." The reason for wonderment is that all of those speaking to them were "Galileans"—the same men of Galilee to whom the angels spoke when Jesus ascended into heaven. Nevertheless, having returned to Jerusalem and having obediently waited for the coming of the Holy Spirit, they now, having been baptized in the Spirit, bear witness to Jesus in a multitude of languages.[12]

Luke enumerates the various nations that were present and who heard of "the mighty works of God" proclaimed in their own languages.[13] All the nations noted were from Judea, north Africa, Asia Minor, and Asia itself, including visitors from Rome. Thus, the world as it was known at the time was present on Pentecost, here in Jerusalem. At the outpouring of the Holy Spirit, the gospel was proclaimed to the ends of the earth; and therefore, a world-wide church came to be.[14]

Being "amazed and perplexed," all the Jews and all the devout men under heaven, asked one another, "What does this mean?" The question does

---

of what took place at the tower of Babel. There, because of their pride, God dispersed all human beings by having them speak different languages, and so a multiplicity of different language-speaking nations came to be (see Gn 11:1-9). However, the Holy Spirit now becomes the unifying means by which all nations become one in Christ Jesus.

12. In Luke's Gospel, Jesus, in his final address to his apostles, tells them that "repentance and forgiveness of sins should be preached in his name to *all nations, beginning in Jerusalem*" (Lk 24:47, emphasis added).

13. That the apostles spoke in many languages so that all nations could hear the good news of Jesus, reverses what took place at the Tower of Babel. There, men, who spoke "one language," wanted to build a tower that would reach to the heavens, but God was displeased because of their arrogance. So, God confused their language "that they may not understand one another's speech." "Therefore, its name was called Babel, because there the Lord confused the language of all the earth; and from there the Lord scattered them abroad over the face of all the earth" (Gn 11:1-9). What now unites all nations and languages is salvation in Jesus. In him all peoples and languages become one.

14. Although the Holy Spirit came down upon representatives of all the presently known nations and peoples, the gospel did not reach the ends of the earth as the event implied. The gospel would be preached in sub-Saharan Africa, Great Britain, Eastern and Northern Europe, Australia, and North and South America only over the course of many centuries. The ends of the earth far exceeded what was anticipated on Pentecost.

not simply pertain to the speaking of various languages. The multiplicity of tongues may have been the catalyst for asking the question, but the speaking in other tongues itself demands a further and deeper explanation. The answer is found in the outpouring of the Holy Spirit, the Spirit who now impels the apostles to declare the mighty deeds of God, the mighty works done by his risen incarnate Son, Jesus Christ—that is what *this* all means. Peter will now step forward to proclaim the fullness of all *this*. However, while most are amazed and perplexed, wondering what it could all mean, some cynically mock. What is taking place, they conclude, is explained by an early morning drinking bout. "They are filled with new wine."

## The Prophetic Fulfillment (Acts 2:14–21)

> But Peter, standing with the Eleven, lifted up his voice and addressed them: "Men of Judea and all who dwell in Jerusalem, let this be known to you, and give ear to my words. For these men are not drunk, as you suppose, since it is only the third hour of the day; but this is what was spoken by the prophet Joel: 'And in the last days it shall be, God declares, / that I will pour out my Spirit upon all flesh, / and your sons and your daughters shall prophesy, / and your young men shall dream dreams; / yes, and on my menservants and my maidservants in those days / I will pour out my Spirit; and they shall prophesy. / And I will show wonders in the heaven above / and signs on the earth beneath, / blood, fire, and vapor of smoke; / the sun shall be turned into darkness / and the moon into blood, / before the day of the Lord comes, the great and manifest day. / And it shall be that whoever calls on the name of the Lord shall be saved.'"[15]

Amid the mockery, Peter stands up with the other eleven apostles and begins to speak. At this juncture, the Eleven, except for a brief period, John, fade into the background, as well as the one hundred twenty others in the upper room. Peter now enters center stage.[16] Moreover, as was noted when he took

15. Unless otherwise noted, all Scripture passages in this section are taken from Acts 2:14–21.

16. This is the first of six sermons that are recounted in Acts. Besides this discourse, Peter delivers four others of various lengths (see Acts 3:12–26, 4:8–12, 5:29–32, 10:34–43). Paul delivers the final discourse in Acts 13:16–41. These six sermons or discourses are, obviously, not the exact verbatim words that Peter and Paul spoke. They do, nonetheless, contain the content of what was proclaimed. They present what came to be termed the *kerygma,* that is, the foundational apostolic teaching proclaimed and confessed within the early church. This practice was common in the ancient world where it was impossible to transcribe or remember a speech word for word. For example, Thucydides wrote, "With reference to the speeches in this history, some were delivered before the war began, others while it was going on; some I heard myself, others I got from various quarters; it was in all cases difficult to carry them word for word

the lead in choosing an apostle to replace Judas, Peter is here again exercising his apostolic primacy. It is Peter who spoke, as he stood "with the Eleven." Luke also specifies that, in speaking to the gathered crowd, Peter lifted up his voice. This "lifting up" of his voice is not only so that Peter could be heard by the large, assembled crowd, but also he is "lifting up" his voice in the Holy Spirit so that his words would also be anointed. It is a prayerful "lifting up." Likewise, if Peter's proclamation is Spirit-filled, then his words will fly on the wings of the Spirit and enter the welcoming ears of his listeners so that they would hear with believing hearts and minds. Peter first addresses those gathered—"Men of Judea and all who dwell in Jerusalem." He, thus, acknowledges the presence of both Jews and Gentiles—all the nations under heaven.[17] He first wants to address the immediate misconception—what "this" does not mean. It must be known, and his hearers need to give an attentive ear to what he says. "For these men are not drunk, as you suppose, since it is only the third hour of the day." Peter and the other eleven apostles, by speaking in various tongues and languages, are not drunk—after all it is only nine o'clock in the morning. Drunkenness is not what "this" means. Rather, Peter professes that what "this" means "is what was spoken by the prophet Joel."[18] Thus, Peter begins the body of his evangelistic discourse by providing a lengthy quotation from the prophet Joel—the interpretive key to "this" present event.

---

in one's memory, so my habit has been to make the speakers say what was in my opinion demanded of them by the various occasions, of course adhering as closely as possible to the general sense of what they really said" (*History of the Peloponnesian War*, 1.22.1).

It should also be noted that this apostolic *kerygma* is in accord with Luke's overall understanding of salvation history, a history of God's actions, beginning with Abraham, progressing throughout the Old Testament, and finding its fulfillment in God's definitive saving acts—those enacted in Jerusalem by his incarnate messianic Son, Jesus Christ. What is now being narrated in the Acts of the Apostles is the further enacting of salvation history, that is, the final age inaugurated by the outpouring of the Holy Spirit in Jerusalem, wherefrom the gospel will be proclaimed to the ends of the earth until the end of time.

17. By referring to the "men of Judea," Peter is alluding to the ancient Judean kingdom ruled by David and Solomon. Later he will address them as "men of Israel," which refers to the patriarch Jacob, who is also called Israel. Jacob had twelve sons from which came the twelve tribes of Israel. Thus, Peter is setting his Pentecost sermon within the context of the whole Old Testament history. Moreover, what is happening at Pentecost, the "this," is the fulfillment of what was anticipated in David's and Solomon's Judean kingdom—the kingdom of God (see Acts 1:3). Likewise, the twelve tribes of Israel now find their prophetic realization in the twelve apostles who will "father" the renewed, Spirit-filled Israel—the church that will be composed of both Jews and Gentiles, men from every nation under heaven.

18. Peter is quoting from Jl 2:28–32. It is unlikely that Peter had memorized verbatim the entire passage from Joel. Nonetheless, he was able to paraphrase it, and, at points, he was able to quote the text itself. Knowing that Peter employed Joel, Luke provides the text of Joel himself, though Peter (Luke) slightly altered the first verse, as we will now see.

The text begins, "And in the last days it shall be, God declares...." However, Joel 2:28 reads, "And it shall come to pass afterwards." Peter wants to specify that what will come to pass "afterwards" is what will take place "in the last days." What is taking place presently on Pentecost, the "this," is the inauguration of the eschatological last days, the breaking in of the end-times. This specification finds its biblical warrant in other prophets. Speaking through Isaiah, God declares, "It shall come to pass in the last days that the mountain of the house of the Lord shall be established as the highest of the mountains and shall be raised above the hills; and all of the nations shall flow to it."[19] With all of the nations under heaven now assembled on the Lord's mountain in Jerusalem, the last eschatological days have arrived, for, as prophesied by Joel, God has poured out his Spirit upon all flesh. Moreover, although Israel had defiled the Lord God's holy name by their sins, and so scandalized his name among the pagans, God will vindicate his holiness. Speaking through Ezekiel, God foretells the coming day when he "will sprinkle clean water upon you, and you shall be clean from all your uncleanness.... A new heart I will give you, and new spirit I will put within you; and I will take out of your flesh the heart of stone and give you a heart of flesh ... and you shall be my people, and I will be your God."[20] By baptizing the apostolic community with Father's promised Spirit, Jesus has cleansed Israel and all nations of their sins and has transformed their stony hearts into hearts imbued with the Holy Spirit, thus eschatologically vindicating his name among the pagans. The apostolic church has become the Father's people, and he has become her God. But what are the signs that "this" is what has taken place?

Joel's prophecy postulates the eschatological last-day-wonders that will take place. Because God has "poured out his Spirit," Israel's sons and daughters, young and old, will see visions, dream dreams, and prophesy. Such visions, dreams, and prophecy are all Spirit-engendered, and thus bear witness to the Spirit's eschatological presence. Moreover, God will work "wonders in the heaven above and signs on the earth beneath." There will be blood, fire, and smoke. The sun will become dark, and the moon will appear as blood. These frightening omens will take place "before the day of the Lord comes, the great and manifest day."[21] Thus, the arrival of the eschatological age will manifest

19. Is 2:2. See also Nm 24:14, Dn 2:28, and Hos 3:5. The Letter to the Hebrews speaks of the beginning of this eschatological age. "In many and various ways God spoke of old to our fathers by the prophets; but in these last days he has spoken to us by a Son, whom he appointed the heir of all things, through whom also he created the world" (Heb 1:1–20). Jesus, the Father's incarnate Son, ushered in the last days by sending forth his Spirit upon the apostolic church.

20. Ez 36:23–28. See also Ez 39:29.

21. For a prophetic description of this pending ominous day of the Lord, see Zec 14. The

contrasting events—the Spirit's gifts of visions, dreams, and prophecy, and the impending great and manifest day of the Lord's final judgment of humankind. Significantly, although Joel's prophecy refers to "God" as "the Lord" when referencing the last day, yet "the Lord" now refers to the risen Jesus. The two angelic men told the "men of Galilee" that "this Jesus, who was taken up from you into heaven, will come in the same way as you saw him go into heaven" (Acts 1:11). As the risen Lord of heaven and earth, Jesus's glorious return is "the great and manifest day," the final day upon which divine judgement will be rendered.[22]

While one must take seriously the portentous day of the Lord's coming, "it shall be that whoever calls on the name of the Lord shall be saved." The crucified Jesus is now the risen Lord, for through his sacrificial death he overcame sin with its curse of death, and in his resurrection, he obtained everlasting life.[23] Thus, on "the great and manifest" last day, by calling on his name, "Jesus," one will obtain salvation.

With the sound as a rushing wind filling the upper room and with tongues of fire appearing upon those who began speaking in other tongues as the Spirit gave them utterance, the devout men from every nation under heaven asked, "What does this mean?" So, through Joel's prophecy, they now know the meaning of "this." "This," what has just occurred, is the inbreaking of a new era upon the world, the age that was preordained from the creation of the world, the age to which the whole of human history was leading, the time prophetically anticipated and foretold throughout Israel's history—the eschatological epoch wherein the Lord Jesus sends, until the end of this age, his Holy Spirit upon the apostolic church. *This* is what Pentecost means. And "this" will find its culmination with the coming of the day of the Lord, when all who call upon the name of Jesus will be saved.

Having interpreted the event of Pentecost, the "this," by means of Joel's prophecy, Peter now provides, in his discourse, a fuller explanation of how all of "this" came to be.

---

book of Revelation references Joel's prophecy of the coming of the last days. "When he [the Lamb, Jesus] opened the sixth seal, I [John] looked, and behold, there was a great earthquake; and the sun became black as sackcloth, the moon became like blood" (Rv 6:12). These signs will presage the second eschatological coming of the Lord Jesus, the sacrificed and risen Lamb, on the last day. See also Rv 8:12.

22. In John's Gospel, Jesus states, "The Father judges no one, but has given all judgment to the Son, that all may honor the Son, even as they honor the Father" (Jn 5:22).

23. The theological significance of declaring Jesus "Lord" will be treated later when Peter quotes Ps 110:1.

## God Made Jesus Both Lord and Christ (Acts 2:22-36)

> Men of Israel, hear these words: Jesus of Nazareth, a man attested to you by God with mighty works and wonders and signs which God did through him in your midst, as you yourselves know—this Jesus, delivered up according to the definite plan and foreknowledge of God, you crucified and killed by the hands of lawless men. But God raised him up, having loosed the pangs of death, because it was impossible for him to be held by it.[24]

As noted previously, although he first addressed his audience as "men of Judea," Peter now addresses them as "men of Israel," thus subsuming into his sermon the whole historical narrative of Judea and Israel as found in the Old Testament. What Peter will now declare concerning Jesus finds it origin in the history of his fellow Jews. Moreover, as he first exhorted his hearers to "give ear to my words," so now Peter urges them to "hear his words," for he is about to tell them how the meaning of Pentecost, the "this," came about. All that has taken place has to do with "Jesus of Nazareth." One might think that Peter would have specified that it had to do with the Son of God becoming man, or with the coming of the Messiah. That Peter specifies that Jesus is from Nazareth accentuates the historical nature of what he is about to declare—a real historical person from a town of their acquaintance, and not about some ethereal person from some mystical realm. Peter reminds them that it was to them that God himself bore witness to this Jesus "through mighty works and wonders and signs in your midst, as you yourselves know." His Jewish listeners cannot deny Jesus's miracles, healings, and exorcisms. He did God's mighty works in their midst. They saw them themselves. The implication is that such mighty deeds manifested that Jesus was sent by God, and therefore was the long-promised and long-expected Messiah. His Jewish brethren ought to have drawn this conclusion, and thus believed in him.[25]

24. Unless otherwise noted, all Scripture passages in this section are taken from Acts 2:22-36. However, because of the length of Peter's discourse, it would be of no benefit to provide the entire text at the onset. Further texts will be incorporated at the appropriate places. Moreover, while Peter will make similar points in future discourses, references to them will not be made at this juncture but at the appropriate time of their theological examination.

25. What Peter reminds his Jewish audience is something that, in John's Gospel, some of them had concluded. When Jesus came to Jerusalem and taught in the temple, some asked if this was not the man whom the Jewish leaders wish to kill but have done nothing. "Can it be that the authorities really believe that this is the Christ?" Some respond negatively, because they know where Jesus is from, Nazareth, but when the Messiah comes no one will know where he is from. Jesus, nonetheless, professes that he was sent, but they do not know the one who sent him. Although they sought to arrest him, no one laid hands on him. "Yet many of the people believed in him; they said, 'When the Christ appears, will he do more signs than

However, "this Jesus, delivered up according to the definite plan and foreknowledge of God, you crucified and killed at the hands of lawless men." From all eternity God foreknew, in accordance with his divine providence, that Jesus, his incarnate Son, would be put to death. He also predestined that Jesus, as the great high priest, would offer himself as the perfect sacrifice for the forgiveness of humankind's sin. Nonetheless, Peter bluntly indicts his fellow Jews, for it was they who crucified and killed him, and they did so by the despicable means of employing the hands of the depraved Romans. There was nothing honorable in their motives nor principled in their actions.

Peter, nonetheless, concludes with a robust declaration. "But God raised him up, having loosed the pangs of death, because it was impossible for him to be held by it." "But," despite all the evil and immorality that surrounded the crucifixion of the man Jesus, and notwithstanding that the Jews themselves were the protagonists of this supreme, premeditated injustice, God raised this Jesus from Nazareth from the dead, by freeing him from its pangs—the seemingly unbreakable and terminal chains of death. The reason God did so was because it was impossible for death to lay hold of him. Death had no authority over Jesus, for by overcoming sin in his all-loving sacrificial death, he vanquished the curse of death. He put death to death, and so was freed from the pangs of death's grasp. It was impossible for God, then, not to raise him from the dead—a resurrection that he rightly merited.

To confirm and corroborate what he just declared, Peter calls upon the prophetic words of no less than the Jews' greatest king—David.

> For David says concerning him, "I saw the Lord always before me, for he is at my right hand that I may not be shaken; therefore, my heart was glad, and my tongue rejoiced; moreover, my flesh will dwell in hope. For you will not abandon my soul to Hades, nor let your Holy One see corruption. You have made known to me the way of life; you will make me full of gladness with your presence."

---

this man has done?" (Jn 7:25-31). Similarly, "many came to him [Jesus]; and they said, 'John did no sign, but everything that John said about this man was true.' And many believed in him" (Jn 10:41-42). Unlike the Baptist, Jesus did work signs and wonders. Significantly, after Jesus raised Lazarus from the dead, the Pharisees and priests were extremely alarmed. "What are we to do? For this man performs many signs. If we let him go on like this, everyone will believe in him, and the Romans will come and destroy both our holy place and our nation" (Jn 11:47-48). Thus, "from that day on they took counsel about how to put him to death" (Jn 11:53). Not only did many who witnessed Jesus's signs believe in him, but even those who refused to believe in him, acknowledged that he indeed worked signs. Peter will now confront his Jewish listeners with the hard truth that, despite witnessing the signs that attested that he was from God, they put Jesus to death.

Peter is quoting Psalm 16:8–11 where David is rejoicing in what God has done and will do for him. David is always in the presence of God, even abiding at the Lord's right hand. He is, therefore, glad and sings the Lord's praises. Because he abides with the Lord, David never loses hope, for the Lord will not forsake his soul to Sheol. Neither will the Lord even let the flesh of his Holy One see decay. Rather, God will always preserve David in his heavenly presence.

Although David is singing about the Lord's goodness to him, Peter will now point out to his listeners that, despite his confidence that God will preserve his soul from Hades and his flesh from corruption, David died. Therefore, Peter concludes that David's words must be prophetic and so apply to someone else, namely Jesus.

> Brethren, I may say to you confidently of the patriarch David that he both died and was buried, and his tomb is with us to this day. Being therefore a prophet, and knowing that God had sworn an oath to him that he would set one of his descendants upon his throne, he foresaw and spoke of the resurrection of the Christ, that he was not abandoned to Hades, nor did his flesh see corruption. This Jesus God raised up, and of that we all are witnesses. Being therefore exalted at the right hand of God, and having received from the Father the promise of the Holy Spirit, he has poured out this which you see and hear. For David did not ascend into the heavens; but he himself says, "The Lord said to my Lord, Sit at my right hand, till I make your enemies a stool for your feet." Let all the house of Israel therefore know assuredly, that God has made him both Lord and Christ, this Jesus whom you crucified.

Peter tells his fellow Jews that the patriarch David died and was buried, and he can confidently do so because they all know that his tomb is still with them.[26] Nonetheless, because of his patriarchal status, David was a prophet, and therefore what he seemingly declared about himself in Psalm 16 applies to Jesus. Moreover, David also knew what God had sworn to him—that one of his offspring would sit upon his throne and reign forever. "Thou [the Lord] hast said, 'I have made a covenant with my chosen one, / I have sworn to David my servant: / I will establish your descendants forever, / and build your throne for all generations'" (Ps 89:3–4). Likewise, "The Lord swore to David a sure oath / from which he will not turn back: / 'One of the sons of your body / I will set on your throne. / If your sons keep my covenant / and my testimonies which I shall teach them, / then their sons also forever / shall sit upon your throne'"

26. Because David was revered as such a great king, he was later numbered among the other three patriarchs—Abraham, Isaac, and Jacob. Because Peter said that David's tomb was still in their midst, the tradition ensued that his tomb was next to the upper room on Mount Zion in Jerusalem. Jews to this day go to this tomb where supposedly David was buried to pray.

(Ps 132:11–12). Because of these oaths, David prophetically knew that they foretold "the resurrection of the Christ," that is, Jesus, and therefore, Jesus Christ "was not abandoned to Hades nor did his body see corruption," as David prophesied in Psalm 16. Rather, "This Jesus God raised up, and of that we are witnesses." By raising up Jesus, God fulfilled what he had sworn to David, for Jesus is of the line of David and as gloriously risen, he now sits on David's everlasting throne.[27] All the apostles are witnesses to Jesus's resurrection.

Moreover, because this Jesus was raised by God, he is, "therefore exalted at the right hand of God," for he has ascended into God's heavenly presence. Likewise, "having received from the Father the promise of the Holy Spirit, he has poured out this which you see and hear." Peter has consistently been employing the word "God," but now, for the first time, he speaks of "the Father" with the implication that this raised and ascended Jesus is his eternal Son. Because Jesus is the Father's resurrected and ascended Son, the Father has given to him the Father's promised Holy Spirit, whom he has now "poured out." This is the "this" that the men of Israel presently "see and hear." Thus, finally, having heard the heavenly sound like the rush of mighty wind, and having seen the tongues as of fire alighting upon all in the upper room, and having heard the Spirit-filled one hundred twenty speaking their own languages, the men of Israel, know what this all means. "This" means that Jesus of Nazareth, who was attested to by God by mighty works, wonders, and signs, and whom the Jews killed and had crucified by the Romans, and whom the Father raised from the dead, this Jesus, in accord with the prophesies of David and the divine promises made to him, has poured out his Holy Spirit. What the men of Israel have seen and heard is the inbreaking of the new and everlasting eschatological age—the kingdom of God of which Jesus, as the Father's exalted incarnate Son, is king. What Peter has just told his fellow Jews is that the history of salvation history, which began with the patriarchs, has now achieved its goal in the risen Jesus Christ, the man from Nazareth.

Peter concludes his Pentecost discourse by again reminding his listeners that the deceased David, unlike Jesus, "did not ascend into the heavens; but he himself says, 'The Lord [*Kurios*] said to my Lord [*to Kurio mou*], Sit at my right hand, till I make your enemies a stool for your feet.'"[28] Within the Old Testament, to speak of two "Lords" is astonishing, for the Jewish religion was noted

27. In Luke's Gospel, the angel Gabriel informs Mary that, since the son to be born of her will be the Son of the Most High, "the Lord God will give to him the throne of his father David, and he will reign over the house of Jacob forever; and of this kingdom there will be no end" (Lk 1:32–33).

28. He quotes Ps 110:1. Psalm 110 is the most quoted psalm in the New Testament.

for its singular belief in one God.[29] For David to say that he heard "the Lord" speak "to my Lord" implies that David's Lord is distinct from "the Lord" who is speaking to his "Lord," yet, because they are both called "Lord," they are both equally God. Although such a declaration would be inexplicable within the Old Testament context, with the coming of Jesus as the Father's incarnate Son, the text assumes an unprecedented clear meaning, though a new mystery comes to light—that of the Trinity.[30] Both the Father and the Son are fully divine, and so both can be rightly designated "Lord." This is the understanding that Peter is professing, and the truth that he wants his Jewish brethren to believe. The risen Jesus, the Father's incarnate Son, is Lord and as so equally divine as his Father, and thus sits at the Father's right hand upon the Father's heavenly throne. There the Son-Lord is to wait until his Father-Lord makes a footstool for his feet, that is, vanquishes all of those who refuse to acknowledge that Jesus is truly Lord.

Thus, Peter concludes his Pentecost discourse with this bold call to faith. "Let all the house of Israel therefore know assuredly that God has made him both Lord and Christ, this Jesus whom your crucified." The whole house of Israel, all Peter's Jewish brethren, and not simply some or most, are to be committed to the belief that God, that is, their God, has designated this man Jesus, the man whom they crucified, both Lord and Christ. Jesus, as the Father's messianic incarnate Son, is definitively Lord, for through his death and resurrection, he is the universal Savior. As Christ and Lord, he has poured out his Holy Spirit. All of the above, from the onset of Peter's discourse to its

29. God revealed to Moses his divine name as *Eheyeh Asher Eheyeh*—I Am Who Am or He Who Is (see Ex 3:13–14). Because the divine name, shortened to Yahweh or to the tetragrammaton, YHWH, was regarded as too sacred to be uttered, it was replaced by the Hebrew word *Adonai* ("Lord"). In the Greek Septuagint, the Hebrew for "I Am Who Am" was rendered as *ego eimi ho on* or I Am (*ego eimi*), and *Adonai* was rendered as Kurios. In John's Gospel, we find Jesus referring to himself as "I Am" (*ego eimi*; see Jn 8:28, 8:58, and 12:32). Because Jesus appropriated the divine name to himself, he was accused of blasphemy.

30. In the post-apostolic church, the church Fathers wrestled with the question as to how God can be one and the Father and the Son both be equally God. There were various inadequate attempts at addressing this issue, but the Council of Nicaea (AD 325) declared that the Son of God was the only begotten Son, who "was God from God, light from light, true God from true God, begotten and not made, of one substance (*homoousion*) with the Father." In this creedal definition, the council professed that the one God is the Father and the Son, for they both together equally share the one divine nature. Subsequently, the question of the Holy Spirit came to the fore. The First Council of Constantinople (AD 381) declared that "the Holy Spirit, the giver of life, who proceeds from the Father," is "with the Father and the Son worshiped and glorified." Because the Holy Spirit proceeds from the Father, and so is worshiped and glorified in communion with the Father and the Son, he is fully divine as well, for he shares in their one divine nature.

completion, is the answer to the question that the Jews and the devout men from every nation under heaven asked, "What does *this* mean?"

## What Shall We Do? (Acts 2:37-42)

> Now when they heard this they were cut to the heart, and said to Peter and the rest of the apostles, "Brethren, what shall we do?" And Peter said to them, "Repent, and be baptized every one of you in the name of Jesus Christ for the forgiveness of your sins; and you shall receive the gift of the Holy Spirit. For the promise is to you and to your children and to all that are far off, everyone whom the Lord our God calls to him."[31]

Peter, having concluded his Pentecost discourse, Luke immediately narrates the response of those who heard him—"they were cut to the heart." This cutting to the heart was threefold. First, they were convicted of the evil they had done in crucifying Jesus and handing him over to lawless men, the Romans. Second, they rejoiced to hear that Jesus, whom they put to death, the Father raised up and exalted at his right hand. Third, they were overawed and astounded at knowing that the heavenly sound like that of rushing wind and the appearance of tongues as of fire signified the outpouring of the Holy Spirit upon all in the upper room. Within this emotionally enthused and spiritually animated context, they asked "Peter and the rest of the apostles, 'Brethren, what shall we do?'" Significantly, they call Peter and the other apostles "brethren." They are "brethren" in that they are all ethnically Jews. However, they are not religiously "brethren," for they have not yet professed their faith in Jesus, and they have yet to be baptized in the Holy Spirit. Nonetheless, there is hope in referring to Peter and the apostles as "brethren"—this is what they ardently want to be, but they are unaware as to how this hoped-for affiliation can come about. So, they asked the "brethren" "what shall we do?" that is, what do we need to do to become "brethren" with you? Peter informs them, "Repent, and be baptized every one of you, in the name of Jesus Christ for the forgiveness of your sins; and you shall receive the gift of the Holy Spirit."[32] To

31. Unless otherwise noted, all scripture passages in this section are taken from Acts 2:37-42. The remainder of these verses will be later added to the text.

32. To be baptized "in the name Jesus Christ" should not be seen as different from, or even contrary to, what Jesus commands his apostles to do in Matthew's Gospel. There Jesus commissioned them to preach the gospel to all nations, "baptizing them in the name of the Father and of the Son and of the Holy Spirit" (Mt 28:19). To be baptized "in the name of Jesus Christ" is to be baptized in the Father's promised Holy Spirit, for Jesus is the Father's risen, Spirit-filled incarnate Son (see Acts 2:32-33). Moreover, such an understanding is in accord with Joel's prophecy, where "whoever calls on the name of the Lord shall be saved" (see Acts 2:21).

become "brethren" within the apostolic community, they must first repent of their sins, and this act of repentance must be accompanied with being baptized in the name of Jesus Christ.

There is, then, a twofold conjoined act that they must perform. To be baptized in the name of Jesus Christ implies that one believes that the risen Jesus is the promised Spirit-filled Christ, and so the universal Savior and risen Lord. Moreover, to be baptized in his name means to die and rise with him, and to receive the free gift of the Holy Spirit who cleanses one of sin and makes one holy. Unlike those who received John's baptism, which only symbolized the forgiveness of sins, those baptized in the name of Jesus Christ and by Jesus Christ are truly forgiven and interiorly made righteous. For as the risen, messianic Spirit-filled Christ, Jesus is empowered to baptize in the Holy Spirit those who believe in him.[33] Thus, the "name" of Jesus, which means, "YHWH-Saves," is synonymous with who he is as the Father's divine Son, and what he has accomplished through his death and resurrection—salvation. One reaps these saving benefits, as Peter declares, through repentance and faith-filled baptism in the Holy Spirit. Through the acts of repentance and baptism in the Holy Spirit, his fellow Jews will then become, with the apostolic community, authentic "brethren" in Christ Jesus.

Peter also tells those seeking baptism that "the promise is to you and to your children and to all that are far off, everyone whom the Lord our God calls to him." The promise of being baptized with the Holy Spirit is not only for those present, but it is also for the children. As will be seen later in Acts, entire households will be baptized.[34] Moreover, this promise is also for "those who are far off"—the Jewish diaspora and to the far-off Gentiles.[35] Thus, "everyone

In baptism, one calls on the name of the Lord Jesus Christ. Paul was baptized by calling on the name of Jesus (see Acts 22:16). Jesus is the risen Lord, and anyone who, upon being baptized, calls upon his name will be saved. Additionally, as will be seen later, the apostles work miracles "in the name of Jesus."

33. At the onset of the Acts of the Apostles, Luke distinguishes between the way John baptizes, that is, "with water," and the way Jesus will baptize, that is, "with the Holy Spirit" (Acts 1:5). Moreover, later in Acts, when Paul comes to Corinth, he asks "some disciples" if they received the Holy Spirit when they came to believe. They responded that they "never even heard that there is a Holy Spirit." They were baptized in "John's baptism." Paul informed them that John baptized in preparation for the one who was to come, Jesus. "On hearing this, they were baptized in the name of the Lord Jesus. And when Paul laid his hands upon them, the Holy Spirit came on them; and they spoke with tongues and prophesied" (Acts 19:1-6).

34. See Acts 10:44-48, 16:14-15, and 16:29-34.

35. Paul declares that Jesus, through his saving blood, broke down the "dividing wall" between Jews and Gentiles, making them "one body" and created "in himself one new man in place of two." Thus, Christ Jesus "came and preached peace to you [the Ephesian Gentiles] who

whom the Lord our God calls to him" is eligible to be baptized in the Holy Spirit. Since he is speaking to Jews, Peter, by referencing "the Lord *our* God," is referring to the Lord God of Israel, YHWH. He is the one who is summoning the foreordained to faith in Jesus Christ, his risen incarnate Son, for only Jesus baptizes in his promised Holy Spirit.

Luke now sums up what took place after Peter's Pentecost discourse and with regard to his fellow Jews wishing to be baptized in the Holy Spirit. "And he [Peter] testified with many other words and exhorted them saying, 'Save yourselves from this crooked generation.' So those who received his word were baptized, and there were added that day about three thousand souls." While Peter, within the text, finished speaking, yet Luke informs the reader that Peter continued, at length, to bear witness to Jesus. Such an aside implies, as was noted at the onset of Peter's discourse, that Peter's words are not the very words that he spoke. Rather, they are Luke's rendering of Peter's main arguments and thoughts in words similar to what Peter said. One of the further points that Peter made was that he "exhorted them, saying, 'Save yourself from this crooked generation.'" To be saved from this crooked generation is to be saved from the fallen race of Adam—his entire ancestry, both Jew and Gentile alike. This phrase was first spoken by Moses, and he applied it to the Israelites themselves. After God led Israel out of Egypt, Moses, in his song, declares that the Israelites "dealt corruptly with him [God], they are no longer his children because of their blemish; they are a perverse and crooked generation."[36] Because they turned to other gods, the Israelites blemished themselves, and so became a perverse and crooked generation. It is from this generation, the generation of fallen Adam and from their own unfaithful ancestors, that Peter's Jewish brethren must now save themselves. And they do so, for Luke immediately adds that "those who received his [Peter's] word were baptized." By believing in Jesus and being baptized with the Holy Spirit, they forsook the perverse and depraved generation of this world and entered into the apostolic community born of the Holy Spirit—the church. In so doing, "there were added that day about three thousand souls," that is, about three thousand were added to the brethren.[37] The hope of those who heard Peter's words with faith was fulfilled. They were now brethren with the brethren.

---

were far off and peace to those who were near [the Jews]; for though him we both have access in the one Spirit to the Father." All are now "fellow citizens with the saints and members of the household of God" (Eph 2:13–19).

36. Dt 32:5. Paul exhorts the Philippians to live holy and blameless lives "in the midst of a crooked and perverse generation, among whom you shine as lights in the world" (Phil 2:15).

37. Given the above context where Peter speaks of the Jewish nation becoming a perverse

Being among the brethren, "they held steadfastly to the apostle's teaching and fellowship, to the breaking of the bread and to the prayers." To be among the brethren demanded that one adhere to the apostolic teaching, that is, the *kerygma*, and to be in fellowship with the apostolic community and not in fellowship with the community of the perverse and crooked world. This apostolic teaching and fellowship are most fully enacted and advanced here on earth in the breaking of the bread, for in the Eucharistic liturgical celebration the brethren become one with the risen Lord Jesus Christ, and so become one with one another.[38] Having been baptized with the Holy Spirit, the brethren are ushered into baptism's completion—the Eucharist. This Eucharistic fellowship was further expressed and enhanced by the common prayer together—their Spirit-filled giving of praise, worship, and honor to their Lord Jesus Christ—all to the glory of God the Father.

## Living the Apostolic Life (Acts 2:43-47)

> And fear came upon every soul; and many wonders and signs were done through the apostles. And all who believed were together and had all things in common; and they sold their possessions and goods and distributed them to all, as any had need. And day by day, attending the temple together and breaking bread in their homes, they partook of food with glad and generous hearts, praising God and having favor with all the people. And the Lord added to their number day by day those who were being saved.[39]

Luke speaks of the "fear" that "came upon every soul." This "fear" was not that of terror or dread, but a reverent "fear" of wonder and astonishment, for "every soul" recognized that they now lived in communion with none other than the Lord Jesus Christ, one whom they ought to honor, respect, and worship. Moreover, awe and amazement were further enhanced because of the "wonders and signs" that were "done through the apostles." These "wonders and signs," as

---

and crooked generation by turning to other gods, Luke's noting that "about three thousand" were converted could be theologically significant. When he returned to the Israelite camp, having received the Ten Commandments, Moses found many worshiping the golden calf. In response, Moses ordered the priestly Levites to kill all those who apostatized, "and there fell of the people that day about three thousand men" (Ex 32:28). Thus, the three thousand brethren that were added to the nascent apostolic church reversed the apostacy of the Jewish past—these brethren would be faithful to the new ecclesial community by being baptized into Jesus Christ (see Acts 2:37-41).

38. In Luke's Gospel, the men on the road to Emmaus recognized Jesus "in the breaking of the bread" (Lk 24:28-35).

39. Unless otherwise noted, all Scripture passages in this section are taken from Acts 2:43-47.

will soon become evident, were worked in the name of Jesus and, so replicate the wonders and signs that he himself worked. That the apostles could enact similar miracles in his name caused astonishment. Luke again stresses, as he did previously, that "all believers" gathered "together," but now adds that they "had all things in common." Because they held everything in common, "they sold their possessions and goods and distributed them to all, as any had need." Luke, here, is portraying an "idealized" life of what it practically means for brethren to live with brethren—a community of oneness in every way, where all individual physical needs were met. In other words, they loved one another—a love that was fostered by the Holy Spirit and lived in communion with Jesus Christ their Lord.

Moreover, they daily went to "the temple together." Here, the question arises as to why they went to the temple, for now they abided in the new and living temple—Jesus Christ. In him and through the Spirit, they offered worship to God the Father. The temple, it would seem, was now redundant. At least two interrelated reasons can be offered. First, they were following the example of Jesus himself. He went to the temple to pray to his heavenly Father, and now the apostolic community was doing the same. Second, while in the temple and its holy environs, Jesus preached to the people. The apostles are now but following his example. Chapter three consists of Peter and John "going up to the temple at the hour of prayer," and while there, Peter proclaims the gospel "in the portico called Solomon's."[40]

Although they together went to the temple to pray and evangelize, they broke "bread in their homes," that is, they did not celebrate the Eucharist in public places, such as the temple area, but in the privacy of their own homes. Only those who were baptized could celebrate and partake of Jesus's sacrificed and risen body and blood. Therefore, not having at this nascent stage their own churches, the apostolic community used what they had—their own homes. Moreover, they also partook of a regular meal, sharing their food "with glad and generous hearts, praising God and having favor with all people."[41]

40. Acts 3:1 and 11–12.

41. This arrangement was not without its difficulties. Paul has heard that, when the Corinthians "assemble as a church [*ecclesia*]," there "are divisions" among them. In response to these factions, Paul states, "When you meet together, it is not the Lord's supper that you eat. For in eating, each one goes ahead with his own meal, and one is hungry, and another is drunk. What! Do you not have houses to eat and drink? Or do you despise the church of God and humiliate those who have nothing? Shall I commend you in this? No, I will not."

Paul continues, telling what he has received from the Lord concerning Jesus's institution of the Eucharist. He, then, draws his pointed conclusion. "Whoever, therefore, eats the bread and drinks the cup of the Lord in an unworthy manner will be guilty of profaning the body and

And amid their living the life of faith, "the Lord added to their number day by day those who were being saved." This daily addition of those who were "being saved" appears to imply that some are not being saved. Some reject Christ, and so are not saved. The contrast between those who come to faith and those who do not will be a theme throughout the Acts of the Apostles.

## Conclusion

In chapter two of the Acts of the Apostles, Luke narrates the full meaning of Pentecost, the "this," that is, all the effects that emerged from Jesus pouring out his Holy Spirit upon the apostolic community. With the birth of the church, the apostles, and in particular Peter, began to preach the gospel to all the nations under heaven. Peter's Pentecost discourse resulted in the conversion of Jews and Gentiles alike. They too believed in Jesus and were baptized in the Holy Spirit. They, as spirit-filled and faith-filled brethren, remained faithful to the teaching of the apostles and to fellowship, and to the breaking of bread. Lastly, the Lord Jesus, by continuing to enact his name, YHWH-Saves, daily added members to his church—those born anew in his Spirit. As will now be seen, this growth continues in chapter three through Peter's persistent apostolic preaching of the gospel.

---

blood of the Lord. Let a man examine himself and so eat of the bread and drink of the cup. For anyone who eats and drinks without discerning the body eats and drinks judgment upon himself" (1 Cor 11:18–29). There is here a double, interrelated meaning. If a man does not recognize and acknowledge Christ's real presence in the Eucharist, he is calling down judgment upon himself. Moreover, if a man does not recognize and acknowledge the ecclesial body, that is, those who are sharing in the Eucharist with him, he is equally condemned. This "despising of the church of God" is precisely what the Corinthians are doing. They are partaking of Christ's body and blood, and simultaneously, they are neglecting the poor and the hungry, and so are sinning against both Christ's Eucharistic presence and his presence within his ecclesial body. Thus, they are condemned. This condemnation is a component of the ever-maturing apostolic community of believers, more and more sensitive to the implications of Christ's presence among them.

# *Chapter 3*

## THE HEALING OF THE LAME MAN

With the outpouring of the Holy Spirit on Pentecost and Peter's first evangelistic discourse, which added three thousand converts to the Christian brethren, the Acts of the Apostles immediately narrates the first miracle that Peter performs in the name of Jesus. While on earth, Jesus enacted, on his own authority and in his own name, miraculous signs, and so was *becoming* YHWH-Saves. The apostles now attest that Jesus is indeed YHWH-Saves. The miraculous deeds presently performed by the apostles in Jesus's name, bear witness to Jesus *being* Jesus, the risen Savior and glorified Lord—YHWH-Saves.

### In the Name of Jesus (Acts 3:1–10)

> Now Peter and John were going up to the temple at the hour of prayer, the ninth hour. And a man lame from birth was being carried, whom they laid daily at the gate of the temple which is called Beautiful to ask for alms of those who entered the temple.[1]

Although John will not play a significant role in the Acts of the Apostles, here he is paired with Peter, who will be the chief actor in the healing of the lame man.[2] Earlier, Acts noted that the apostolic community went daily to the tem-

1. Unless otherwise noted, all Scripture passages in this section are taken from Acts 3:1–10. However, because of the length of the healing narrative, it would be of no benefit to provide the entire text at the onset. Further texts will be incorporated in due course.

2. In John's Gospel, Peter and John are often paired. At the last Passover supper, when Jesus speaks of his betrayer, Peter motions to John and tells him to ask Jesus who it is. While John does the asking, because he is laying at Jesus's breast, it is Peter who, in a Petrine manner, straightaway initiates the query (Jn 13:21–26). In subsequent instances, John keeps Peter close at

ple to pray.[3] So now, at the hour of prayer, three in the afternoon, Peter and John are making their way to the temple.[4] Simultaneous to Peter and John entering the temple, "a man lame from birth was being carried, whom they laid daily at that gate of the temple which is called Beautiful to ask for alms of those who entered the temple." It is ambiguous who the "they" are, but in their kindness "they" daily carried the lame man to the Beautiful Gate so that he might beg for alms.[5]

> Seeing Peter and John about to go into the temple, he asked for alms. And Peter directed his gaze at him, with John, and said, "Look at us." And he fixed his attention upon them, expecting to receive something from them. But Peter said, "I have no silver or gold, but I give you what I have; in the name of Jesus Christ of Nazareth, rise and walk."

---

hand. At Jesus's trial before the high priest, Peter "followed Jesus," but it was John, who knew the high priest, who gained entree for Peter to come into the inner court—though it was there that Peter denied that he knew Jesus (see Jn 18:15-17). Likewise, when Mary Magdalene found Jesus's tomb empty, she ran back and informed Peter and John. They ran to the tomb together, but John outran Peter. Nonetheless, he allowed Peter to enter the tomb first (see Jn 20:1-6). When the risen Jesus appeared to some of his disciples, and asked Peter, three times, whether he loved him, John was close at hand. It was John who followed Jesus and Peter, as Jesus was revealing to Peter the type of death he must undergo. Seeing John behind them, Peter inquired about the manner of John's death. Jesus responded by ultimately saying that it was none of Peter's business. Rather, what was important is that Peter follow him (see Jn 21:18-22). In these instances, it is obvious that John considers Peter the prince of the apostles and so head of the church. John's role is to have a brotherly care for Peter. For a fuller theological interpretation of Peter's and John's relationship, see T. G. Weinandy, *Jesus Becoming Jesus: A Theological Interpretation of the Gospel of St. John*, vol. 3 (Washington, DC: The Catholic University of America Press, 2022), 329-33.

Later in Acts, after the apostles in Jerusalem heard that the Samaritans received the gospel, "they sent to them Peter and John." Both Peter and John laid hands upon the Samaritans whereby they were baptized in the Holy Spirit. However, Simon the magician offered Peter and John money so they could give him such apostolic power. In response, it was Peter who rebuked Simon and called him to repentance, for he was bound by iniquity (see Acts 8:14-24). Again, although Peter and John work as a twosome, Peter invariably takes the lead and is the spokesman. In Luke's Gospel, Jesus sends Peter and John to go and prepare a place for them to hold the Passover supper—the Last Supper (see Lk 22:7-13).

3. See Acts 2:46.

4. Twice daily, prayers were offered in the temple during the morning and evening sacrifices. "Now this is what you shall offer upon the altar: two lambs a year old, day by day continually. One lamb you shall offer in the morning, and the other lamb you shall offer in the evening" (Ex 29:38-39). See also Ex 30:7-8 where Aaron is instructed to burn incense before the Lord in the morning and in the evening.

5. It is uncertain as to which gate is named "Beautiful," but it is thought to be the gate that leads from the courtyard of the Gentiles into the interior courts where only Jews were permitted. Thus, the lame man would collect alms from his Jewish brethren.

Being a daily beggar, the lame man was ever alert for someone to give him alms, and so he observed Peter and John before they took notice of him. Immediately upon seeing them, he asked them for alms. Now, having been confronted by the ever-vigilant beggar, Peter "directed his gaze at him, with John." Again, although John sees him as well, Acts accentuates that it is Peter who "directed his gaze." The reason for this emphasis is that it will be Peter, and not John, who will perform the act of healing.

Thus, it is Peter who commands the lame man, "Look at us." Such an instruction at first appears odd since the lame man took notice of Peter and John prior to their seeing him. However, Peter does not want the lame man to observe him and John as merely potential everyday givers of alms, but as men who possess the ability to do something even greater than give money—even lots of money. Obediently, the man did fix his gaze upon them, but only in the hope of receiving something of monetary value. "But Peter said." The "but" is important, for what Peter is about to say and do is not what the man expected. Rather, Peter declared, "I have no silver and gold, but I give you what I have; in the name of Jesus Christ of Nazareth, rise and walk." Peter is not wealthy, and so he is incapable of giving the man any money. However, he does have something, and that he will give to the lame man. Observe, Peter addresses the man directly—"I give *you* what I have." Peter is personally concerned about the lame man's personal wellbeing, and his concern far exceeds the issue of "silver and gold." And, although Peter will heal the man in the name of Jesus, there is an even greater matter that Peter must deal with: that of the lame man's salvation. Peter wishes the healing of the lame man to stir up in him faith in Jesus, which will lead him to be saved. So, Peter directs the lame man "in the name of Jesus Christ of Nazareth, rise and walk." Peter, as an apostle, cannot act on his own authority. To do so would be ineffective. But to act in the name of Jesus Christ of Nazareth, is to act in the name of YHWH-Saves, he who is the divinely promised, Spirit-filled Messiah, he who has died and is now risen. Thus, what Jesus did *in his own name*, Peter now replicates *in Jesus's name*. That name is supremely efficacious.

Given this understanding, what is ironic is that Jesus Christ is from Nazareth. As Peter earlier declared that "Jesus of Nazareth" is the one who worked "mighty wonders and signs" in the midst of all the people, so now "in his name," the name of this man from Nazareth, these same marvelous wonders and signs continue to be worked by Peter and the apostolic church, and for all to see.[6] By attaching "from Nazareth" as the place from where Jesus comes

6. See Acts 2:22–23.

adds historicity to who Jesus is and all that he has salvifically accomplished. As noted in the previous chapter, while Jesus is the incarnate Son of God, he is not some super-celestial being who exists in some ethereal realm—he is from Nazareth, and in the name of this man from Nazareth one can be healed and saved.

> And he took him by the right hand and raised him up; and immediately his feet and ankles were made strong. And leaping up he stood and walked and entered the temple with them, walking and leaping and praising God. And all of the people saw him walking and leaping and praising God, and recognized him as the one who sat for alms at the Beautiful Gate of the temple; and they were filled with wonder and amazement at what had happened to him.

Having commanded the lame man to rise and walk in the name of Jesus Christ of Nazareth, Peter simultaneously took hold of his right hand and pulled him up. That he immediately lifts the lame man to his feet manifests that Peter is certain that the man is healed. This assurance is confirmed, for in the very act of lifting him up by his right hand, the man's ankles and feet are made strong. Moreover, this "lifting up" did not entail Peter strenuously tugging the man off the ground. Rather, Peter's raising up of the man was accompanied by the lame man "leaping up." As Peter held his right hand, the lame man leaped up and began to walk. Not only did he leap up and walk, but he also entered the temple with Peter and John. This joyful leaping into the temple was complemented with joyful praise of God—cheerily worshiping God in the place where he dwelt, for it was now the ninth hour, truly the time for prayer.

Moreover, as Jesus worked miracles for all to see, so the healing of the lame man was for all to see. Thus, everyone in the temple "saw him walking and praising God," and they "recognized him as the one who sat for alms at the Beautiful Gate of the temple." At the Beautiful Gate something delightfully attractive took place, such that all who saw it "were filled with wonder and amazement at what had happened to him." Likewise, as all who beheld Jesus's earthly miracles were amazed, so now everyone who witnessed the healing of the lame man in the name of the heavenly Jesus are astonished. Again, what took place during Jesus's miraculous works is now replicated within the apostolic age.[7] This miraculous healing in the name of Jesus theologically

7. In Luke's Gospel, when Jesus heals the paralytic who was lowered down through the roof, "amazement seized them all, and they glorified God and were filled with awe, saying, 'We have seen strange things today'" (Lk 5:27). See also Mt 9:8 and Mk 2:12.

Interestingly, in John's Gospel when Jesus, at the pool at Bethsaida, healed the man "who had been ill for thirty-eight years," there was no joyful leaping. The man simply took up his pallet and walked. The man showed no excitement, thankfulness, or joy. When confronted by

manifests the presence of the eschatological kingdom of God—the arrival of the salvific messianic age, an age that the risen Jesus himself embodies. Thus, what the prophet Isaiah declared is fulfilled. On the day of the Lord "the eyes of the blind shall be opened, and the ears of the deaf unstopped; the lame man leap like a hart, and the tongue of the dumb sing for joy" (Is 35:5–6). Likewise, while the wicked will be destroyed on the day of the Lord, the righteous "shall go forth leaping like calves from the stall" (Mal 4:2). The leaping, lame man bears witness to the presence of God's kingdom, and so abides in the risen Jesus Christ of Nazareth, the kingdom's king. Through the ministry of the apostles, the kingly Jesus continues his saving eschatological ministry. Moreover, within and through the ever-present apostolic church, Jesus is ever *being* Jesus—YHWH-Saves.

## Why Do You Wonder? (Acts 3:11–16)

> While he clung to Peter and John, all the people ran together to them in the portico called Solomon's, astounded. And when Peter saw it, he addressed the people, "Men of Israel, why do you wonder at this, or why do you stare at us, as though by our own power or piety we had made him walk?"[8]

Because the people saw the lame man walking and leaping, they began to congregate around the healed lame man, who was now sticking closely to Peter and John as they gathered in Solomon's Portico.[9] When Peter saw that a crowd was gathering, he took the opportunity to preach to the assembled people. What is here perceived is a pattern that first began with Jesus himself. The goal of a miracle is not simply for the benefit of the one for whom the miracle is worked, such as healing the blind, the deaf, and the lame. Rather, a miraculous deed is the causal means by which an awe-struck crowd is gathered. A crowd having gathered, Jesus, then, had the opportunity to preach the good news, of which

---

the Jews who wanted to know who healed him, the man did not even know Jesus's name, but later, when he did find out that it was Jesus, the man told the Jews. Because Jesus worked this miracle on the sabbath, and called God his Father, the Jews sought to kill him (see Jn 5:1–18). Thus, the healing of the unresponsive and indifferent man became the catalyst for the Jewish authorities wanting to put Jesus to death.

8. Unless otherwise noted, all Scripture passages in this section are taken from Acts 3:11–16. However, because of the length of Peter's discourse, it would be of no benefit to provide the entire text at the onset. Further texts will be incorporated in due course.

9. The portico, named after King Solomon, who first built the temple, was a colonnade along the eastern side of the temple mount. Jesus had taught there (see Jn 10:22–24). The apostles and early Christian community often subsequently gathered there as well to pray and evangelize (see Act 5:12–13).

the miracle is a sign—the presence of God's salvific kingdom. Peter, following Jesus's example, now begins to preach the gospel to those who were amazed at his ability to heal the lame man in the name of Jesus Christ. Peter may not have realized it at the time, but, by his example, he taught the apostolic church, for all ages, a theological and pastoral principle. Miracles always provide the best occasions for preaching the Gospel—they are attention-getters.[10]

So, Peter addressed the people, "Men of Israel, why do you wonder at this, or why do you stare as us, as though by our own power or piety we had made him walk?" Although Peter has not surprisingly taken the lead by addressing the people, he speaks in terms of "we," that is, himself and the ever-silent John. Thus, even though Peter is the one who commanded the lame man to stand up, he tells the men of Israel that they should not stare at "*us*" for it was not by "*our* own power or piety we made him walk." The implication is that it was not simply Peter who performed the act of healing, but that the John, by his mere presence, was also instrumental. The act of healing was an apostolic event, a power that belonged to the entire apostolic ministry of the apostles, which included Peter *and* John, and not the consequence of only one man's singular ability. All ecclesial acts, such as miraculous healings, are performed by and on behalf of the one apostolic church, even if one man is enacting the acts, and thus the "we" and the "our."

Peter first inquires, with some irony, as to why they "wonder at this." If they had their religious wits about them, they would have immediately recognized, and so would not have been surprised at all, that it was "in the name of Jesus Christ of Nazareth" that "this" healing took place. Only an act performed in Jesus's name would comprise the power necessary for such a miraculous healing. They should, therefore, not "stare" at Peter and John, for neither possess the power nor the holiness to make the lame man walk. They need to look to someone else to find the source of their wonderment—Jesus Christ.

Now, importantly, Peter addresses the crowd as "men of Israel." When first addressing those gathered on Pentecost, he referred to them as "men of Judea," and later as "men of Israel." By speaking to them in such a manner, Peter is deliberately reminding them as to who they truly are—members of an entire Jewish history that is found in the whole of their ancient scriptures. They are God's chosen people. Being the chosen race of God, they ought to

10. Miraculous deeds enacted in the name of Jesus continue to be today the best preludes for the preaching of the gospel, both for the renewal of the faith among believers and for eliciting faith among the unevangelized. This pattern is so not only among contemporary Protestant and Catholic evangelists, but also among the saints throughout the history of the church, many of whom were noted for their ability to heal the sick in the name of Jesus.

expect and anticipate, and thus not be shocked at, what the Lord their God has done and continues to do for them. With this prelude, Peter proceeds to address the "men of Israel" by calling to mind what the God of their fathers has recently done in their very midst.

> The God of Abraham and of Isaac and of Jacob, the God of our fathers, glorified his servant Jesus, whom you delivered up and denied in the presence of Pilate, when he decided to release him. But you denied the Holy and Righteous One, and asked for a murderer to be granted to you, and killed the Author of life, whom God raised from the dead. To this we are witnesses. And his name, by faith in his name, has made this man strong whom you see and know; and the faith which is through Jesus has given this man his perfect health in the presence of you all.

In the above, Peter is making two very significant theological points. First, the God of Abraham, Isaac, and Jacob has "glorified" Jesus his "servant."[11] By referring to Jesus as God's "servant," Peter is alluding to the Suffering Servant Songs in Isaiah. "Behold my servant, whom I uphold, my chosen one, in whom my soul delights" (Is 42:1). Likewise, "Behold, my servant shall prosper, he shall be exalted and lifted up, and shall be very high" (Is 52:13). God has glorified his servant, for his servant was "despised and rejected by men, a man of sorrows, and acquainted with grief." The suffering servant was "wounded for our transgressions, he was bruised for our iniquities; upon him the chastisement that made us whole, and with his stripes we were healed." Nonetheless, "it was the will of the Lord to bruise him; he has put him to grief; when he makes an offering for sin, he shall see his offspring, he shall prolong his days."[12] Jesus, by assuming the sin of the world and offering himself as a pure sacrifice, won God's forgiveness. The God of the people's fathers was so pleased with Jesus, his suffering servant, that he raised Jesus gloriously from the dead. Thus, Peter is affirming that Jesus, both in his death and in his resurrection, has fulfilled Isaiah's prophetic words.

Second, ironically, God's glorification of his servant was made possible by the very people Peter is speaking to. They not only "delivered up" Jesus, but they also "denied" him in the very presence of Pilate, even when he wanted to release him. Thus, they, as Jews, betrayed one of their own into the hands

11. By speaking of the God of Abraham, Isaac, and Jacob, Peter is recalling God's words to Moses at the burning bush. "I am the God of your father, the God of Abraham, the God of Isaac, and the God of Jacob" (Ex 3:6). Subsequently, God will reveal the God of Moses's fathers is "I Am Who Am," He Who Is (Ex 3:14).

12. Is 53:3, 5, and 10. See also Is 49:1-7, 50:4-11, and the whole of Is 53. Later in Acts 8:26-35, Philip will also interpret the Suffering Servant Songs in the light of Jesus.

of their most hated enemies, the Romans. Moreover, in so doing, they "denied the Holy and Righteous One," and instead clamored for the release of "a murderer," Barabbas, and so "killed the Author of life." Note the ironic contrast. They insisted upon the release of one who was condemned for maliciously taking the lives of others, and "denied the Holy and Righteous One"—"the Author of life." As the Son of God incarnate, Jesus was filled with the Holy Spirit, and therefore, was righteous in his sinlessness. Similarly, the God of their fathers created all things through his Son, who is the Father's life-giving Word.[13] Moreover, as witnessed on Pentecost, Jesus is the author of *new* life, for he sent his Holy Spirit upon all who believed in him—thus making them holy and righteous like himself. However, despite the evil that the Jewish people perpetrated against Jesus, the holy and righteous author of life, "God raised" him from the dead.

Although his audience rejected Jesus and had him crucified, Peter now declares that he and silent John can testify to his resurrection. "To this we are witnesses." Moreover, it is precisely because Jesus is risen that "his name, by faith in his name, has made this man strong whom you see and know." Peter accentuates the revelational significance of the name of Jesus. First, the name Jesus is powerful in and of itself, for Jesus is gloriously risen. Second, therefore, by faith in the one who bears the name Jesus, miracles can be performed by enacting them in his name. One only needs to observe the healed lame man, one whom all the people know, to conclude that it is "through faith in Jesus" that the lame man is now in "perfect health in the presence of you all." Having addressed the immediate issue of the crowd's amazement at the lame man being healed in the name of Jesus, Peter proceeds to provide a deeper theological understanding of who Jesus is and of his salvific importance.

## Fulfilling the Words of the Prophets (Acts 3:17–26)

> And now, brethren, I know that you acted in ignorance, as did also your rulers. But what God foretold by the mouth of all the prophets, that his Christ should suffer, he thus fulfilled. Repent therefore, and turn again, that your sins may be blotted out, that times of refreshing may come from the presence of the Lord, and that he may send the Christ appointed for you, Jesus, whom heaven must receive until the time for establishing all that God spoke by the mouth of his holy prophets from of old.[14]

13. See Jn 1:1–4 and Heb 1:2.

14. Unless otherwise noted, all Scripture passages in this section are taken from Acts

So, Peter now wishes his Jewish brethren to know that the evil deeds they and their leaders enacted against Jesus, they did in ignorance. Peter addresses the Jewish crowd, "brethren," and he does so for a twofold reason. First, they are all Jews, and second, as his Jewish brethren, Peter wants to speak to them as a brother Jew, and so win their fraternal consideration and approval as to what he is about to proclaim. Thus, with empathy, Peter acknowledges their and their rulers' ignorance in relationship to what woefully happened to Jesus. They did not know what they were doing.[15]

Although the Jews and their rulers were irresponsibly ignorant, yet what they did fulfilled God's purposes, for he foretold what happened through the prophets, that is, "that his Christ should suffer." The immediate prophesies that come to mind are the very ones Peter alluded to previously, that is, Isaiah's Suffering Servant Songs. God's anointed one, the long-anticipated Christ, was to suffer so that sins might be forgiven, and in so suffering, God raised him from the dead. Because the Christ has come, Peter calls the people to repent, to turn back to righteousness, so that their sins "may be blotted out." If they do so, "times of refreshing may come from the presence of the Lord, and he may send the Christ appointed for you, Jesus." For Peter, these "times of refreshing" refer to the living waters of baptism wherein the new life of the Holy Spirit will blot out their sins and make them holy.[16] This will be accomplished because God the Father, the Lord, will send them the Christ he has given them, that is, the risen Jesus. The enactment of Peter's exhortation

---

3:17–26. Again, however, because of the length of Peter's remaining discourse, it would be of no benefit to provide the entire text at the onset. Further texts will be incorporated in due course.

15. The blame for Jesus's unjust crucifixion resides more with the Jewish leaders than the Jewish populace at large. It was the chief priests, scribes, and Pharisees who plotted to kill Jesus. At Jesus's trial before Pilate, they whipped up the crowd to demand Jesus's condemnation and death. See Mt 27:20–23, Mk 15:11, and Lk 23:13–25.

Paul makes a similar declaration to Peter's. Paul speaks of God's wisdom versus the wisdom of the world. None of the rulers of this age grasped the wisdom of God, "for if they had, they would not have crucified the Lord of glory" (1 Cor 2:8). Lacking God's wisdom, and so in their ignorance, the Jews put Jesus, "the Lord of glory" to death.

Moreover, the crucified Jesus himself acknowledged that those who were killing him were ignorant and so the Father should forgive them. "Father, forgive them; for they know not what they do" (Lk 23:34). Interestingly, only Luke's Gospel contains this passage, and it is very much in accord with what Peter states in Luke's Acts of the Apostles.

16. Peter's exhortation is in keeping with Jesus's words to Nicodemus in John's Gospel. "Truly, truly, I say to you, unless one is born of water and the Spirit, he cannot enter the kingdom of God. That which is born of the flesh is flesh, and that which is born of the Spirit is spirit" (Jn 3:5–6). Moreover, Jesus tells the Samaritan woman that the water he will give will "become in him a spring of water welling up to eternal life" (Jn 4:14). Baptism in the Holy Spirit inaugurates "the times of refreshing."

would fulfill what was spoken by Isaiah the prophet, "Wash yourselves; make yourselves clean; remove the evil of your doing from my eyes; cease to do evil, learn to do good ... though your sins are like scarlet, they shall be white as snow; though they are red like crimson, they shall become like wool" (Is 1:16–18).

Now, Jesus, the Father's appointed Christ, is he "whom heaven must receive until the time for establishing all that God spoke by the mouth of his holy prophets from of old." Although the gloriously risen and heavenly ascended Jesus is present as the appointed Christ, yet he must also remain in heaven until the end of time comes when all that God foretold by the ancient prophets is fulfilled. Thus, the present times of refreshing will find their eschatological fulfillment when the ascended Jesus returns at the end of time. Nonetheless, because Jesus, the Christ, is present and now active through the apostolic church, those who are baptized in the Holy Spirit already abide in God's eschatological kingdom. For Peter, this can be confirmed through the words of Moses and the other holy prophets.

> Moses said, "The Lord God will raise up for you a prophet from your brethren as he raised me up. You shall listen to him in whatever he tells you. And it shall be that every soul that does not listen to that prophet shall be destroyed from the people." And all the prophets who have spoken, from Samuel and those who came afterwards, also proclaimed these days.

Jesus is the future prophet of whom Moses spoke.[17] Precisely because Jesus is "the prophet," Peter is implying that his Jewish brethren, the very brethren from whom Jesus was chosen, must listen to him. If they do not do so, they will no longer truly be members of the Jewish people, that is, members of God's chosen race. In denying God's Spirit-filled prophet, one rejects the God who sent him, that is the God of their fathers. Likewise, not only did Moses, but also all the prophets, beginning with Samuel, foretell "these days," that is "the times of refreshing" that are now present because the risen prophet Jesus Christ has sent forth the Holy Spirit upon all who believe in him.

In this light, Peter concludes by reminding his Jewish brethren of the dignity they possess as God's chosen people, and so the blessings that God wishes to bestow upon them.

17. See Dt 18:15–19. Some of what Peter quotes is literally taken from Deuteronomy, though the latter part is a briefer summary.

In John's Gospel, some of the Jews considered Jesus to be the "the prophet." When they heard Jesus speak of the coming Holy Spirit, "the people said, 'This is really the prophet.' Others said, 'This is the Christ'" (Jn 7:39–41). To be "the prophet" is to be "the Christ," the one who baptizes in the refreshing waters of the Holy Spirit.

> You are the sons of the prophets and of the covenant which God gave to your father, saying to Abraham, "And in your posterity shall all the families of the earth be blessed." God, having raised up his servant, sent him to you first, to bless you in turning every one of you from your wickedness.

Peter reminds his audience that they are the sons, and so the beneficiaries, of the prophets and of the covenant which he made with their ancestors. They know the prophetic words God spoke to them—words that have now been fulfilled in Jesus, who as a son of Abraham, is the incarnate Son of God.[18] Moreover, as Jews, beginning with their progenitor father Abraham, they possessed a covenantal relationship with God, thus making them singularly his chosen people. Not only are they blessed through this covenantal relationship, but they, in turn, will be the divine means by which all peoples and nations will be blessed by God.[19] Peter concludes by fondly reminding his Jewish brethren that as descendants of Abraham, Jesus is the supreme blessing not only for them but also for all nations—for all who believe in him. Thus, God, having "raised up his servant," Jesus, "sent him to you first, to bless you in turning every one of you from your wickedness."[20] On this encouraging note, Peter concludes his discourse.

18. In John's Gospel, the Jews sarcastically ask Jesus if he "is greater than our father Abraham, who died?" Jesus responds by saying, "Your father Abraham rejoiced that he was to see my day; he saw it and was glad." The Jews retort, "You are not yet fifty years old, and have you seen Abraham?" To which Jesus declares, "Truly, truly, I say to you, before Abraham was, I am [*ego eimi*]" (Jn 8:56–58). Jesus, as a Jew, is a son of Abraham, and so one in whom Abraham would rejoice, for Jesus would not simply be his son, but he would be the incarnate He Who Is, he who existed eternally before Abraham.

The author of the Letter to the Hebrews speaks of Abraham and other Jewish ancestors as "all died in faith, not having received what was promised, but having seen it and greeted it from afar" (Heb 11:13). Thus, with far-seeing faith, Abraham joyfully greeted Jesus's coming "from afar."

19. See Gn 22:15–18.

20. Peter's declaration that Jesus came first to the Jews is confirmed in Matthew's Gospel. Jesus informs the Canaanite woman who wants him to deliver her daughter from a demon, "I was sent only to the lost sheep of Israel" (Mt 15:24). See also Matthew 10:6 where Jesus sends the Twelve to preach the gospel only "to the lost sheep of the house of Israel."

Paul follows this same pattern. He always first preaches the gospel in synagogues. "I am not ashamed of the Gospel: it is the power of God for salvation to everyone who has faith, to the Jews first and also to the Gentiles" (Rom 1:16). Only after the Jews refused to believe in Jesus does Paul then preach to the Gentiles (see Acts 13:44–48). See also Acts 13:5 and 14; 13:14; 14:1; 17:1, 10, and 17; 18:5 and 19.

## Conclusion

Little needs to be said by way of conclusion to chapter three of the Acts of the Apostles. The healing of the lame man in the name of Jesus precipitated the gathering of an amazed crowd, which in turn, occasioned Peter's discourse at Solomon's Portico. Because the God of Abraham, Isaac, and Jacob raised his servant Jesus from the dead, those who have faith in him now possess the power to enact miracles in his name—the Holy and Righteous One, the Author of life. Thus, Peter's Jewish brethren are called to repentance and faith in Jesus as their Savior and Lord, for he is the prophet promised by Moses. Through their faith in Jesus, they will experience this present time of refreshment in the Holy Spirit. They, in turn, will become a blessing to all nations as declared by Abraham.

However, as Peter and John were addressing the people, trouble was brewing. Priests, the temple captain, and the Sadducees were annoyed that they were "proclaiming in Jesus the resurrection of the dead" (Acts 4:1-2). What transpired because of this maddening proclamation is the subject matter of Acts, chapter four.

# *Chapter 4*

## THE ARREST OF PETER AND JOHN

In chapter three of the Acts of the Apostles, Peter and John healed a lame man "in the name of Jesus Christ of Nazareth" (Acts 3:6). This miracle precipitated the gathering of a large crowd in Solomon's Portico in the temple, whereupon Peter proclaimed that Jesus, whom they crucified, the God of Abraham, Isaac, and Jacob, raised gloriously from the dead. Therefore, Peter's Jewish brethren are called to repentance and faith in Jesus as their Savior and Lord, for he is the prophet promised by Moses. By coming to believe in Jesus, they are, in turn, to become a blessing to all nations as declared by Abraham.

As noted previously, Peter's and John's proclamation of Jesus's resurrection infuriated the priests, the temple captain, and the Sadducees. Chapter four of the Acts of the Apostles now narrates what transpired next—the arrest of Peter and John.

### Peter and John Arrested (Acts 4:1-12)

> And as they were speaking to the people, the priests and captain of the temple and the Sadducees came upon them, annoyed because they were teaching the people and proclaiming in Jesus the resurrection from the dead. And they arrested them and put them in custody until the next day, for it was already evening. But many of those who heard the word believed; and the number of the men came to about five thousand.[1]

1. Unless otherwise noted, all Scripture passages in this section are taken from Acts 4:1-12. However, because of the length of this present narrative, it would be of no benefit to provide the entire text at the onset. Further texts will be incorporated in due course.

We find, then, three groups of people who enacted the arrest of Peter and John—the priests, the head of the police who guarded the temple area, and the Sadducees. Importantly, the Sadducees, who were members of the priestly nobility, did not believe in a resurrection.[2] Thus, they, more than the other priests and the temple guards, were outraged with Peter and John, "because they were teaching the people," and specifically because they were "proclaiming in Jesus the resurrection from the dead." The theological implication is not only that Jesus himself is risen from the dead, but also that those who presently abide in him, through faith and baptism, will rise gloriously from the dead as well. It is this twofold, inter-related profession of the resurrection that the Sadducees found appalling, and so adamantly wanted Peter and John to be detained. That being the case, "they arrested them and put them in custody until the next day, for it was already evening." By specifying the late hour of the day, Luke adds historical veracity to the entire narrative. Luke also provides, at this juncture, an aside. "But many of those who heard the word believed; and the number of the men came to about five thousand."

Because the people "heard the word," many believed. What is the nature of the "word" that they heard? Specifically, it is the "apostolic" word, for it was articulated by Peter, the prince of the apostles, in company with the apostle John, Jesus's beloved disciple. The "word" that was taught was, then, the foundational apostolic Christian kerygma—particularly that the crucified-Jesus died for humankind's sin, and that he has been raised from the dead, so that those who believe in him might attain eternal life. The apostle Peter, having first proclaimed the apostolic "word," established it as the kerygmatic

2. To trap Jesus, the Sadducees, as narrated in Mark's Gospel and the other two Synoptic Gospels, asked Jesus about the resurrection from the dead. They proposed what would appear to them an absurd scenario. In accordance with the law of Moses, if a husband dies without bearing any children, his brother should raise up children on his behalf. Now, there were seven brothers, all of whom died without providing any children. The woman herself died. "In the resurrection whose wife will she be? For the seven had her as wife?" Jesus reprimands them for neither knowing Scripture nor the power of God. In heaven there is no marriage. "As for the dead being raised, have you not read in the book of Moses, in the passage about the bush, how God said to him, 'I am the God of Abraham, and the God of Isaac, and the God of Jacob'? He is not God of the dead, but of the living; you are quite wrong" (Mk 12:18-22). See also Mt 22:23-33 and Lk 20:27-40. By mentioning Moses and the bush, Jesus is alluding to the fact that the God of Abraham, Isaac, and Jacob is He Who Is (*Ego Eimi*). God is the God of the living because he is existence itself—he who is simply *ipsum esse*.

Interestingly, as we will eventually examine, Paul precipitated a brawl between the Pharisees, who do believe in the resurrection, and the Sadducees, who do not, by professing at a trial before the Roman tribune that he did believe in the resurrection. Obviously, Paul is referring to Jesus's resurrection and the resurrection of those who believe in him (see Acts 23:6-10).

apostolic "word" for all ages. This apostolic "word" may become more fully comprehended and more fully expressed throughout the coming centuries, but it will not be altered and cannot be changed because of its apostolic nature. It embodies the faith-filled teaching of the apostles themselves.[3]

The trial of Peter and John having been postponed because of the lateness of the day, Luke, after his side remarks, once more picks up the sequence of the narrative.

> On the next day their rulers and elders and scribes were gathered together in Jerusalem, with Annas the high priest and Caiaphas and John and Alexander, and all who were of the high-priestly family. And when they had set them in their midst, they inquired, "By what power or by what name did you do this?" Then Peter, filled with the Holy Spirit, said to them, "Rulers of the people and elders if we are being examined today concerning a good deed done to a cripple, by what means this man was healed, be it known to you all, and to all the people of Israel, that by the name of Jesus Christ of Nazareth, whom you crucified, whom God raised from the dead, by him this man is standing before you well. This is the stone which was rejected by you builders, but which has become the cornerstone. And there is salvation in no one else, for there is no other name under heaven given among men by which we must be saved."

What gathered the next day was the Sanhedrin, that is, the highest Jewish court. Though it would be obvious, Luke specifies that it was held in Jerusalem, the Jewish capital, and so he accentuates its supreme judicial authority. Moreover, Luke enumerates all those who were present. This enumeration highlights not only the eminence of the judges present, but also the seriousness of the charges leveled against Peter and John, charges that would require such a prominent judicial assembly. Annas the high priest is the first named. Although the Roman authorities had replaced him in AD 15, the Jewish authorities continued to accept him as the legitimate high priest. Caiaphas is named next. He was the son-in-law of Annas, and the present high priest appointed by the Romans in AD 18. John's identity is ambiguous. He is thought to be the son of Annas, and he would assume the office of high priest in AD 36, becoming Caiaphas's successor. Luke notes that "all were of the high-priestly family"—a rather Jewish mafia. Moreover, this judicial assembly was, for the most part, the same court that condemned Jesus. "So, the band of soldiers and their captain and the officers of the Jews seized Jesus and bound him. First,

3. Luke notes that those who believed "the word" were about five thousand men. After Peter's Pentecost discourse, Luke stated that "there were added that day about three thousand souls" (Acts 2:41). In mentioning these rather large numbers, Luke wants to testify to the significant rapid growth of the nascent church.

they took him to Annas; for he was the father-in-law of Caiaphas, who was high priest that year" (Jn 18:12-13). Judicially, the deck was stacked. The court that condemned Jesus was not about to exonerate Peter and John for proclaiming that the once-condemned Jesus is risen, and that all who believe in him will also rise to everlasting life.

The members of the Sanhedrin having assembled, "they had set them in their midst," and asked, "By what power or by what name did you do this?" In one sense they already knew the answers to the questions they asked, for they arrested Peter and John because they healed the cripple by the power that resided in the name of the risen Jesus, and because of their subsequent proclamation concerning the resurrection. Nonetheless, such questions were mandatory within a trial setting. The accusatory charges had to be properly ascertained. Such questions did, however, provide Peter with the immediate opportunity to give his interpreted defense of the miraculous event, and he did so "filled with the Holy Spirit."[4]

Peter first acknowledges that those to whom he is speaking are "rulers of the people and elders," thus respectfully recognizing their rightful authority. He then wants to be clear about the nature of the charges laid against him and John, that is, that they are "being examined today concerning a good deed done to a cripple," and "by what means this man was healed." Peter makes evident the obvious. No one can deny that the healing of the cripple was a "good deed." Thus, there is no criminality contained in that "good deed." As to the means by which this good deed was done, "be it known to you all, and to all of the people of Israel, that by the name of Jesus Christ of Nazareth, whom you crucified, whom God raised from the dead, by him this man is standing before you well." Peter wants all those assembled, as well as all the Jewish people, to be assured that the good deed was done in the name of Jesus Christ of Nazareth, the very one whom they have crucified.[5] Peter employs the exact same words he used when enacting the miracle—that it was done in the name of "Jesus" who is the Spirit-anointed "Christ," and who is from Nazareth.[6] By

4. That Peter speaks under the inspiration of the Holy Spirit is in keeping with what Jesus had declared. His disciples will be taken before councils, governors, kings, and synagogues to bear witness to his name. However, they should not be anxious about what they are to say, for what they are to say will be given to them, "for it is not you who speak, but the Spirit of your Father speaking through you" (Mt 10:16-20). See also Mk 13:9-13 and Lk 12:11-12.

5. By including "all the people of Israel" whom he wants to be told of the miracle, Peter manifests that he believes that such knowledge would help elicit faith among his Jewish brethren—both in the present and in the future. Thus, what Luke narrates in the Acts of the Apostles is evangelistic in intent, for the conversion of both Jews and Gentiles alike.

6. See Acts 3:6.

noting that Jesus is from Nazareth, Peter accentuates that Jesus is a historical figure who is from a specific geographical location. Although it may be surprising and incongruous that a historical person from Nazareth is the long promised and presently anticipated Messiah, and that it was by the Spirit-imbued power of his name that this healing was enacted, nonetheless, that is what took place. That the enactment of the miracle was in the name of Jesus of Nazareth attests that he is indeed the Christ. Moreover, as he did previously, Peter curtly observes that his accusers crucified Jesus who is the Christ.[7] However, despite their condemnation of Jesus, "God raised him from the dead"; and it is by the power of the risen Jesus Christ that the cripple "is standing before" them healed.[8] In the light of who Jesus is, what Peter is doing is contrasting the accusations against him and John with the lack of faith among the assembled rulers and elders. If they believed in Jesus as the risen Christ, the present allegations would be resolved immediately —of course a cripple can be healed in the name of Jesus the Christ. Everyone should simply rejoice in the "good deed done." However, what we perceive here at the onset of the apostolic preaching of the gospel is something that will transpire throughout the course of the church's history. In rejecting Jesus as the Christ, the good deeds done by Christians are often interpretated as threats to the wellbeing of those who do not believe, and so the faithful are incessantly persecuted.

Having professed that Jesus of Nazareth is the Christ, Peter declares, "This is the stone which was rejected by you builders, but which has become the cornerstone." Peter is referencing Psalm 118:22. The Psalmist is initially distressed because his enemies have surrounded him on all sides. Yet, he knows that the Lord is his salvation. Thus, "the stone which the builders rejected has become the head of the corner. This is the Lord's doing; it is marvelous in our eyes. This is the day which the Lord has made; let us rejoice and be glad in it."[9] Obviously, Jesus is that "stone" that the unbelieving Jews have rejected.[10]

7. See Acts 3:13–16.

8. The observation that "this man is standing before you well" implies that the man is present at the trial.

9. Ps 118:3 and 22–24.

10. Peter is likely remembering and calling attention to Jesus's parable of the wicked tenants, which some of the Jewish leaders present may have heard Jesus give. In that parable, Jesus tells of a vineyard owner who leased his vineyard to tenants. However, when he sent his various servants to collect the produce, the tenants not only refused to provide the fruit, but they also beat the servants. So, the owner decides that he will send his "beloved son," thinking that they will respect him. Nevertheless, they kill the son so as to inherit the vineyard themselves. The owner then destroys the tenants and says that he will give it to others. At which point, Jesus quotes Psalm 118:22. The vineyard owner is the Father, and Jesus is his beloved

Nonetheless, while the Jewish leaders crucified him, the Lord, by raising Jesus up, has made him the cornerstone of his temple—the church. The risen Jesus, then, is the cornerstone of the living temple, and all who believe in him become Spirit-filled worshippers of the Father.[11] This is the marvel at which all should rejoice, for this day of Jesus's resurrection was made by the Lord. With a tinge of sarcastic irony, Peter refers to the Jewish leaders as "you builders." They are to be builders in two senses. First, as Sadducees, they were in charge of overseeing the present re-building of Herod's temple, a task that was underway from 19 BC to AD 63.[12] Second, as Sadducees, they should also be "build-

---

Son whom he sent. Although the Jewish authorities refused to accept Jesus, the Father will make him the cornerstone. The Jews perceived that Jesus "had told the parable against them." Moreover, they realized that "the vineyard" would be given to the Gentiles. In response, the Jewish leaders attempted to arrest him, but for fear of the multitude they did not do so (see Mt 22:23–33, Mk 12:1–12, and Lk 20:27–38).

11. Peter more fully elaborates upon this notion in his first letter. "Come to him, to that living stone, rejected by men but in God's sight chosen and precious; and like living stones be yourselves built into a spiritual house, to be a holy priesthood, to offer spiritual sacrifices acceptable to God through Jesus Christ. For it stands in Scripture: 'Behold, I am laying in Zion a stone, a cornerstone chosen and precious, and he who believes in him will not be put to shame.' To you therefore who believe, he is precious, for those who do not believe, 'The very stone which the builders rejected has become the cornerstone'" (1 Pt 2:4–7).

12. In John's Gospel, when Jesus cleansed the temple, the Jews asked, "What sign have you to show us for doing this?" In response, Jesus declared, "Destroy this temple, and in three days I will raise it up." To which, the Jews retorted, "It has taken forty-six years to build this temple, and will you raise it up in three days?" At this juncture the Evangelist adds an aside. "But he spoke of the temple of his body" (Jn 2:18–21).

The temple was the building wherein God dwelt. Moreover, within the temple, sacrifices were offered to God. Now, Jesus in saying that if this physical temple is destroyed, he will raise it up in three days, for, as John attests, Jesus, as the Son of God incarnate, is the true temple. His body is the new and living temple, for the Son dwells in that body. Thus, with the coming of the Son of God as man, to come into the presence of God one must come into Jesus's presence—one must abide in him. Likewise, as the Son of God incarnate, Jesus is the new perfect high priest who offers the perfect sacrifice of himself for the forgiveness of sins. Because of his perfect sacrifice, Jesus will rise from the dead in three days. Again, the irony is that Peter and John, within Solomon's Portico, healed the cripple in the name of the risen Jesus Christ, he who is the cornerstone that the Jews rejected, but whom God raised up on the third day, thus making him the ever-living cornerstone of the new temple. What Jesus prophetically declared in John's Gospel has now been fulfilled as narrated in the Acts of the Apostles. The narrative link between the two events is John himself, for he was present at both events. Moreover, because Jesus is the new living temple, wherein he offered himself as the most perfect sacrifice, the stone temple became redundant, having been superseded by Jesus himself. The temple was destroyed by the Romans in AD 70, and there has never been an attempt to rebuild it. From a Christian perspective, this absence of an attempt is theologically important for it bears witness to the truth that the risen Jesus is the everlasting temple in whom his Father is worshiped in communion with the Holy Spirit.

ers" in a spiritual sense, that is, they ought to be building up the spiritual life of the Jewish people. Although they are building the physical temple, they are not aiding in building the spiritual temple, for they have rejected the very cornerstone of that living temple—Jesus Christ.

Peter brings to conclusion his discourse by emphatically declaring the salvific significance of Jesus. "And there is salvation in no one else, for there is no other name under heaven given among men by which we must be saved." Beginning with Peter and John healing the cripple *in the name of Jesus Christ of Nazareth*, Peter has focused on the power of Jesus's name, both within his sermon to the gathered crowd in Solomon's Portico and in his defense before the Sanhedrin.[13] Jesus's name is so powerful that Peter now professes that there is salvation in no one else. Rather, in no other name under heaven or on earth can one be saved.

The name Jesus (in Hebrew, *Joshua*) means YHWH-Saves.[14] This is a divinely given name. The angel Gabriel told Mary that she would conceive and bear a son by the overshadowing of the Holy Spirit, "and you shall call his name Jesus" (Lk 1:30–31). In Matthew's Gospel, "an angel of the Lord appeared to Joseph in a dream," and told him that he need not be afraid to take Mary as his wife, "for that which is conceived in her is of the Holy Spirit; she shall bear a son, and you shall call his name Jesus, for he will save his people from their sins" (Mt 1:20–21). Because Jesus is conceived by the overshadowing of the Holy Spirit, he possesses the Holy Spirit from the moment of his conception, that is, from within his very coming to be, and thus he is, from the moment of his conception, the Spirit-anointed Christ.[15] Of utmost significance is the name of the son conceived in Mary's womb by the Holy Spirit. The one who bears the name, Jesus, will enact his name, YHWH-Saves, and so save the Jewish people as well as the Gentiles from their sin. Jesus will gradually enact his name. Through his earthly ministry—his preaching, healings, miracles, exorcisms, Jesus ever increasingly becomes Jesus. In his sacrificial death

13. See Acts 3:6 and 16; 4:7, 10, 17–18.

14. The book of Sirach states, "Joshua, the son of Nun was mighty in war, and was the successor of Moses in prophesying. He became, in accordance with his name, a great savior of God's elect" (Sir 46:1). Note that while Joshua was named such from birth, he only enacted his name later, that is, when he saved God's people. As we will now see, the same is true of Jesus. He is named Jesus from his conception, but he will only gradually enact his name as YHWH-Saves.

15. The Holy Spirit, then, does not come to dwell in Jesus from without as is the case with those who are baptized. To clarify, when Jesus was baptized by John, and the Spirit descended upon him, that descending-Spirit was the Father's "commissioning Spirit," that is, the Spirit that empowered Jesus to inaugurate his saving ministry—his Father's saving work.

and glorious resurrection, Jesus definitively becomes Jesus, for, through these salvific acts, humankind is freed from sin and death, and so is able to obtain everlasting life.[16] Moreover, having ascended into heaven, the risen Jesus is empowered to send forth his Holy Spirit upon the church, and upon those who come to faith in him and are baptized. Here we now perceive that Jesus is acting as Jesus—YHWH-Saves. The healing of the cripple in his name manifests and testifies to the salvific power of Jesus's name, and thus discloses that one can only obtain salvation in Jesus and in no other name. Jesus is, then, the definitive Lord and universal Savior. His name holds primacy both in heaven and on earth.[17]

## Speaking in Jesus's Name (Acts 4:13-22)

> Now when they saw the boldness of Peter and John, and perceived that they were uneducated, common men, they wondered; and they recognized that they had been with Jesus. But seeing the man that had been healed standing beside them, they had nothing to say in opposition.[18]

When Peter finished his discourse on the salvific power of Jesus's name, the members of the Sanhedrin were surprised by Peter's and John's boldness, for they recognized that they were not learned but "uneducated and common men." This un-educatedness made them "wonder." What could account for their boldness, conviction, and clarity of thought? Luke, as previously noted, provides the answer. Peter was filled with the Holy Spirit.[19] Moreover, though

16. For a fuller theological account of Jesus becoming Jesus, see my three volumes: *Jesus Becoming Jesus: A Theological Interpretation of the Synoptic Gospels* (Washington, DC: The Catholic University of America Press, 2018); *Jesus Becoming Jesus*, vol. 2, *A Theological Interpretation of the Gospel of John: Prologue and Book of Signs* (Washington, DC: The Catholic University of America Press, 2021); and *Jesus Becoming Jesus*, vol. 3, *A Theological Interpretation of the Gospel of John: The Book of Glory and the Passion and Resurrection Narratives* (Washington, DC: The Catholic University of America Press, 2022).

17. Because the Son of God humbled himself in becoming man and in dying on the cross, the Father exalted him and "bestowed on him the name which is above every other name." Therefore, "every knee should bow" and "every tongue confess that Jesus Christ is Lord to the glory of God the Father" (Phil 2:5-11). Similarly, because Jesus is the creator of all and because he is "the first born from the dead," he is "pre-eminent," both in the order of creation and in the order of redemption, "for in him the fullness of God was pleased to dwell" (Col 1:15-20).

18. Unless otherwise noted, all Scripture passages in this section are taken from Acts 4:13-22. However, because of the length of this present narrative, it would be of no benefit to provide the entire text at the onset. Further texts will be incorporated in due course.

19. See Acts 4:8.

Luke is here describing the historical perception of the present assembled Jews, this scenario would be replicated throughout history. Yes, there will be learned and noble Christians who will proclaim the gospel and be persecuted for so doing, yet the vast majority of those who will boldly proclaim the gospel and who will be maltreated throughout the course of history will be common, uneducated folk—to the amazement of their persecutors. They, too, will be inspired by the Holy Spirit.

Though the members of the assembled Jews wondered at Peter's and John's rhetorical ability, they did recognize that they had been followers of Jesus, which may, so they thought, account for their confident proclamation. Jesus himself, as Annas and Caiaphas were aware, boldly proclaimed the good news, and for this reason, they crucified him.[20] Nonetheless, amid their wondering, they saw the man who had been healed standing with Peter and John, and so they thought it prudent not to say anything "in opposition" to the miraculous deed done in Jesus's name.

> But when they had commanded them to go outside of the council, they conferred with one another, saying, "What shall we do with these men? For that a notable sign has been performed through them is manifest to all the inhabitants of Jerusalem, and we cannot deny it. But in order that it may spread no further among the people, let us warn them to speak no more to anyone in his name."

The members of the council were facing a conundrum, and so they sent Peter and John, and the cured cripple outside to confer among themselves on how they might best address the challenge that confronted them. They were befuddled as to what to do with Peter and John. On the one hand, they could not deny that a remarkable "sign" was enacted, and that everyone in Jerusalem was aware of it.[21] So, they could not pretend or deny that it happened. On the other hand, they could not allow this vexing and threatening situation to continue, and so spread further. So, their solution was to forbid Peter and John to speak to anyone "in his name." That they thought Peter and John would obey such a command demonstrates how naïve they were, as will be demonstrated

20. See Acts 3:13–5 and particularly Acts 4:10.

21. In using the word "sign" to denote the miracle, the council is employing a "Johannine" term. In his Gospel, John designates Jesus's seven miracles as "signs," for they signified or manifested his divinity. The present healing of the cripple is a "sign" in that it signifies or attests to Jesus's resurrection, and thus, to the power that resides in his name. While we may assume that Luke is accurately narrating the conversation among the council, we can also conclude that Luke is aware of its Johannine significance, for John would have been, as we have noted previously, the source of Luke's account.

shortly. Moreover, what is more significant is that they did not say that Peter and John cannot preach any longer in Jesus's name, but rather "in *his* name." They found the name of "Jesus" so repugnant that they could not even say it. Psychologically and emotionally, they simply wanted Jesus and his name to vanish from the face of the earth. However, that was impossible, for Jesus had gloriously risen from the dead. Thus, his name is imbued with everlasting salvific power, as demonstrated by the "sign" that Peter and John performed—the "sign" that initiated the conundrum in which the Sanhedrin presently finds itself.

> So, they called them and charged them not to speak or teach at all in the name of Jesus. But Peter and John answered them, "Whether it is right in the sight of God to listen to you rather than to God, you must judge; but for we cannot but speak of what we have seen and heard." And when they had further threatened them, they let them go, finding no way to punish them, because of the people; for all men praised God for what had happened. For the man on whom this sign of healing was performed was more than forty years old.

Luke narrates that, having called Peter and John back into their presence, the assembled Jews, as they had decided, forbade them "to speak or teach at all in the name of Jesus." The "at all" means that not only were they prohibited from speaking of Jesus publicly, such as in Solomon's Portico as they had been doing, but they were also banned from teaching in his name privately behind closed doors. All this proselytizing must cease immediately and forever.

In responding, Peter and John placed the burden of the rightness of their judgment back upon the Sanhedrin. They must judge whether, in the sight of God, it is right for Peter and John to obey God or them. As for Peter and John, they are obliged to declare what they "have seen and heard."[22] What they have heard is all that Jesus taught them throughout his public ministry and after his resurrection. Moreover, they must profess what they have seen, that is, the risen glorified Jesus, and so the one in whom there is the forgiveness of sins and eternal life, for in no other name is there salvation.[23] Thus, the Sanhedrin utterly failed in their attempt at finding a solution to their conundrum. They further threatened Peter and John, but to no effect. In the end, they released them, both because they could not find suitable punishment and for fear of the people who gave glory "to God for what happened"—the healing of the cripple

22. Because of the Holy Spirit, the apostles will bear witness to Jesus "in Jerusalem, and in all of Judea and Samaria and to the end of the earth" (Acts 1:8).

23. At the onset, Luke informs the reader of Acts that the risen Jesus appeared multiple times to the apostles over a forty-day period (see Acts 1:3).

in the name of Jesus.[24] The cured cripple himself became a living "sign" of the salvific power of Jesus's name.[25]

## Rejoicing Among the Spirit-Filled Brethren (Acts 4:23-31)

> When they were released, they went to their friends and reported what the chief priests and the elders had said to them. And when they heard it, they lifted their voices together to God and said, "Sovereign Lord, who made the heaven and the earth and the sea and everything in them, who by the mouth of our father David, your servant said by the Holy Spirit, 'Why did the Gentiles rage, and the peoples imagine vain things, against the Lord and against his Anointed'—for truly in this city there were gathered together against your holy servant Jesus, whom you anointed, both Herod and Pontius Pilate, with the Gentiles and the people of Israel, to do whatever your hand and your plan had predestined to take place."[26]

Having been released, Peter and John immediately "went to their friends." Luke does not enumerate who these friends were, but it is presumed, given the context, that they were fellow Christians living in Jerusalem. Upon their arrival, they told their Christian friends all that "the chief priests and the elders said to them." What they said was that Peter and John were not allowed to proclaim the resurrection of Jesus, nor teach in Jesus's name. Surprisingly, in hearing what appears to be bad news, the fellow Christians of Peter and John "lifted up their voices together to God" in jubilant declarative praise. They realized that such threats of persecution were the fulfillment of Jesus's own prophecy, as noted above—that his disciples would be taken before councils, governors, kings, and synagogues to bear witness to his name.[27] In the midst of such threatening persecution, they could then rejoice, for such harassment was the result of their faithful testimony to Jesus as Lord and Savior.

24. In Mark's Gospel, the Jewish authorities wanted to arrest Jesus but did not because they feared the people (see Mk 12:12).

25. After stating that the Jewish council was afraid of the people, Luke concludes, "For the man on whom the sign of healing was performed was more than forty years old." The "for" thus causally conjoins the council's fear with the age of the healed cripple. Why the council's fear of the people is causally related to the age of the man healed is very abstruse. The only reason I can think of is that, because the man is over forty years old, he could incite the people to riot against the council members, if they had unjustly punished Peter and John.

26. Unless otherwise noted, all Scripture passages in this section are taken from Acts 4:23-31. However, because of the length of this present narrative, it would be of no benefit to provide the entire text at the onset. Further texts will be incorporated in due course.

27. See Mt 10:16-20, Mk 13:9-13, and Lk 12:11-12.

So, they joyfully declared that their "Sovereign Lord" was he "who made the heaven and the earth and the sea and everything in them." Significantly, they began their prayer to the sovereign Lord not in reference to Jesus as the incarnate Son, nor to his salvific death and resurrection, but to the eternal God's work of creation. The sovereign eternal Lord is primordially the Creator, for the act of creation, the making of heaven, earth, and seas, is the first and the foundation of all his further acts. Only within the order of creation will the Father send his Son into the world, and only within this created order will his incarnate Son save humankind from sin and death by dying on the cross and rising from the dead. Moreover, as the Father's gloriously risen Son, Jesus will send forth his Holy Spirit upon those who believe in him, and so establish his church. What began in God's sovereign act of creation is presently being fulfilled within the nascent Christian community, a fellowship that is rejoicing in the privilege of being able to suffer on behalf of Jesus and his gospel, all of which is part of their sovereign Lord's eternal plan.

Their sovereign Lord spoke through the very "mouth" of their "father David," who was also "the servant" of their Lord. Since King David spoke on behalf of God, he spoke "by the Holy Spirit." That the Christians, in their prayer, specified that David spoke by the Holy Spirit is theologically telling. The Acts of the Apostles begins with the risen Jesus ascending into heaven, and, from his heavenly throne, he pours out the Holy Spirit upon the apostles on Pentecost. The Holy Spirit is the supreme fruit of Jesus's death and resurrection—the end for which the Father sent his Son into the world. By acknowledging that King David spoke under the inspiration of the Holy Spirit implies that the Holy Spirit was proleptically active within the whole of salvation history. The sovereign Lord's eternal plan, wherein Jesus's future death and resurrection made it possible for him to send forth the Holy Spirit, allowed for the Holy Spirit to be already active from the moment of God's primordial act of creation. In the light of Jesus, the whole of human history is never devoid of the Holy Spirit.

What, then, did David, the Jews' father and the Lord's servant, prophetically declare by the Holy Spirit? "Why did the Gentiles rage, and the peoples imagine vain things? The kings of the earth set themselves in array, and the rulers were gathered together, against the Lord and against his Anointed." The friends of Peter and John were quoting Psalm 2:1–2. The Psalmist finds it inexplicable that the earth's kings and the rulers would mobilize and array themselves against God and his anointed king. They do so to rebelliously "burst their bonds asunder and cast their cords from us." However, the Lord who "sits in heaven laughs; the Lord has them in derision." In his wrath and fury, he will, nonetheless, "set my king on Zion, my holy hill." He will declare to his anointed, "You are my son, today I have begotten you. Ask of me, and I will make the nations your heritage, and the ends of the earth your possession. You shall break them with a rod of iron and dash them in pieces like a potter's vessel." Thus, if the kings are "wise," they will "serve the Lord with fear," lest, in the Lord's anger, they be destroyed (Ps 2:3–12).

The prayer continues by observing that "truly in this city there were gathered together against your servant Jesus, whom you anointed, both Herod and Pontius Pilate, with the Gentiles and the people of Israel, to do whatever your hand and your plan had predestined to take place." What David prophesied has been fulfilled in their very own city, Jerusalem. Those who gathered together against God's anointed king, Jesus, were both Gentiles and Jews; and they did so under the Jewish king, Herod, and the Roman Gentile ruler, Pilate. Although the prayer of the friends of Peter and John is condemnatory of the actions of Gentiles and the peoples of Israel, yet, surprisingly, the prayer accentuates that such condemnatory deeds were in accordance with God's eternal predestined plan. That these evil actions were divinely foreordained does not lessen the guilt of those who performed them, for they did them freely, though it does manifest that God reigns sovereignly even over the evil that men and women may freely enact.[28]

Having noted that what the Gentiles and Jews did to Jesus was in accordance with the prophetic word of their father, King David, the prayer concludes by asking God's favorable protection.

> And now, Lord, look upon their threats, and grant your servants to speak your word with boldness, while you stretch out your hand to heal, and signs and wonders are performed through the name of your holy servant Jesus.

What precipitated the threatening actions of the Jews was Peter and John healing the cripple in the name of Jesus Christ of Nazareth, and their subsequent proclaiming the gospel with boldness. Remarkably, the Christians in

28. This notion of freely doing what was predestined is also seen with regard to Judas Iscariot, in whom Satan entered (see Lk 22:3). In chapter one of Acts, Peter stated, "Brethren, the scripture had to be fulfilled, which the Holy Spirit spoke beforehand by the mouth of David, concerning Judas who was guide to those who arrested Jesus" (Acts 1:16). As the killing of Jesus was predestined in accordance with what was spoken by the Spirit-filled mouth of David, so Judas's betrayal of Jesus also fulfilled the scriptures (see also Jn 17:12). Nonetheless, in both instances, the evil acts were done freely. The question remains, What Scripture passage did Judas's betrayal fulfill? The Psalmist states, "Even my bosom friend in whom I trusted, / who ate my bread, has lifted his heel against me" (Ps 41:9).

Jerusalem do not beseech the Lord to bring an end to the persecution. Rather, they ask that they be allowed to continue to speak his word with boldness, while he stretches out his healing hand, so as to continue to work wondrous signs; miraculous signs that are enacted in the name of Jesus, his holy servant-Son. In other words, the apostolic church in Jerusalem desires that God empower her with the Holy Spirit so that she might continue to proclaim confidently that there is no redemption apart from Jesus Christ, and that in his name alone is there salvation. God immediately answered this ardent request.

> And when they had prayed, the place in which they were gathered together was shaken; and they were filled with the Holy Spirit and spoke the word of God with boldness.

When the friends of Peter and John completed their prayer, the house where they had gathered shook. The coming of the Holy Spirit upon them was the cause of this earthquake-type shaking. Having been filled with the Holy Spirit, they, in answer to their prayer, boldly proclaimed God's word. This event, sometimes referred to as "the little Pentecost," resembles the coming of the Holy Spirit upon the apostles on Pentecost. Then there was a heavenly rushing sound like a mighty wind which filled the house. Tongues of fire rested upon the heads of the apostles. Whereupon, having been filled with the Holy Spirit, they "began to speak in other tongues, as the Spirit gave them utterance" (Acts 2:1–4). Presently, the shaking of the house manifests the coming of the Holy Spirit upon them, causing them to proclaim boldly God's word. In both instances, the outpouring of the Holy Spirit is the impetus that compels those who have received the Spirit to preach the gospel. Within the contemporary church this is witnessed in the Charismatic Renewal. Those who are baptized in the Spirit immediately proclaim boldly that Jesus is the universal Savior and definitive Lord. Such testimony is in keeping with Jesus's promise to his apostles. When they receive the Holy Spirit, "you shall be my witnesses in Jerusalem and in all of Judea and Samaria and to the end of the earth" (Acts 1:8).

What we perceive thus far in chapter four of the Acts of the Apostles is Jesus *being* Jesus, that is, enacting his name as YHWH-Saves. He does so through the instrumentality of church as the apostolic community. It is Peter and John who heal the cripple in his name, and who proceed to bear witness to his resurrection, and thus that in him alone is salvation. Moreover, the friends of Peter and John, the nascent Jerusalem church, boldly proclaim, amid persecution, God's word by the power of the Holy Spirit, that is, that the sovereign Lord's anointed one is Jesus Christ. Thus, not only is Jesus YHWH-Saves, but God the Father, who anointed Jesus as the Spirit-filled Christ, is also YHWH-Saves. Similarly, the Holy Spirit is YHWH-Saves, for it is through, with, and in him that Jesus, the Christ, enacts his Father's salvific work. The apostolic church is, therefore, the salvific presence of the entire Trinity. It is, thus, the sacrament, the saving, efficacious sign, wherein and through which the persons of the Trinity, each according to his distinct identity, enact humankind's salvation. Moreover, by being a member of the apostolic church, one partakes of and so reaps the benefits of the Trinity's saving acts—acts wherein Jesus is being Jesus as the Father's risen, Spirit-filled, incarnate Son.

## The Communal Life of the Apostolic Church (Acts 4:32–37)

> Now the company of those who believed were of one heart and soul, and no one said that any of the things which he possessed was his own, but they had everything in common. And with great power the apostles gave their testimony to the resurrection of the Lord Jesus, and great grace was upon them all.[29]

Luke, at this juncture, interrupts his historical narrative concerning the activity of Peter and John. He inserts a brief description of the communal life of the apostolic church.[30] Of first importance is the unity of "heart and soul" among the believing brethren. This oneness was founded upon their unity of faith—they all believed the one gospel proclaimed by the apostles. The manner in which this one faith manifested itself was by everything being owned in common. Unity of faith fostered one common life—a testimony that they all belonged to the one living body of Christ. Together, they were brothers and sisters in Christ.

Moreover, within this community of faith, the apostles powerfully bore witness "to the resurrection of the Lord Jesus, and grace was upon them all." Once again, Luke accentuates that this harmony of faith resided in their belief in Jesus, who was their risen divine Lord (Yahweh). Because of their faith in

29. Unless otherwise noted, all Scripture passages in this section are taken from Acts 4:32–37. However, because of the length of this present narrative, it would be of no benefit to provide the entire text at the onset. Further texts will be incorporated in due course.

30. Earlier Luke noted the attributes that defined the first Christians. "And they held steadfastly to the apostles' teaching and fellowship, to the breaking of the bread, and to the prayers" (Acts 2:42). Here there is a theological emphasis—loyalty to the apostolic teaching, which, in turn, fostered Christian fellowship, which, then, fully expressed itself in the Eucharistic liturgy and in their common prayer. What is now primarily emphasized is the common communal life that flows from their unity of faith.

the Lord Jesus, the Holy Spirit continued to pour an abundance of grace upon them. Again, this grace manifested itself in their communal apostolic life.

> There was not any one needy among them, for as many as were possessors of lands or houses sold them, and brought the proceeds of what was sold and laid it at the apostles' feet. Thus, Joseph who was surnamed by the apostles Barnabas (which means, Son of encouragement), a Levite, a native of Cyprus, sold a field which belonged to him, and brought the money and laid it at the apostles' feet.

None were poor or needy among them, for those who were affluent sold their possessions and gave them to the apostles. Whereupon the trusted apostles would distribute the communal contributions. Luke provides, as an example, a man named "Joseph." What is fascinating is that Luke describes him in detail, thus indicating that he must have been a well-known and respected person. Although his name is Joseph, the apostles gave him the surname of "Barnabas," which presumably defined his personality. He was a "son of encouragement." Amid the trials and persecutions of the early Christian community, he must have stood out as one who reassured his brothers and sisters to be steadfast in the faith; and he must have done so with great confidence and cheer. Moreover, he was a Levite, and thus part of the Jewish priestly class. Being such, the other Jewish believers would have trusted him and his witness to the gospel. Lastly, Luke also informs the reader that Barnabas was from Cyprus. Now, this man sold his field and gave the money to the apostles. Nonetheless, why did Luke choose this particular man to highlight?

As we will see, after his conversion, Paul wanted to visit the Christian community in Jerusalem. The disciples, however, "were all afraid of him," for they doubted his discipleship. Barnabas, nonetheless, befriended him, and "brought him to the apostles." Barnabas spoke of Paul's conversion and "how at Damascus he preached boldly in the name of Jesus" (Acts 9:26–27). Moreover, when persecution broke out after the martyrdom of Stephen, some disciples went to Antioch where they successfully preached the gospel. When news of this success reached Jerusalem, "they sent Barnabas to Antioch," "for he was a good man, full of the Holy Spirit and of faith." From there he went in search of Paul at Tarsus and brought him to Antioch. Together, "for a whole year they met with the Church and taught a large company of people" (Acts 11:22–26). Subsequently, the church in Antioch, at the inspiration of the Holy Spirit, commissioned Barnabas and Paul and sent them out on Paul's first missionary journey.[31] Sadly, Paul and Barnabas later separated. They separated be-

31. See Acts 13:1–3.

cause of a dispute over John Mark, who had earlier deserted Paul and Barnabas during that first missionary journey. Barnabas wanted to take John Mark with them on the second missionary journey, but Paul refused to accept him. Thus, Barnabas took John Mark with him to Cyprus, and Paul set off on his second missionary journey.[32]

Although Luke paints a glowing picture of the communal life among the first Christians in Jerusalem, the above dispute between Paul and Barnabas testifies that such was not always the case. Moreover, as we will shortly see in chapter five of the Acts of the Apostles, not everyone was willing to place all their money into the common pot. Because of this reluctance, Luke's lustrous portrayal of the emerging Jerusalem community may be somewhat idealized—what the church should be, but never fully is. Only in heaven will all believers be "of one heart and soul," for only then will the body of Christ be made perfect in the love of the Holy Spirit.

## Conclusion

In the above theological interpretation of chapter four of the Acts of the Apostles, we found Peter and John being detained because of their bold preaching of the gospel, specifically that the crucified Jesus is gloriously risen. The members of the Sanhedrin demanded that they cease preaching in the name of Jesus. However, they testified that they were compelled to proclaim what they heard and saw. Instead of becoming alarmed by such threats, Peter and John, joined by the Jerusalem Christian community, rejoiced amid the persecution. They would not be bullied into silence. They would boldly bear witness to Jesus Christ, their risen Lord and Savior. In this perilous atmosphere, the Christian community lived a common life of faith and of communal care for one another.

We find in chapter five of Acts the strains within this communal Christian life. The apostles will continue to perform acts of healing in Jesus's name, and they will once again be arrested and placed on trial. This will again cause rejoicing among the Jerusalem Christians. With that in mind, we will continue to theologically interpret Luke's historical narrative.

32. See Acts 15:36–41.

## *Chapter 5*

# TRIBULATIONS AND SUCCESSES

In chapter four of the Acts of the Apostles, Peter and John are detained because of their preaching. The Sanhedrin demanded that they cease preaching in the name of Jesus. However, instead of becoming alarmed, Peter and John, joined by the Jerusalem Christian community, rejoiced amid the persecution. They would not be frightened, but rather they would boldly bear witness to Jesus Christ, their risen Lord and Savior.

What we will now find in chapter five of Acts are the tribulations that the early apostolic church continues to experience, both from within and from without. The apostles also continue to perform acts of healing in Jesus's name, and they are, again, arrested and placed on trial. Once again, such hardship occasions rejoicing among the Jerusalem Christians. With the above in mind, we can continue our theological interpretation of Luke's historical narrative.

## Ananias and Sapphira (Acts 5:1–11)

> But a man named Ananias with his wife Sapphira sold a piece of property, and with his wife's knowledge he kept back some of the proceeds and brought a part and laid it at the apostles' feet. But Peter said, "Ananias, why has Satan filled your heart to lie to the Holy Spirit and to keep back part of the proceeds of the land? While it remained unsold, did it not remain your own? And after it was sold, was it not at your disposal? How is it that you contrived this deed in your heart? You have not lied to men but to God." When Ananias heard these words, he fell down dead. And a great fear came upon all who heard of it. The young men rose and wrapped him up and carried him out and buried him.[1]

1. Unless otherwise noted, all scripture passages in this section are taken from Acts 5:1–11.

In chapter four Luke informs the reader that "the company of those who believed were of one heart and soul, and no one said that any of the things which he possessed was his own, but they had everything in common" (Acts 4:32). Presently, it appears that Ananias and Sapphira gave the impression that they willingly contributed all their possessions as well. However, having "sold a piece of property," Ananias, "with his wife's knowledge" retained some of the proceeds, and "brought only part and laid it at the apostles' feet." Peter, under the inspiration of the Holy Spirit, perceived Ananias's and Sapphira's deception, and so he confronts Ananias. It was Satan who filled his heart, and, in so doing, induced him "to lie to the Holy Spirit," and thus deceitfully "to hold back part of the proceeds of the land." Peter continues to explain the moral implications of the situation. As long as the property remained unsold, it belonged to Ananias. Even after he sold it, the proceeds belonged to him, and he could do with them as he wished.[2] If such implications are the case, why then, Peter asks, did Ananias contrive this demonic deception? "You have not lied to men but to God." Here, here are irreconcilable enemies—Satan and the Holy Spirit, who is God.

Satan is the father of lies. In John's Gospel, Jesus declares that Satan "was a murderer from the beginning, and has nothing to do with the truth, because there is no truth in him. When he lies, he speaks according to his nature, for he is a liar and the father of lies."[3] Thus, Ananias fell prey to Satan's deceit and

---

However, because of the length of this present narrative, it would be of no benefit to provide the entire text at the onset. Further texts will be incorporated in due course.

2. In his Second Letter to the Corinthians, Paul instructs the Corinthians on how they should approach the collection that was being taken up for the impoverished Christians in Jerusalem. He noted that the Christians in Macedonia "gave according to their means, and beyond their means, of their own free will." Since the Corinthians excel in every way, Paul exhorted them to be "gracious" in this work as well. Paul was not demanding that they contribute, but he hoped that they would live up to their generous reputation. Again, Paul stated the basic principle, "Each one must do as he has made up his mind, not reluctantly or under compulsion, for God loves a cheerful giver. And God is able to provide you with every blessing in abundance, so that you may always have enough of everything and may provide in abundance for every good work... Thanks be to God for his inexpressible gift!" (2 Cor 8:1–9:15).

For Paul, love obliges generosity, and such gracious giving needs to be given freely, and in accord with one's means. There should be no sense of compulsion or reluctance, but the gift should be accompanied by joy, for, as God has joyfully given all graces, so he joyfully loves a cheerful giver. Ananias was not a cheerful giver. Rather, he was a deceitful giver, and God, therefore, was not pleased.

3. Jn 8:44. In the book of Genesis, it is Satan, disguised as a serpent, who deceives Adam and Eve, and, in so doing, they committed the first sin (see Gn 3:1–8). Moreover, as implied in what Jesus states, Satan is a murderer for he provoked Cain to kill his brother Abel, the first murder and murderer after the fall of Adam and Eve.

lied. In so doing, he assumed the nature and character of Satan himself. However, although he thought he was deceiving Peter, Ananias was really lying "to the Holy Spirit," which is impossible, since the Holy Spirit, as God, is the Spirit of truth.[4]

God the Father is the fount of all truth. As the Father's Word, the Son possesses the fullness of truth as the perfection of his Father's image. The Holy Spirit possesses the fullness of truth, and so is the Spirit of truth, for he proceeds from the Father, the source of all truth, and from the Son who, as the Father's Word, perfectly reflects the truth of the Father. The Father and Son mutually love one another in the love of the Holy Spirit, for, as the Spirit of Truth, he engenders, and so accentuates, the truth that they fully and lovingly share with one another. Thus, Ananias did not lie "to men but to God"—the Holy Spirit of Truth. Abruptly, and quite unexpectedly, Luke informs the reader that, upon hearing Peter's words, Ananias "fell down and died."

Death, as the punishment for lying to the Holy Spirit, may, at first sight, seem rather extreme. However, to attempt to deceive the Holy Spirit, who is the Spirit of Truth, can be interpreted as blasphemy against the Holy Spirit. In Matthew's Gospel, Jesus decidedly declares, "I tell you, every sin and blasphemy will be forgiven men, but the blasphemy against the Spirit will not be forgiven."[5] To attempt to deceive the Holy Spirit, the Spirit of truth, is to blaspheme the Spirit, to sin against the very nature of who the Spirit is. Thus, such a sin is unforgiveable, for it transgresses the very Spirit in whom one can be forgiven. Thus, the wages of such a sin is death—and so Ananias "fell down and died." As noted above, Jesus calls Satan a murderer. Although Satan did not directly kill Ananias, yet he was fully under Satan's power and authority, and so he suffered the malediction that accrued to him, that is, death. Ananias's physical death confirmed that he was in league with the primordial murderer—Satan himself.

Now, with the sudden death of Ananias, "great fear came upon all who heard of it." I believe this "great fear" is twofold. First, those who heard of Ananias's death, both Christians and non-believers, which death was a result of his lying to Peter, stood in awe of Peter and the apostles. So significant were the apostles within the apostolic community that to lie to them was the same as lying to the Holy Spirit, and was deserving of death. Secondly, this awe was also imbued with "great fear." A lesson was learned—one does not fool around with the apostles. If one does, one does so at one's own risk. You may get into

4. See Jn 14:16–17, 14:26, 15:26, and 16:7–11.

5. Mt 12:31. See also Mk 3:28–30 and Lk 12:10.

trouble, and you may even end up dead. Why? The apostles speak and act on behalf of the risen Lord Jesus Christ, and they do so with the authority and power of none other than the Holy Spirit. They possess a Spirit-commissioned authority given to them by Jesus himself, and so a divine reckoning is warranted. Thus, ironically, the death of Ananias became a fearful, awe-inspiring endorsement of the truth of the apostolic gospel.

Luke concludes his narrative concerning Ananias and his death in a very practical manner. "The young men rose and wrapped him up and carried him out and buried him." Despite his deadly sin, the body of Ananias was treated with great respect. He was buried in a proper Jewish manner. That the men who buried him were "young" testifies to the historicity of the entire event. Luke is informing the reader exactly what John had witnessed and later conveyed to him.

After Ananias's burial, Luke continues by narrating what transpired concerning Sapphira.

> After an interval of about three hours his wife came in, not knowing what had happened. And Peter said to her, "Tell me whether you sold the land for so much." And she said, "Yes, for so much." But Peter said to her, "How is it that you have agreed together to tempt the Spirit of the Lord? Listen, the feet of those that have buried your husband are at the door, and they will carry you out." Immediately she fell down at his feet and died. When the young men came in, they found her dead, and they carried her out and buried her beside her husband. And great fear came upon the Church, and upon all who heard of these things.

So, after about three hours, Sapphira came into the place where the apostles were residing. Unbeknownst to her is the death of her husband. Peter, as he did with Ananias, initiated the questioning. Peter asked her whether she and her husband "sold land for so much," though Luke does not inform the reader as to the exact amount. More than likely, John forgot what the exact amount was, though he did know at one point. Sapphira confirms that Peter accurately knows the correct amount. Little did she know that, in so saying, she condemned herself, a condemnation that brought with it the sentence of death. Having replied in the affirmative, Peter then asked her the rhetorical condemnatory question. "How is it that you have agreed together to tempt the Spirit of the Lord?" In cahoots with her husband, they together attempted to deceive Peter, pretending to have given him all the proceeds from their sale of the land, when they were retaining some of the profit. Moreover, in so doing, they were tempting "the Spirit of the Lord," that is, the Spirit of the Lord Jesus

Christ. How did their deceit "tempt" the Spirit? Can the Spirit be tempted? Obviously, the Spirit of Truth cannot be tempted to tell a lie. However, the couple, by attempting to deceive Peter, was also tempting the Spirit in that they presumed or hoped that the Spirit would remain silent and not divulge their ruse. However, the Holy Spirit, being the Spirit of truth, never consented to their attempt at tempting him to remain silent. Rather, Peter immediately recognized that the whole scheme was a satanic plot, and thus a falsehood that was not only perpetrated against him, but also a "lie to the Holy Spirit." The Spirit of Truth, and not the father of lies, won the day.

Peter then instructs Sapphira to pay heed. "Listen, the feet of those that have buried your husband are at the door, and they will carry you out." With the clomping of the approaching feet and the creaking of the opening door, Sapphira, immediately, "fell down at his (Peter's) feet and died." Having died in the same manner as her husband, the young men "carried her out and buried her beside her husband." Together they contrived their deception, so together they are buried.

Luke, once again, informs the reader that "great fear came upon the whole Church, and upon all who heard of these things." The "things" that were heard were the deaths of Ananias and Sapphira. Their deaths occasioned "great fear," both within and without the church. As already noted earlier, this "great fear" was the recognition of the awesome authority and power of the apostles.

Of theological significance is Luke's employing, for the first time, the Greek word *ekklēsia* (church) which designates an assembly or congregation. It appears twenty-three times in the Acts of the Apostles.[6] Within Greek secular literature it denoted a social or political gathering, but in the Old Testament it refers to a worshiping community.[7] Thus, in the New Testament, *ekklēsia*, following the Old Testament usage, specifies the gathering of the worshiping Christian community both here on earth and in heaven.[8]

## The Healing of Many (Acts 5:12-16)

> Now many signs and wonders were done among the people by the hands of the apostles. And they were all together in Solomon's Portico. None of the rest dared join them, but the people held them in high honor. And more than

6. See, for example, Acts 8:1, 8:26, 14:23 and 27, 15:3 and 22, and 18:22.

7. See Dt 9:10, Jos 8:35, and 1 Kgs 8:65.

8. In the remainder of the New Testament, it appears ninety-one times. See, for example, Mt 16:18 and 18:17, Rom 16:16, 1 Cor 1:2, Eph 3:10 and 5:23, and Heb 12:22-23.

> ever believers were added to the Lord, multitudes both of men and women, so that they even carried out the sick into the streets, and laid them on beds and pallets, that as Peter came by at least his shadow might fall on some of them. The people also gathered from the towns around Jerusalem, bringing the sick and those afflicted with unclean spirits, and they were healed.[9]

Having finished telling the disturbing events surrounding Ananias and Sapphira, Luke proceeds on a happier note. The apostles continued to work "many signs and wonders among the people." The wondrous signs bear witness to Jesus's resurrection, for they were worked in his name. Such signs were performed among "the people," that is, among the entire population living in Jerusalem, since the apostles were gathered openly in Solomon's Portico. Luke notes that "none of the rest dared to join them, but the people held them in high honor." Who are the "none of the rest?" It would appear that Luke is referring to the populace that were not Christian. Even non-believers esteemed the apostles. That such is the case, can be discerned by what Luke states immediately following. "And more than ever believers were added to the Lord, multitudes both men and women." Because the apostles were held in such high regard, they, by their personal integrity and by their preaching, converted many people "to the Lord," that is, to Jesus, who is the risen, incarnated, divine Son of God, and so the Lord (YHWH). So great was the number of conversions that Luke speaks of "multitudes," and accentuates that these multitudes were composed of "men and women."[10] This encouraging development was not a feminine phenomenon due to the masculine charm of the apostles.

Because of the signs and wonders worked by the apostles, the people "even carried out the sick into the streets and laid them on beds and pallets." The hope was that, even if the apostles could not heal them all individually, "at least Peter's shadow might fall on some of them." At first, such frenzied activity may appear to be excessive enthusiasm. However, it rather testifies to the people's ardent faith—a faith that trusts that even Peter's shadow, a silhouette of the person, contains the healing and saving power of Jesus. Not only did the people of Jerusalem bring out the ailing, but the people from the surrounding towns also brought "the sick and those afflicted with unclean spirits, and they were healed." Significantly, all these apostolic healings and exorcisms replicate Jesus's signs and wonders. The risen Jesus continues his salvific work, and he

9. Unless otherwise noted, all scripture passages in this section are taken from Acts 5:12-16.

10. Here Luke is once more highlighting the phenomenal growth of the early church. See Acts 2:41, 2:47, 4:4, 6:7, 11:21, 11:24, and 21:20. Such growth was a sign of the work of the Holy Spirit—engendering faith in Jesus as Lord and Savior.

does so now through his apostles within his Spirit-empowered church. To be the church of Jesus Christ is continually to make present, throughout the ages, his saving work. The risen Jesus continues to be Jesus—YHWH-Saves.

## The Arrest and Imprisonment of the Apostles (Acts 5:17–32)

> But the high priest rose up and all who were with him, that is, the party of the Sadducees, and filled with jealousy they arrested the apostles and put them in the common prison. But at night an angel of the Lord opened the prison doors and brought them out and said, "Go and stand in the temple and speak to the people all the words of this Life." And when they heard this, they entered the temple at daybreak and taught.[11]

The popularity of the apostles, as they preached in Solomon's Portico, did not go unnoticed by the temple's high priest, Annas or Caiaphas, and the priestly party of the Sadducees. They observed all that was taking place—the signs and wonders, the teaching, and the ever-growing number of people, even from outside of Jerusalem. They were not happy, and Luke informs the reader as to why—they were jealous. The temple, including Solomon's Portico, was under the purview of the priestly class, but now it had been commandeered by the apostles and their animated devotees. As with the earlier preaching of Peter and John, the Jewish leaders concluded that such mutinous activity had to cease. So "they arrested the apostles and put them in the common prison." However, their incarceration was short-lived.

At night "an angel of the Lord opened the prison doors and brought them out." This is the first of a number of interventions by an angel, whereby the apostles are provided divine aid or instruction.[12] Having supernaturally opened the doors, the angel brings them out and gives them a charge. They are to return to the temple, the very place where they were arrested, and proclaim to the people "all of the words of this Life." Here, the word "Life" possesses a twofold interrelated meaning. First, the words of this "Life" are those words that give life, that is, that Jesus is risen and so is alive. Second, by believing that the risen Jesus is the Father's incarnate Son, one obtains everlasting

11. Unless otherwise noted, all scripture passages in this section are taken from Acts 5:17–32. However, because of the length of this present narrative, it would be of no benefit to provide the entire text at the onset. Further texts will be incorporated in due course.

12. See Acts 8:26, 10:3–6, 12:7–10, 12:23, and 27:23–24. We have seen that the title "Lord," as a divine name, has been applied to Jesus. Here it is generically applied to simply "God."

life—all those who believe in Jesus as Lord and Savior will also rise gloriously from the dead. The apostles obeyed the angel's instructions. At daybreak, they once more entered the temple and began to preach the gospel of life. All of this was unbeknownst to the high priest and his court.

> Now the high priest came and those who were with him and called together the council and all the senate of Israel, and sent to prison to have them brought. But when the officers came, they did not find them in prison, and they returned and reported. "We found the prison securely locked and the sentries standing at the doors, but when we opened it, we found no one inside."

Everything was in order. The priests were in attendance, the council was present, even Israel's senate was at hand. Moreover, normality governed the prison. It was securely locked, and the guards were attentively standing watch. What was abnormal was that the prison was empty—"no one was inside." "Now when the captain of the temple and the chief priests heard these words, they were perplexed about them, wondering what this would come to." Upon hearing the account of the locked but empty prison, the authorities were befuddled and mystified, not simply by the unexplainable mystery of the prison being empty, but more so by its future implications—"what would this come to." They soon obtained their answer.

"And some one came and told them, 'The men whom you put in prison are standing in the temple and teaching the people.'" The situation was back to where it began. Because the apostles were teaching in the temple, they were arrested and put into prison. Having been set free by an angel, they took up where they left off—they were once again in the temple teaching the people. God's word will not be imprisoned.[13]

Upon hearing this distressing news, "the captain with the officers went and brought them, but without violence for they were afraid of being stoned by the people." In the end, there is irony. For fear of being stoned by ordinary people, the armed temple guard peaceably brought the apostles back to the Jewish authorities. Obviously, the apostles would not have put up a struggle, which would have precipitated violence. It is "the people" that was of concern. Significantly, the temple guard were fearful of being "stoned." In the Old Testament, stoning was the punishment for blasphemy. "He who blasphemes the

13. Psalm 50:3 declares, "Our God comes, he does not keep silence." More pertinent are Paul's words. "Remember Jesus Christ, risen from the dead, descended from David, as preached in my gospel, the gospel for which I am suffering and wearing fetters like a criminal. But the word of God is not fettered" (2 Tm 2:8–9). The voice of the risen Jesus will never be silenced. For all ages, the apostolic church will proclaim the good news of Jesus Christ, even in chains.

name of the Lord shall be put to death; all the congregation shall stone him" (Lv 24:16). By arresting the apostles for proclaiming Jesus to be the Spirit-filled, risen Son of God the Father, the unbelieving temple guards were, indirectly, committing blasphemy, and so they justly should be stoned by all the people. To blaspheme the proclaimer is to blaspheme the proclaimed.

> And when they had brought them, they set them before the council. And the high priest questioned them, saying, "We strictly charged you not to teach in this name, yet here you have filled Jerusalem with your teaching and intend to bring this man's blood upon us."

Although Luke informs the reader that the council "questioned" the apostles, whom they set before them, the Jewish authorities, in fact, accused them of disobeying what they had previously proscribed. The apostles continued "to teach in this name," and in so doing they have unbearably "filled Jerusalem" with their teaching, that is again, that Jesus is the risen Lord and Savior, and that apart from his name there is no salvation. What is worse is that the apostles "intend to bring this man's blood upon" them. Noticeably, the council members appear purposely to refuse to refer to Jesus by his name. They refer to "this name," and "this man," but not to "Jesus" as the name of this man. They find the name, Jesus, agonizing to hear or insufferable to say. Why? They are filled with guilt and refuse to admit it. That is why they are so distraught by the apostles intending "to bring this man's blood upon" them. Earlier, within their prayer to the "sovereign Lord," the Jerusalem Christians declared that, though Jesus was the Lord's anointed servant, "both Herod and Pontius Pilate, with the Gentiles and the peoples of Israel" condemned and crucified Jesus (Acts 4:27). Moreover, the council members likely cringingly remember what they, and the frenzied crowd that they had whipped up, declared when Pilate washed his hands and avowed himself innocent of Jesus's blood. "His blood be on us and on our children."[14] Presently, they refuse to acknowledge that they clamored for Jesus's crucifixion and death, and even called down his blood upon them. Rather, they find it utterly repugnant and totally objectionable that the apostles now intend to hold them accountable for Jesus's blood. The members of the Jewish council were attempting to rewrite history that they might assuage their guilt and so lessen their culpability in the shedding of Jesus's blood.

14. Mt 27:24–25. The irony is that, although the Jewish leaders want to take responsibility for Jesus's death by calling down his blood upon them, they are calling down upon themselves the blood by which they would be saved. Obviously, the whole Jewish nation is not guilty in condemning and crucifying Jesus, but only those who actively sought Jesus's death.

> But Peter and the apostles answered, "We must obey God rather than men. The God of our fathers raised Jesus whom you killed by hanging him on a tree. God exalted him at his right hand as Leader and Savior; to give repentance to Israel and forgiveness of sins. And we are witnesses to these things, and so is the Holy Spirit whom God has given to those who obey him."

In response to their once more being arrested and being taken before the Sanhedrin, Peter, as head of the apostles and speaking on their behalf, lays down a foundational principle. They, with the implication that it applies to all Christians, "must obey God rather than men." If there arises an irreconcilable difference between what the secular government or the prevailing society demands and what God commands, Christians must be obedient to God.[15]

Peter next delineates what God has done in relation to Jesus. "The God of our fathers," the God not only of Peter and of the apostles, but also of all the Jews, and thus the God of Abraham, Isaac, and Jacob, that God "raised Jesus whom" the members of the Sanhedrin "killed by hanging him on a tree."[16] Although the Jewish leaders crucified Jesus, the God of their very own fathers raised him from the dead. Moreover, their God "exalted him at his right hand as Leader and Savior," and he did so to allow Israel to repent and so receive forgiveness. Peter's remarks interweave two contrasting truths—what "the God of our fathers" has done, and what Jewish leaders have done. Although the Jews rejected Jesus by hanging him "on a tree," God "exalted him this right hand," and thus made him "Leader and Savior."[17] God did this so that Israel,

15. Over the centuries, many Christian martyrs put this principle into practice. Thomas More is an excellent example. Before being decapitated, he declared, "I die the king's good servant, and God's first." Thomas More and Peter were of one mind.

16. Peter is alluding to Deuteronomy 21:22-23. And if a man has committed a crime punishable by death and he is put to death, and you hang him on a tree, his body shall not remain all night upon the tree, but you shall bury him the same day, for a hanged man is accursed by God; you shall not defile your land which the Lord your God gives you for an inheritance. The practice of hanging an executed criminal on a tree was to deter God's wrath (see Nm 25:4). Paul, in his Letter to the Galatians, applies this to Christ and states, "Christ redeemed us from the curse of the law, having become a curse for us—for it is written, "Cursed be everyone who hangs on a tree"—that in Christ Jesus the blessings of Abraham might come upon the Gentiles, that we might receive of the Spirit through faith." Jesus, by hanging on the cross, bore the curse of sin. However, by offering up his life as a loving sacrifice to the Father, he freed humankind from the curse of sin, and won for us the new life of the Holy Spirit, the Spirit we receive when we believe in Jesus Christ as our Lord and Savior.

17. The risen Jesus, upon his ascension into heaven, comes to sit at his Father's right hand in glory, and in so doing, is exalted by the Father as the Leader and Savior of all of humankind. Jesus can be seen as "Leader" in two ways. First, as Ruler and Lord, Jesus leads all who believe in him to salvation. Second, in John's Gospel, Jesus declares, "I am the way, and the truth, and the life; no one comes to the Father, but by me" (Jn 14:6). As the Father's incarnate Word, Jesus

that is, all the Jews, might obtain forgiveness of their sins through the gift of repentance.

Having professed all that the God of the Jewish fathers has done for Jesus, Peter draws his conclusion. "And we are witnesses to these things, and so is the Holy Spirit whom God has given to those who obey him." Peter and the apostles, as well as the Holy Spirit, bear testimony to all that they have seen concerning Jesus—the "things" that he had just delineated. Peter's reference to the Holy Spirit is theologically significant.

In John's Gospel, Jesus tells his apostles that, while he was still with them, he has taught them many "things." "But the Counselor, the Holy Spirit, whom the Father will send in my name, he will teach you all things, and bring to your remembrance all that I have said to you" (Jn 14:26). The Holy Spirit is the one who will ensure that the apostles teach "all things," and that they will remember all that Jesus taught them. Subsequently, Jesus, again, informs the apostles that when he sends the Counselor from the Father, "even the Spirit of truth, who proceeds from the Father, he will bear witness to me; and you also are witnesses, because you have been with me from the beginning" (Jn 15:26–27). Here, the Holy Spirit of truth will bear witness to Jesus as will the apostles, for they were with him from the onset of his salvific ministry. Now, in his above statement, it is as if Peter was remembering what Jesus told the apostles as found in John's Gospel. They can now bear witness to all "these things" concerning Jesus because they were with him "from the beginning." They can do so because the Holy Spirit is presently teaching and reminding them of all that Jesus said and did. Thus, the Holy Spirit, the Spirit of truth, is performing the tasks that Jesus prophesied that he would do. Similarly, by the power of the Holy Spirit, the Spirit of truth, the apostles are enacting the charges that Jesus assigned to them—that of bearing witness to all that he said and did from the beginning.

Peter states that not only are the apostles bearing witness to Jesus, but that the Holy Spirit himself is also testifying to Jesus. The question arises, Does the Holy Spirit bear witness apart from the apostles, as seemingly implied by Peter's statement? The Holy Spirit himself, apart from the apostles, does attest to Jesus in that Jesus is the one who sends the Holy Spirit upon the apostles and, in so doing, founds his apostolic church. Thus, within Jesus's very act of sending forth of the Holy Spirit, the Spirit in and through whom the church comes

---

fully manifests the truth of the Father, and thus, leads us to the Father. In so doing, we come to share in the Father's divine life as his children. "No one has ever seen God; the only-begotten Son, who is in the bosom of the Father, has made him known" (Jn 1:18).

to be, the Spirit himself is, in turn, simultaneously attesting to, and so confirming, the truth that Jesus is truly risen, for if he were not risen, he would not be able to establish his Spirit-filled church. In the very act of Jesus pouring out the Holy Spirit, the Holy Spirit reciprocally attests to Jesus's salvific Lordship.

Peter concludes his declaration by noting that "God has given" the Holy Spirit, "to those who obey him." What are "those" who obey so that the Father might give them the Holy Spirit? They must possess the obedience of faith—they must believe that Jesus is the Father's Spirit-filled, incarnated Son, the one whom the Father raised gloriously from the dead and the one who is now exalted at the Father's right hand. Such an obedient act of faith manifests that the Father has imbued the believer with the Holy Spirit.

All that Peter declared, in the above, is very reassuring and uplifting for those who believe. However, as Luke will now inform the reader, for those who refuse to believe, Peter's testimony incites outrage.

## Gamaliel's Calming Wisdom (Acts 5:33-42)

> When they heard this, they were enraged and wanted to kill them. But a Pharisee in the council named Gamaliel, a teacher of the law, held in honor by all the people, stood up and ordered the men to be put outside for a while.[18]

So angered by what Peter said, the members of the Sanhedrin wanted to kill the apostles. However, a Pharisee named Gamaliel stepped into the breach. Luke proceeds to provide a fulsome chronicle of Gamaliel's integrity.[19] As "a teacher of the law," he was "held in honor by all the people." As a member of the Sanhedrin, he requested that Peter and the other apostles be removed. Once outside, he addressed other council members. First, he cautions them not to do anything rash, lest they later regret what they did. "Men of Israel, take care what you do with these men." Next, he provides recent historical events that illustrate and support his caution.

> For before these days Theudas arose, claiming to be somebody, and a number of men, about four hundred, joined him; but he was slain and all who followed him were dispersed and came to nothing. After him Judas the Galilean

18. Unless otherwise noted, all scripture passages in this section are taken from Acts 5:33-42.

19. Gamaliel lived around the years AD 20-50. So honored was he in Jerusalem that he received the title, "raban" (our teacher), rather than the normal title of "rabbi" (teacher). He is also remembered by the early church as the teacher of Paul prior to his conversion. Paul boasted that he studied "at the feet of Gamaliel" (Acts 22:3).

> arose in the days of the census and drew away some of the people after him; he also perished, and all who followed him were scattered.[20]

With this historical background in place, Gamaliel draws his considered, cautionary conclusion.

> So, in the present case I tell you, keep away from these men and let them alone; for if this plan or this undertaking is of men, it will fail; but if it is of God, you will not be able to overthrow them. You might even be found opposing God!

What history has taught Gamaliel, and which he wants the Sanhedrin to take on board, is that, if the teaching of Peter and the apostles is of human origin, it will inevitably fail. It may appear to be thriving now, but such present enthusiasm will not be able to sustain itself. Moreover, if what "these men" are saying is true, especially if it is from God, then no matter how hard their attempts to squash it, such efforts will not succeed. Worst of all, if it is of divine origin, they will find that they are opposing God himself, and thus engaging in a battle that cannot be won, and for which one can even be condemned. Therefore, the Sanhedrin should not only "avoid" the apostles, but they should also leave "them alone." On the one hand, Gamaliel is simply providing his Jewish brethren wise counsel. On the other hand, one may also discern, by his choice of words and by the calming manner with which he spoke, that Gamaliel was sympathetic to what Peter and the apostles were teaching, and that he may even have been open to believing the gospel.[21]

"So, they took his advice, and when they had called in the apostles, they beat them and charged them not to speak in the name of Jesus, and let them go." Well, the advice that the Jewish leaders took, was not exactly what Gamaliel intended. They did not avoid the apostles nor leave them alone. Moreover, Gamaliel did not advise that they "beat" the apostles, nor did he suggest that they forbid the apostles to preach in Jesus's name, an order that Peter and the

20. There is a later Theudas, but nothing is known of the Theudas of which Gamaliel speaks. The Jewish historian, Josephus, writes that Judas the Galilean orchestrated a revolt against the Roman occupation in AD 6. His teaching gave rise to Zealot party between AD 44 and 46. The Zealots attempted to liberate Israel from the Romans in the Jewish Wars (AD 66–70). This rebellion was crushed by the Romans. As for the "census" mentioned, this was not the census taken up by Caesar Augustus at the time that Jesus was born in Bethlehem, but a later census prescribed for tax purposes in AD 6.

21. There is no early historical written record that asserts that Gamaliel became a Christian. However, there is a later ecclesiastical tradition that claims that Gamaliel became a Christian. Photios I of Constantinople (ca. 820–893), claimed that Peter and John baptized him, together with his son Abibon.

apostles had already refused to do. It would appear that the more hotheaded members of the Sanhedrin partially, though significantly, had their way. The apostles were not killed, but they left bloodied and bruised. Nonetheless, they did release the apostles, for which Gamaliel was assuredly pleased.

"Then they left the presence of the council, rejoicing that they were counted worthy to suffer dishonor for the name." As with the release of Peter and John earlier, so now the apostles left the Sanhedrin "rejoicing."[22] They rejoiced, for they were found worthy to suffer for the name of Jesus. In the eyes of the world, such suffering was a "dishonor," but among Christians it was indeed an "honor," for it imitated Jesus's own suffering. Moreover, although they were consistently forbidden to preach in Jesus's name, yet "every day in the temple and at home they did not cease teaching and preaching Jesus as the Christ." Throughout Jerusalem, not only publicly but also within their own homes, the apostles continued to proclaim that Jesus is the Christ. By designating that Jesus is the "Christ," the apostles were accentuating, in the midst of the Jewish Sanhedrin's opposition, that Jesus is the long-awaited, Spirit-filled Jewish Messiah, sent by the God of their fathers—Abraham, Isaac, and Jacob.

Although Luke, in chapter five, has focused on the apostles' and the Spirit's testimony that Jesus is the risen, Spirit-filled Christ, what lies within this narrative is Jesus being Jesus—YHWH-Saves. Amid their successes and tribulations, the apostles, through their apostolic and ecclesial ministry of healing and preaching, all of which is done in Jesus's name, were enacting Jesus's own salvific works, and so bearing testimony that he is the risen, ever-acting Lord and Savior.

Having focused on the apostles' interaction with their own Jewish brethren, Luke, in the following chapter, turns to the apostles' relationship with the Hellenists in their midst, and to the continued persecution of the church with the arrest of Stephen, the first martyr.

22. See Acts 4:1–31.

# *Chapter 6*

# THE HELLENISTS AND STEPHEN'S ARREST

Having told of the scandalous behavior of Ananias and Sapphira, the many healings performed by the apostles, and their subsequent arrest and trial, Luke next narrates the concerns found among the Jewish Hellenists in Jerusalem—the unintended lack of charity shown toward their widows. This matter was rectified by the appointment of seven deacons who were to care for the widows' needs. Luke also provides the circumstances under which Stephen, one of the newly ordained deacons, was arrested by members of the synagogue of Freedmen on charges of blasphemy. With this brief overview in mind, we can theologically examine the texts themselves.

## Seven Are Chosen to Serve (Acts 6:1-7)

> Now in these days when the disciples were increasing in number, the Hellenists murmured against the Hebrews because their widows were neglected in the daily distribution. And the Twelve summoned the body of disciples and said, "It is not right that we should give up preaching the word of God to serve tables. Therefore, brethren, pick out from among you seven men of good repute, full of the Spirit and of wisdom, whom we may appoint to the duty. But we will devote ourselves to prayer and to the ministry of the word."[1]

What appears to have precipitated this present concern among the Hellenists was the increase of disciples taking place in Jerusalem.[2] Prior to this

1. Unless otherwise noted, all Scripture passages in this section are taken from Acts 6:1-7. However, because of the length of this present narrative, it would be of no benefit to provide the entire text at the onset. Further texts will be incorporated in due course.

2. Here Luke is once more highlighting the phenomenal growth of the early church. He

complaint, everything was freely held in common and distributed by the apostles according to the various needs.[3] With the ever-increasing influx of converts, what had once been a loving disorganized band of enthusiastic believers now needed to be organized if that communal charity and mutual care for one another was to persist. The disgruntled, murmuring Hellenists were the first to recognize the necessity for this orderliness—"their widows were neglected in the daily distribution."[4]

In the face of this injustice, "the Twelve summoned the body of the disciples." Significantly, Luke does not say that "the apostles" convened the disciples, but "the Twelve." In so doing, Luke is accentuating that these twelve men held a singular authority within the Christian community. Having been appointed by Jesus himself, they possessed a unique hierarchical rank within the church.[5] It was "the Twelve," then, who gathered the Jerusalem brethren, and resolved what should be done concerning the widows of the Hellenists.

> It is not right that we should give up preaching the word of God to serve tables. Therefore, brethren, pick out from among you seven men of good repute, full of the Spirit and of wisdom, whom we may appoint to this duty. But we will devote ourselves to prayer and the ministry of the word.

---

previously noted this growth in Acts 2:41, 2:47, and 4:4. He will do so again at the end of this chapter, Acts 6:7.

3. See Acts 4:32–35.

4. Although the Jerusalem Church was composed entirely of Jews, it was made up of two groups. There were Hebrew Christians who spoke Aramaic and were residents of Palestine. There were also Hellenists who spoke Greek. They were more than likely part of the former diaspora who had immigrated to Jerusalem from various parts of the Roman empire. On Pentecost, the Galilean apostles spoke Hebrew, but everyone heard them in their own language, for "there were dwelling in Jerusalem Jews, devout men from every nation under heaven" (Acts 2:5). It should also be noted that the care of widows was always a concern both in the Old and New Testaments. See Dt 24:19 and 26:12, 1 Tm 5:3–8, and Jas 1:27.

Since the apostles later protested that they were not commissioned "to serve tables," it would appear that "the daily distribution" pertained to the allotting of food to the widows of the Hellenists. The Greek word "to serve" is *diakonein*, thus, those who were later ordained "to serve" bore the title "deacon." See, for example, Phil 1:1.

5. Not surprisingly, in his Gospel, Luke distinguishes the hierarchical nature of the Twelve from that of the rest of Jesus's disciples. "In those days he went out into the hills to pray; and all night he continued in prayer to God. And when it was day, he called his disciples, and he chose from them twelve, whom he named apostles" (Lk 6:12–13, see also Mt 10:1–4 and Mk 3:13–19). In the context of prolonged prayer, although Jesus summoned all "his disciples," he specifically chose "twelve, whom he named apostles." Only on the Twelve did Jesus confer apostolic authority.

Here, the apostles assert three things.[6] First, the singular ministry of the apostles was to pray and to preach the gospel. As apostles, they were required to pray on behalf of the nascent church and to preach God's word—the ministry that Jesus commissioned them to undertake. Second, the entire Jerusalem community was to choose from among them "seven men," who were reputable, Spirit-filled, and wise. That the virtue of wisdom is signaled out among the other possible virtues is interesting. Wisdom is a practical virtue. To be wise is to know what needs to be done given the circumstances—often complex. Wisdom involves, then, astutely heeding the concerns of all parties involved, so that all are content with the proposed resolution. Simple intellectual knowledge or romantic, euphoric enthusiasm will not suffice. Third, once the disciples have made their decision as to whom the seven will be, the apostles will "appoint" them to this duty.

Here, we find, for the first time, a foundational ecclesial principle. The Christian community can rightly pick whom they wish to govern or assist them, but only the apostolic ecclesial authorities can appoint them. This is the theological basis, as we will see shortly, for the Sacrament of Ordination. The local Christian community can rightly recommend whom they desire to be ordained, either as deacons, priests, or bishops. However, only those who hold apostolic authority, founded upon their being successors of the apostles, that is, bishops, are empowered to administer the Sacrament of Ordination.

In response to the apostles, Luke states, "And what they said pleased the whole multitude, and they chose Stephen, a man full of faith and of the Holy Spirit, and Philip, and Prochorus, and Nicanor, and Timon, and Parmenas, and Nicolaus, a proselyte of Antioch."[7] So, the Jerusalem faithful were happy with the apostles' proposal. That being the case, they chose the seven men who were to serve the needs of the Hellenists' widows. Of the seven, Stephen holds pride of place, for Luke informs the reader that he "was full of faith and of the Holy Spirit." By emphasizing his Spirit-filled faith, Luke directs the reader's attention to Stephen, since he will become the focus of the immediately ensuing narrative.

6. Obviously, not all of the Twelve could have said the above in unison. While one would expect that it was Peter who was the spokesman, yet what he determined would have been in accord with the minds of the other apostles. He spoke on their behalf, and thus exercised the apostolic authority of all twelve.

7. Since the concern at hand is the care of widows of the Hellenists, not surprisingly the seven chosen men bear Greek names. Nicolas is designated "a proselyte of Antioch." A proselyte was a Gentile who converted to Judaism. So, the Gentile, Nicolas, having become a Jewish believer, subsequently became a Christian, and is now chosen to be a deacon.

The Jerusalem church "set these seven men before the apostles, and they prayed and laid their hands upon them." Prayer, accompanied by the laying on of hands, signified the consecrating or commissioning of a person. In the Old Testament, God told Moses "to take Joshua, a man in whom is the Spirit, and lay your hand upon him." In so doing Moses "shall commission him" in the sight of the congregation. By laying his hands upon Joshua, Moses will "invest him" with some of his authority, so "that all of the congregation of the people of Israel may obey" (Nm 27:18-23). In the New Testament, Paul exhorts Timothy "not to neglect the gift you have, which was given you by prophetic utterance when the elders laid their hands upon you" (1 Tm 4:14). In the same manner, the apostles were to lay their hands on the seven men, and in so doing, they ordained them deacons—those who would serve within the Hellenist community.[8]

Luke concludes this present narrative by stating, "And the word of God increased; and the number of the disciples multiplied greatly in Jerusalem, and a great many priests were obedient to the faith." On all fronts, everything was advancing. The proclamation of God's word, the gospel of Jesus Christ, was intensifying, and, therefore, the number of converts in Jerusalem was rapidly swelling. Luke, as we have noted, has emphasized this precipitous growth several times previously. What is significantly new is that "many priests were obedient to the faith." This is surprising since it was the priests, "filled with jealousy," who had Peter and John arrested and put on trial. Here, we perceive that there must not have been unanimity among the priestly class—some of them even become Christians by obediently coming to faith in Jesus.

At this juncture, Luke begins his lengthy narration of Stephen's arrest and his proclamation of the gospel, all of which concludes with his being stoned to death.

## The Arrest of Stephen (Acts 6:8-15)

> And Stephen, full of grace and power, did great wonders and signs among the people. Then some of those who belonged to the synagogue of Freedmen (as it was called), and of the Cyrenians, and of Alexandrians, and of those from Cilicia and Asia, arose and disputed with Stephen. But they could not withstand the wisdom and the Spirit with which he spoke.[9]

8. The irony is that the deacons, having been ordained to serve, immediately worked miracles, preached the gospel, and baptized. Luke first narrates this expanded ministry with regards to Stephen (Acts 6:8-7:60) and then with Philip (Acts 8:4-40).

9. Unless otherwise noted, all Scripture passages in this section are taken from Acts 6:8-15.

Previously, Luke informed the reader that Stephen was "a man full of faith and of the Holy Spirit."[10] Now he describes Stephen as one "full of grace and power." This grace is that of the Holy Spirit, who empowered him to work "great wonders and signs among the people." Thus, the deacon Stephen was emulating the apostles, who also worked signs and wonders—they enacted many healings in the name of Jesus. Although Stephen, as a Hellenistic Jew, was ordained a deacon to care for the widows of the Hellenists, his ensuing working of miraculous signs caught the attention of other Hellenistic Jews, those who belonged to what was termed the synagogue of the Freedmen. These Hellenistic Jews were likely freed Roman slaves who emigrated back to Jerusalem from Italy. Moreover, this synagogue was also composed of Hellenistic Jews from North Africa—Cyrene and Alexandria. Others were from the Roman provinces in Asia Minor—Cilicia and Asia. In light of his being a Christian, conflict ensued between Stephen and his fellow Hellenistic brethren.

In the course of these heated disputes, the men of the synagogue of Freedmen "could not withstand the wisdom and the Spirit with which he spoke." Because Stephen spoke with Spirit-filled wisdom, he confounded those who opposed him. They were unable to win the debate, and so resorted to subterfuge.

> Then they secretly instigated men, who said, "We have heard him speak blasphemous words against Moses and God." And they stirred up the people and the elders and the scribes, and they came upon him and seized him and brought him before the council, and set up false witnesses who said, "This man never ceases to speak words against this holy place and the law; for we have heard him say that this Jesus of Nazareth will destroy this place, and will change the customs which Moses delivered to us." And gazing at him, all who sat in the council saw that his face was like the face of an angel.

The men of the Synagogue of Freedmen, on the sly, found some men who were willing to lie, and so bring false charges of blasphemy against Stephen—that he spoke "against Moses and God."[11] Because such blasphemous charges excited "the people and the elders and the scribes," Stephen was "seized" and "brought before the council," that is, the Sanhedrin. Before the council, further false charges were brought forth. He was denounced for speaking against "this holy place," that is, the temple, and "the law." Specifically, he was heard

---

However, because of the length of this present narrative, it would be of no benefit to provide the entire text at the onset. Further texts will be incorporated in due course.

10. See Acts 6:5.

11. As we noted earlier, those who blaspheme God are to be stoned. Ultimately, Stephen will be stoned.

saying "that this Jesus of Nazareth will destroy this place, and will change the customs which Moses delivered to us."[12]

This charge that Jesus will destroy the temple has an earlier complex literary history. All the Synoptic Gospels narrate that Jesus cleansed the temple.[13] However, none of them recount that Jesus said anything about the destruction of the temple and that he would rebuild it in three days.[14] In the Gospels of Matthew and Mark, after Jesus was arrested, he was brought before the council.[15] The council sought false witnesses so that they might put him to death, but they found none. According to Matthew, two finally came forward. They claimed, "This fellow said, 'I am able to destroy the temple of God, and to build it in three days'" (Mt 26:61). In Mark's Gospel, "some" claim to have heard Jesus say "I will destroy this temple that is made with hands, and in three days I will build another, not made with hands."[16] Similarly, onlookers beneath his cross mocked Jesus. "You who would destroy the temple and build it in three days, save yourself!"[17] Since the Synoptic Gospels do not narrate an occasion where Jesus may have made such declarations, even if falsely interpreted, from where did they arise? The only source available is that found in John's Gospel.

John, in greater detail than found in the Synoptics, tells of Jesus cleansing the temple. The Jews ask, "What sign have you to show us for doing this?" By what authority has Jesus cleansed the temple? In reply, Jesus answered, "Destroy this temple, and in three days I will raise it up." To which the Jews said, "It has taken forty-six years to build this temple, and will you raise it up in three days?" The Evangelist, then, added an interpretive editorial comment. "But he spoke of the temple of his body. When therefore he was raised from the dead, his disciples remembered that he had said this" (Jn 2:13–22).

12. Once again, Jesus is designated as coming from Nazareth. The concern is that this man from Nazareth is said to be risen and is threatening to destroy the temple and the law of Moses. The unbelieving Jews are in a quandary. On the one hand, that such a man from Nazareth is now risen is incredible, and so not to be believed. Yet, on the other hand, if he is risen, there is the real threat that he will destroy the temple and abolish the law of Moses.

13. See Mt 21:12–13, Mk 11:15–17, and Lk 19:45–46.

14. Prior to entering Jerusalem, Jesus did predict the destruction of the temple, but he was referring to the destruction caused by the Romans in AD 70. See Mt 24:1–2, Mk 13:1–2, and Lk 5–6.

15. This is the same council with the same members before which Stephen is presently seated.

16. Mk 14:58. Luke, in his Gospel, does not narrate a similar event, though he must have known of this false accusation since, as seen above, he narrates that such a false accusation was made at Stephen's trial.

17. Mt 27:40. See also Mk 15:29.

In the light of this Johannine account, we see that Jesus never said that he would destroy the temple as such, though he was accused, as seen above, of often saying that he would, including at Stephen's present trial. Stephen is charged with the blasphemous crime of declaring that "Jesus of Nazareth will destroy this place," and in so doing Jesus "will change the customs which Moses delivered to us."[18] The risen Jesus is now a threat to the entire Jewish religion, making it redundant. The irony is that there is truth in what they fear.

Jesus, as the Spirit-filled incarnate Son of God, lovingly offered himself to the Father as the perfect sacrifice, the Passover sacrifice of the new and everlasting covenant. In so doing, Jesus has become, in rising from the dead on the third day, the living, everlasting temple, not made by human hands, in whom all who believe in him and so abide in him, can offer, in Spirit and truth, perfect worship of the Father. What Moses taught, and what the temple and the sacrifices prefigured, have now been fulfilled in Jesus's sacrificial death and glorious resurrection—an abundance of everlasting life in communion with the most holy Trinity. What the unbelieving Jewish council feared, unacknowledged by them, has already taken place. As the expected, Spirit-filled Messiah, Jesus has become, through his death and resurrection, Savior and Lord—not only of Jews, but also of Gentiles as well.

Luke concludes this portion of Stephen's trial on an uplifting note. Amid all the enraged accusations against Stephen, the members of the council were looking upon him. "And gazing at him, all who sat in the council saw that his face was like the face of an angel." If taken literally, Luke's depiction of Stephen cannot be true. Angels are not bodily, so they do not possess faces, though they do have distinct identities. What Luke is attempting to describe is Stephen's angelic appearance—his face aglow with divine light, love, and serenity.

## Conclusion

In the preceding chapters of the Acts of the Apostles, Luke narrated the ministry of the apostles, particularly that of Peter and John. Having been filled with the Holy Spirit, they proclaim the gospel, and they work miracles in the name of Jesus. Thus, Jesus is being Jesus through their Spirit-imbued, apostolic ministry. Now, in chapter six, that apostolic office has been expanded to include

18. Because the accusation against Stephen at his trial is similar to the charge against Jesus at his trial, that of Jesus declaring that he would destroy the temple, we perceive that Stephen is replicating Jesus's own saving work. This imitation will become more evident when Stephen is eventually stoned. As a disciple, Stephen has taken up his cross and followed Jesus.

the seven ordained deacons. They, too, publicly announce the good news that the crucified Jesus has gloriously risen. Luke, specifically, focuses on Stephen. Not only did he, by the power of the Spirit, work signs and wonders, but he also professed that Jesus is alive. Jesus, therefore, is now also acting through Stephen and his fellow deacons. Through them, Jesus is enacting his name—YHWH-Saves. Thus, what Jesus could not do prior to his death, when he was still becoming Jesus, he is now able to accomplish, as the risen Jesus, through his Spirit-founded church. Through the church's ecclesial, apostolic ministry, Jesus is able to be Jesus. He enacts his name, and so is able to bring salvation to the whole world, throughout all ages.

# Chapter 7

## STEPHEN'S DISCOURSE AND STONING

Chapter six concluded with the arrest of Stephen and his interrogation by those belonging to the synagogue of the Freemen. Because they "could not withstand" his wisdom, they "secretly instigated men" to accuse of him of "blasphemous words against Moses and God." They, then, brought him before the Sanhedrin. Once again "false witnesses" came forward and declared that Stephen said that "Jesus of Nazareth will destroy this place [the temple] and will change the customs which Moses delivered to us" (Acts 6:8-14).

In chapter seven, Luke provides Stephen's lengthy discourse in response to the allegations laid against him. Not surprisingly, Stephen focuses primarily on the history and significance of Moses, and God's covenantal relationship beginning with Abraham. At the end, the Jews, who were in attendance, were outraged at what they heard, and so they stoned Stephen to death. In this context, we can now turn to the text itself.

### God's Promise to Abraham (Acts 7:1-5)

> And the high priest said, "Is this so?" and Stephen said: "Brethren and fathers, hear me. The God of glory appeared to our father Abraham, when he was in Mesopotamia, before he lived in Haran, and said to him, 'Depart from your land and from your kindred and go into the land which I will show you.' Then he departed from the land of the Chaldeans and lived in Haran. And after his father died, God removed him from there into this land in which you are now living; yet he gave him no inheritance in it, not even a foot's length, but promised to give it to him in possession and to his posterity after him, though he had no child."[1]

1. Unless otherwise noted, all Scripture passages in this section are taken from Acts 7:1-5.

Having been accused of blasphemy against God and Moses, and having been denounced, though falsely, for declaring that Jesus will destroy the temple and the Mosaic customs, the high priest asked Stephen, "Is this so?" The high priest may have expected a "yes" or "no" answer. However, Stephen recognized that he could not reply adequately to the charges laid against him unless he placed them within the entire historical context of God's interaction with the Jewish people—beginning with Abraham. For Stephen, as God acted throughout the history of the Jewish people, so the risen Jesus continues being Jesus throughout history through the apostolic ministry of the church—this is what he wants his present listeners to acknowledge in faith.

Stephen begins by personally acknowledging those before him. He addresses his accusers as "brethren and fathers." While he is the accused and the members of the Sanhedrin are the accusers, yet they are all Jews, and so they are "brethren." Stephen wants to assure them that he does not see them as his enemies, and he hopes that they do not see him as their enemy. Moreover, he recognizes their religious status. Because they belong to the priestly class, and he does not, they are his "fathers," those whom he must respect and honor. Nonetheless, he reverently asks them to "hear" him, to heed what he is about to say. With this introduction, Stephen begins his discourse.[2]

While Abraham, "our father," was still "in Mesopotamia, before he lived in Haran," "the God of glory appeared to" him. Notice that Stephen once again places himself among his Jewish "brethren." Abraham is not only their "father," but his as well; and so together they form part of a long Jewish lineage, one that goes back to the onset of their founding father—Abraham. Stephen describes God as "the God of glory." The God of the Jews is the most glorious God, for there is no one greater, more magnificent, more holy, or more luminous than he. As "He Who Is," (YHWH), God is singular in his deity. Therefore, "Ascribe to the Lord (YHWH), O heavenly beings, / ascribe to the Lord glory and strength. / Ascribe to the Lord the glory of his name; / worship the Lord in his holy array" (Ps 29:1-2). It is none other than this God who first appeared and spoke to their father, Abraham.

---

However, because of the length of this present narrative, it would be of no benefit to provide the entire text at the onset. Further texts will be incorporated in due course. Stephen's extended address should not be taken as his exact words. Nor should one presume, then, that what he states contains no historicity. Rather, the theological and historical content of Stephen's discourse is accurate even though his words may not be verbatim.

2. Stephen will now retell the salvific history of the Jewish people. In so doing, he is imitating what has been done also in the Old Testament. For example, the book of Sirach recounts God's saving deeds (see Sir 44–51). The book of Wisdom does something similar (see Wis 10–12).

Moreover, Stephen is alluding to the book of Genesis, chapters 11-36, and he will continue to do so. Stephen is here alluding to Genesis 11:31 where it is said that Abram left from "Ur of the Chaldeans to go into the land of Canaan, but when they came to Haran, they settled there."[3] Next Stephen quotes Genesis 12:1 where God tells Abram to depart from Haran and his kindred and go "into the land which I will show you." Abraham is not simply to "go to" the land, but "to go into" the land. The land that God will show Abraham will be his land—his rightful, God-given possession. So, this is what Abraham did. Stephen recounts that Abraham left the land of the Chaldeans and then lived in Haran, but that after his father died, "God removed him from there into this land in which you are now living; he gave him no inheritance in it, not even a foot's length, but promised to give it to him in possession and to his posterity after him, though he had no child." Once more, Stephen is referencing Genesis 12:4-7, where God first appeared to Abraham and told him to pass through the land of Canaan, but then promised him that he would give the land "to your descendants." Thus, as Stephen emphasized, God at first did not even give Abraham "a foot's length," but he did promise to give the land "to him in possession and to his posterity after him, though he had no child." Surprisingly, Stephen does not develop the theological significance of Abraham being childless. Since Abraham had no heir, there would be no "posterity" to whom God could give the land promised. Only because Abraham and Sarah, "miraculously," conceived Isaac in their old age, as God foretold, was God able to fulfill his promise that Abraham's posterity would inherit the land.[4] Thus, Stephen accentuates that, because of God's faithfulness to Abraham and his posterity, and because of Abraham's obedience of faith in God's word to him, the Jews, whom he now addresses, are presently living in that very land. Their feet are standing where God did not give Abraham "a foot's length." The hidden question is "Will the present Jewish landowners be as faithful to God as was Abraham their father—will they acknowledge Jesus as their messianic Savior and Lord?"

## Egypt and the Enslavement of the Israelites (Acts 7:6-8)

Having narrated the historical and theological significance of God's call to Abraham, Stephen proceeds swiftly to the Jews' enslavement in Egypt.

3. Ur is in Mesopotamia.

4. See Gn 21:1-3.

> And God spoke to this effect, that his posterity would be aliens in a land belonging to others, who would enslave them and ill-treat them four hundred years. "But I will judge the nation which they serve," said God, "and after that they shall come out and worship in this place." And he gave a covenant of circumcision. And so Abraham became the father of Isaac, and circumcised him on the eighth day; and Isaac became the father of Jacob, and Jacob of the twelve patriarchs.[5]

Now the God of glory not only spoke to Abraham, he also foretold that Abraham's posterity would become "aliens in a land belonging to others," that is, Egypt. There, they would be enslaved and mistreated for "four hundred years." In this summary, Stephen refers to a number of historical events and numerous passages, those concerning Jacob, and Joseph and his brothers. Stephen will shortly elaborate on this story in full, a sad story at first, but one that will become salvific. Nonetheless, in time, the Israelites became slaves in Egypt, though God would eventually set them free through his mighty deeds and the leadership of Moses. Moreover, God made a covenant with his people; the sign of which was circumcision.

> And God said to Abraham, "As for you, you shall keep my covenant, you and your descendants after you throughout their generations. This is my covenant, which you shall keep, between me and you and your descendants: Every male among you shall be circumcised. You shall be circumcised in the flesh of your foreskins, and it shall be a sign of the covenant between me and you." (Gn 17:9–11)

Within this historical context, Stephen quotes Exodus 3:12, where God declared to Moses that he would "judge the nation which they serve," that is, he will condemn Egypt. Moreover, "I will be with you; and this shall be the sign for you, that I have sent you: when you have brought forth the people out of Egypt, you shall serve God upon this mountain."[6]

This historical synopsis concerning Abraham leads Stephen to his summary conclusion. "And so Abraham became the father of Isaac, and circumcised him on the eighth day; and Isaac became the father of Jacob, and Jacob of the twelve patriarchs." The three original patriarchs, Abraham, Isaac, and Jacob, all of whom were faithful to the covenant and were thus circumcised, gave

5. Unless otherwise noted, all Scripture passages in this section are taken from Acts 7:6–8.

6. Ex 3:12. Stephen's own words are an abridged form of this passage. Also keep in mind, The mountain upon which God spoke to Moses is Mount Horeb. Traditionally, this mountain is also called Mount Sinai. It is upon this mountain, then, that God made a covenant with Moses and the Israelites (see Ex 24:3–8).

rise to the prodigy of Abraham—the twelve sons of Jacob, to whom Stephen now bestows the title of "patriarch." Normally the title "patriarch" is reserved to Abraham, Isaac, and Jacob. By including Jacob's twelve sons within this patriarchal hierarchy, Stephen wants to accentuate to his Jewish listeners that they, too, as members of the priestly elite, belong to this revered and illustrious ancestry. Therefore, they must now also be faithful to this divine salvific history, a history that finds its culmination in Jesus Christ.

Having spoken of the four hundred years that the Israelites were in Egypt, Stephen proceeds to rehearse this entire history. This history was marked by Israel's stubborn unfaithfulness—an obstinacy that is now exemplified in his unbelieving Jewish listeners.[7]

## The Redemptive Stories of Joseph and Moses (Acts 7:9–34)

Stephen first speaks of Joseph being sold into slavery by his brothers and taken to Egypt. The brothers' rejection of Joseph is Stephen's first example of someone who is a divinely appointed "savior," and yet is scorned. Joseph, thus, becomes a prefigurement of Jesus, who was also despised and rejected. Nonetheless, Joseph eventually held a high position next to Pharoah. When famine gripped the land, Joseph's brothers came to him to receive grain. Having revealed himself to his brothers, Joseph had them bring their father, Jacob, and their families to Egypt.[8] Importantly, Stephen notes that "as the time of the promise drew near, which God had granted to Abraham, the people grew and multiplied in Egypt till there arose another king who did not know Joseph" (Acts 7:17–18). The "promise" to Abraham that Stephen is referring to is that of possessing the "promised" land. The sign of the promise's near fulfillment is perceived in Israel's growth and identity as a people. This growth as a recognizable people precipitated Pharaoh's fear, and his resultant decision to enslave them. Ironically, this enslavement would become the catalyst for the fulfillment of God's promise to Abraham. God heard their cry and delivered them from their Egyptian slavery, whereupon the Israelites journeyed to the "promised land," thus fulfilling God's pledge to Abraham.[9]

7. Because Stephen narrates this history in some detail, though he is selective, I will not quote the whole of his discourse. I presume that the present readers are well acquainted with the various stories.

8. Stephen is referencing Genesis 37–50.

9. Stephen is referencing Ex 3:7–12.

Stephen, then, provides a rather lengthy summary of Moses's entire life. Having been adopted by Pharoah's daughter, "Moses was instructed in all wisdom of the Egyptians, and he was mighty in his words and deeds" (Acts 7:22). Exodus does not mention Moses's education, nor his youthful mighty words and deeds. Subsequently, Moses "supposed that his brethren understood that God was giving deliverance to them by his hand, but they did not understand." Instead, they cynically asked, "Who made you a ruler and a judge over us?"[10] So, once more, as the Israelites rejected the divinely appointed Moses, so now the Sanhedrin has rejected Jesus, the divine Spirit-anointed Christ. Stephen is, once again, alluding to Moses's prefigurative emulation of Jesus. As the disciples on the road to Emmaus said to Jesus, whom they did not recognize, when he asked them what they were discussing, "[those things] concerning Jesus of Nazareth, who was a prophet mighty in deed and word before God and all of the people, and how our chief priests and rulers delivered him up to be condemned to death, and crucified him.'"[11] Again, like Moses, Jesus was, and continues to be, rebuffed by the priests and rulers.

Significantly, Stephen narrates the event wherein God commissioned Moses as the leader and redeemer of the Israelites. While Moses was on Mount Sinai, an angel appeared to him in a burning bush. As Moses drew near, the Lord said to him, "I am the God of your fathers, the God of Abraham and of Isaac and of Jacob."[12] God informs Moses that he "has surely seen the ill treatment of my people that are in Egypt and heard their groaning." Therefore, he "will come down to deliver them." He will free his people from slavery by sending Moses to Egypt. At this juncture in his discourse, Stephen accentuates what he has already stated and intensifies his condemnatory conclusion of Israel's past rejection of God and all those whom he had sent for their saving benefit.[13]

10. Acts 7:25 and 27. Stephen is referencing Ex 2:11–14.

11. Lk 24:19–20. See also Lk 2:46–47.

12. Interestingly, although Stephen narrates that God told Moses that he is the God of Abraham, Isaac, and Jacob, he does not also relate that God also revealed to Moses his divine name—YHWH, He Who Is. Here, Stephen's main concern is that, in refusing to accept Moses, the Israelites refused to accept the God of their ancestors. As will become evident, as the Israelites refused Moses and the Lord God, so now Stephen's Jewish listeners have rejected Jesus as their Savior and Lord, and in so doing, they have also rejected the God of their patriarchal ancestors. Stephen is referencing Ex 3:1–10.

13. Because of its importance, I will now resume quoting Stephen's discourse in full.

## Israel's Rejection of Moses and the Infidelity of the Israelites (Acts 7:35–43)

> This Moses whom they refused, saying, "who made you a ruler and a judge?" God sent as both ruler and deliverer by the hand of the angel that appeared to him in the bush. He led them out, having performed wonders and signs in Egypt and at the Red Sea, and in the wilderness for forty years.[14]

By referring to him as "this Moses," Stephen is stressing that even though "this" man was sent to Egypt by none other than God, yet the Israelites, in their stubbornness, refused to accept him as their "ruler and judge."[15] Moreover, it was to "this Moses" that a heavenly angel spoke in the burning bush. Furthermore, it was "this Moses" who, with extraordinary "wonders and signs," led the Israelites out of Egypt. Even the Red Sea divided at Moses's command, and all passed through on dry land. Finally, it was "this Moses" who, for forty years, led the whole Israelite people through the desert.[16] To Stephen's mind, what more could God have done for his people through "this Moses?" Yet, incredible as it may appear, they rejected him as their ruler and judge. Stephen has yet to complete what "this Moses" did, so as to bring ever-increasing discomfort to his listening, but unbelieving, Jewish brethren.

> This is the Moses who said to the Israelites, "God will raise up for you a prophet from your brethren as he raised me up." This is he who was in the congregation in the wilderness with the angel who spoke to him at Mount Sinai, and with our fathers; and who received living oracles to give us. Our fathers refused to obey him, but thrust him aside, and in their hearts, they turned to Egypt, saying to Aaron, "Make for us gods to go before us; as for this Moses who led us out from the land of Egypt, we do not know what has become of him." And they made a calf in those days and offered sacrifice to the idol and rejoiced in the work of their hands.

So significant is "this Moses" that he foretold that "God will raise up for you a prophet from your brethren as he raised me up." Stephen is quoting Deuteronomy 18:15, where Moses also noted that the people would heed this

14. Unless otherwise noted, all Scripture passages in this section are taken from Acts 7:35–43. However, because of the length of this present narrative, it would be of no benefit to provide the entire text at the onset. Further texts will be incorporated in due course.

15. Stephen employs "this" four times when referring to Moses. In so doing, he is actuating both the divinely established importance of Moses and the Jewish people's subsequent rejection of him.

16. Stephen is referencing Ex 2:14, 7:3, and 14:21–22.

future prophet. Within the same context of this present quoted prophecy, God also declares through Moses, "I will raise up for them a prophet; and I will put my words in his mouth, and he shall speak to them all that I command him. And whoever will not give heed to my words which he shall speak in my name, I myself will require it of him."[17] Christians, as Stephen well knew, believe that Jesus is the prophet foretold by Moses. However, his interlocutors have refused to listen to the God-given words of that "prophet," and so God will himself hold them accountable.

Concerning Jesus as the fulfillment of God's promise to raise up a prophet, John's Gospel is of theological significance. That Jesus is the anticipated "prophet" is professed in John's Gospel, and in a manner that exceeds all expectations. After Jesus enacted the miracle-sign of the multiplication of the loaves, the crowd concluded, "This is indeed the prophet who is to come into the world!" (Jn 6:14). Likewise, because of Jesus's teaching, the people said, "This is indeed the prophet" (Jn 7:40). Moreover, in Moses's prophecy, God said that he would put his words in the mouth of "the prophet," and that he would speak all that he commanded him. Again, in John's Gospel, Jesus declares, "My teaching is not mine, but his who sent me" (Jn 7:16). Likewise, "When you have lifted up the Son of man, then you will know that I am he, and that I do nothing on my own authority but speak thus as the Father taught me."[18] Similarly, "For I have not spoken on my own authority; the Father who sent me has himself given me commandment what to say and what to speak. And I know that his commandment is eternal life. What I say, therefore, I say as the Father has bidden me" (Jn 12:49-50). In these passages, Jesus emphasizes that he was sent from the Father, and, therefore, he speaks not by his own authority but declares only what the Father has commanded him to say. Thus, Jesus is "the prophet" foretold by Moses, but he is such in a manner that differs in kind and not simply in degree from all the previous prophets and from even that of the anticipated prophet that God had promised. The Father sent his eternal Word, and the Father's eternal Word became incarnate. As the Word incarnate, Jesus, by the very nature of who he is, speaks the Father's word, a word that gives everlasting life. Thus, in refusing to accept Jesus as the prophet whom God would raise up, the Jews have denied the Father's Word incarnate, and, because of this, the Father will hold them accountable.

17. Dt 18:18-19. Peter previously quoted this same passage when preaching to the Jews in Solomon's Portico. See Acts 3:22-23.

18. Jn 8:28. See also Jn 8:26.

Not only is "this Moses" the one who spoke of the future prophet that God would raise up, but he is also the one "who was in the congregation in the wilderness with the angel who spoke to him at Mount Sinai, and with our fathers; and received living oracles to give us." First, Stephen informs his Jewish listeners that Moses was with "the congregation" (*ekklēsia*) in the desert.[19] Previously, Luke spoke of the great numbers that had been added to "the whole Church" (*ekklēsia*).[20] As we noted then, the term *ekklēsia* designates an "assembly" or "congregation." Within the Old Testament, this understanding particularly refers to a group of people assembled in worship. Thus, Stephen perceives that, in the wilderness, Moses was with the Israelite worshiping congregation or assembly. Moreover, in denoting this Jewish worshiping community as an *ekklēsia*, Stephen recognizes it, and he wants his listeners to appreciate it, as a prophetic anticipation of the Christian church. Jesus is the founder of the *ekklēsia*, and he founded it by pouring out his Holy Spirit upon the apostles at Pentecost. This church is now the new congregation or assembly that worships God, in communion with the risen Jesus, through the indwelling of the Holy Spirit. Thus, as Moses was with the Israelite congregation in the desert, so Jesus, is now actively present amid his church. Within the Christian *ekklēsia*, Jesus is, then, *being* Jesus, that is, he is enacting his name as the divine Lord, YHWH-Saves. He is the new Moses who leads the Christian people from the slavery of sin and death into the promised heavenly *ekklēsia*—the kingdom of God.

Second, "this Moses," while with the Israelite congregation in the wilderness, was also with "the angel who spoke to him at Mount Sinai, and with our fathers; and he received the living oracles to give to us." Although Exodus does not reference an angel speaking to Moses, it does tell of God speaking to Moses on Mount Sinai.[21] Moreover, Stephen reminds his priestly listeners that God also spoke "with our fathers." They, too, heard God speaking to them, and so were under divine obligation to heed what he commanded, for he was giving them, through Moses, "living oracles." Normally, one does not speak of oracles being living, for they are simply composed of words. For Stephen,

19. In these verses, Stephen is referencing Ex 19 and 20, Dt 5:1-22, and Dt 6:4-25.

20. See Acts 5:11.

21. See again, Ex 19 and 20, Dt 5:1-22, and Dt 6:4-25. Later, Exodus states, "Thus, the Lord used to speak to Moses face to face, as a man speaks to his friend" (Ex 33:11). The angel that Stephen references could be the eternal Son of God. This is, I believe, highly unlikely. More probable is that he had in mind "the angel of the Lord" who appeared to Moses at the burning bush, though it is the Lord God himself who spoke to Moses, "I am the God of your father, the God of Abraham, the God of Isaac, and the God of Jacob" (Ex 3:2-6).

though, what God revealed to Moses and what Moses spoke to "the fathers" of the Jewish nation was lifegiving. Keeping God's covenantal commandments engenders life, for in doing so, those who obey them grow in their relationship with the living God. Therefore, Moses was giving these lifegiving oracles "to us" for Israel's benefit.

However, Stephen once again declares that the Sanhedrin's Jewish ancestors, "our fathers," "refused to obey him, and thrust him aside, and in their hearts they turned to Egypt." Instead of obeying him, they "murmured against Moses and Aaron." Moreover, their hearts' desire was to return to Egypt. "Would that we had died in the land of Egypt! Or would that we had died in the wilderness! Why does the Lord bring us into this land, to fall by the sword? Our wives and our little ones will become prey; would it not be better for us to go back to Egypt?" (Nm 14:2-3). Not only did the Israelites wish to return to Egypt where they thought that they had a better life, but they also desired to resume worshiping the Egyptian pagan gods. They said to Aaron, "Make for us gods to be before us; as for this Moses who led us out from the land of Egypt, we do not know what has become of him."[22] So "they made a calf in those days, and offered sacrifice to the idol and rejoiced in the work of their hands."[23] In making a golden calf with their own hands, to which they joyfully worshiped, the Israelites abandoned the God who eternally is and so is not made, the God who saved them from the Egyptians. Instead of worshiping the true God, they worshiped idols.[24] Because of their infidelity, God

22. Stephen is quoting, almost verbatim, Ex 32:1. The reason that the people did not know what had become of "this Moses," is that he remained on Mount Sinai "forty days and forty nights" (Ex 24:18; see also Dt 9:9).

23. Stephen is referencing Ex 32:2-6. Historically and theologically significant is that God made a covenant with the Jewish people. This covenant was ratified when Moses sacrificed a bull and sprinkled the blood on the altar. Whereupon the people declared, "All that the Lord of has spoken we will do, and we will be obedient." In response, Moses sprinkled the blood upon the people and then said, "Behold the blood of the covenant which the Lord has made with you in accordance with these words" (Ex 24:4-8). Then God commanded that Moses come to him upon the mountain where he gave him "the tablets of stone" which contained the commandments and the law (Ex 24:12). In less than forty days, the people were unfaithful to the covenant, and asked Aaron to make a god for them to which they could offer sacrifice. The worshiping of the golden calf was the first offense committed against God and the covenant by the Jewish nation. The subsequent history would be a history of the Jewish people being unfaithful to God and to the covenant. Stephen is recalling this history of infidelity to the consternation of his Jewish brethren.

24. Prior to entering the Promised Land, Joshua exhorted the Israelites, "Now therefore fear the Lord, and serve him in sincerity and in faithfulness; put away the gods which your fathers served beyond the River, and in Egypt, and serve the Lord" (Jos 24:14). Ezekiel, speaking on behalf of God, also recalled the infidelity of their Jewish ancestors. "And I said to them,

wanted to destroy them, but Moses stood in the breach and begged God to forgive them, lest the Egyptians say that God brought them out of Egypt only to destroy them. Moreover, Moses reminded God of the promise he made to Abraham, that he would multiply his descendants as the stars of the heaven and give them the land that he had promised.[25] Because of Moses's supplicant prayer, "the Lord repented of the evil which he thought to do to his people."[26]

Nonetheless, Stephen reminds his Jewish brethren of what God did.

> But God turned and gave them over to worship the host of heaven, as it is written in the books of the prophets: "Did you offer to me slain beasts and sacrifices, forty years in the wilderness, O house of Israel? And you took up the tent of Moloch, and the star of the god of Rephan, the figures which you made to worship; and I will remove you beyond Babylon."[27]

Instead of God attempting to free the Jewish people from their sinful idolatry, he turned away from them and "gave them over" to worshipping false heavenly gods. He let them wallow in their sinfulness. There is no greater punishment than to let sinners perdure in their sins, and so ultimately face God's righteous condemnation.[28] In so doing, Stephen states that such was in accord with what was "written in the book of the prophets." Stephen quotes Amos 5:25–27. Amos is both looking back and forward. Because the Israelites worshiped false gods during the forty years they wandered in the wilderness in the past, their future will be one of exile in Babylon. The implication is that the intervening years between their wilderness infidelity and their Babylonian captivity were years of betrayal as well. Thus, in giving them over to the worship of false gods, such as Moloch and Rephan, God gave them over to

---

Cast away the detestable thing your eyes feast on, every one of you, and do not defile yourselves with the idols of Egypt; I am the Lord your God. But they rebelled against me and would not listen to me; they did not every man cast away the detestable things their eyes feasted on, nor did they forsake the idols of Egypt" (Ez 20:7–8).

25. See Ex 32:7–13.

26. Ex 32:14. The Psalmist declares, "They made a calf at Horeb / and worshiped a molten image. / They exchanged the glory of God / for the image of an ox that eats grass. / They forgot God, their Savior, / who had done great things in Egypt, / wondrous works in the land of Ham, / and terrible things by the Red Sea. / Therefore, he said he would destroy them—/ had not Moses, his chosen one, / stood in the breach before him, / to turn away his wrath from destroying them" (Ps 106:19–23).

27. The god Moloch is first mentioned in Leviticus. "You shall not give your children to devote them by fire to Mo'lech, and so profane the name of your God" (Lv 18:21). Rephan refers to the Egyptian star god, Saturn.

28. Even though God could be known through the things he created, the Gentiles refused to honor him, and so Paul declared that God gave them up to the sinful passions and desires. See Rom 1:19–32.

their enslavement in Babylon. Ironically, God freed the Israelites from their slavery in Egypt, and then made a covenant with them, only to have them live a life of infidelity which resulted in their becoming slaves in Babylon.

## God's Continual Faithfulness Through the Ages (Acts 7:44–50)

Stephen continues his discourse by narrating the ways that God continued to be faithful to his chosen people.

> Our fathers had the tent of witness in the wilderness, even as he who spoke to Moses directed him to make it, according to the pattern that he had seen. Our fathers in turn brought it in with Joshua when they dispossessed the nations which God thrust out before our fathers. So it was until the days of David, who found favor in the sight of God and asked leave to find a habitation for the God of Jacob. But it was Solomon who built a house for him. Yet the Most High does not dwell in houses made by hands; as the prophet says, "Heaven is my throne, and earth my footstool. What house will you build for me, says the Lord, or what is the place of my rest? Did not my hand make all these things?"[29]

Stephen continues by reminding the members of the Sanhedrin what "our fathers" had. First, they "had the tent of witness in the wilderness, even as he who spoke to Moses directed him to make it, according to the pattern that he had seen." In the book of Exodus, God specified exactly how the tent or tabernacle that contained the ark of the covenant, and so the earthly dwelling place of God, was to be constructed. "According to all that I show you [Moses] concerning the pattern of the tabernacle, and of all its furniture, so you shall make it."[30] That Stephen designates that the tent is a "tent of witness" indicates that it bears witness to God's unseen presence in their midst as he journeys with them in the wilderness. Thus, for Stephen, God was ever close to "our fathers." Second, Moses having constructed the tabernacle, "our fathers in turn brought it in with Joshua when they dispossessed the nations which God thrust out before our fathers." Although Stephen does not tell of the miraculous manner in which the Israelites entered the promised land, a miracle that replicated the crossing of the Red Sea dry shod, his Jewish brethren would be well acquainted with it.

29. Unless otherwise noted, all Scripture passages in this section are taken from Acts 7:44–50.

30. Ex 25:9. For all the specifics, see Ex 25–30.

> So, when the people set out from their tents, to pass over the Jordan with the priests bearing the ark of the covenant before the people, and when those who bore the ark had come to the Jordan, and the feet of the priest bearing the ark were dipped in the brink of the water (the Jordan overflows all its banks throughout the harvest), the waters coming down from above stood and rose up in a heap far off, at Adam, the city that is beside Zarethan, and those flowing down toward the sea of the Arabah, the Salt Sea, were wholly cut off; and the people passed over opposite Jericho. And while all Israel were passing over on dry ground, the priests who bore the ark of the covenant of the Lord stood on dry ground in the midst of the Jordan, until all the nation finished passing over the Jordan.[31]

Thus, as Moses led the people out of Egypt by passing through the miraculously parted Red Sea, so Joshua led the people into the promised land through the miraculously parted river Jordan—the terminus of the journey through the wilderness. By entering the promised land, God's oath to Abraham was fulfilled. "Go from your country and your father's house to the land that I will show you. And I will make you a great nation, and I will bless you, and make your name great … and by you all the families of the earth shall be blessed" (Gn 12:1–3).

Interestingly, Stephen first says that Joshua and the Israelites brought the ark of the covenant "when they dispossessed the nations." This purging of the nations initially appears to be solely a human achievement. However, Stephen immediately adds, "which God thrust out before our fathers." Thus, while the Israelites overthrew the nations, they did so only because God drove them out as "our fathers" advanced. Only with God's help and the presence of the ark of the covenant were the Israelites assured of taking possession of the land of promise.

Now, as the Israelites took possession of the land, there was no fixed abode where the ark of the covenant was enshrined. Stephen notes that this changed during the time of King David and Solomon. "So it was until the days of David, who found favor in the sight of God and asked leave to find a habitation for the God of Jacob. But it was Solomon who built a house for him." Although David was esteemed by God and asked to build a dwelling "for the God of Jacob," yet it was Solomon who built the temple wherein was placed the ark of the covenant. By referring to "the God of Jacob," Stephen is referencing Psalm 132.

31. Jos 3:14–17. There are other instances in the Old Testament where the ark of the covenant was employed to enact miraculous deeds. For example, carrying the ark of the covenant, Joshua and the Israelites, at God's command, marched around the walled city of Jericho for six days, and on the seventh day, they were able to conquer the city, the walls having crumbled (see Jos 6:1–21).

> Remember, O Lord, in David's favor, all the hardships he endured; / how he swore to the Lord and vowed to the Mighty One of Jacob, / "I will not enter my house or get into my bed; / I will not give sleep to my eyes or slumber to my eyelids, / until I find a place for the Lord, a dwelling place for the Mighty One of Jacob." (Ps 132:1-5)

David, embarrassingly, dwelt in a house of cedar, but according to the Psalmist, because of this discomfiture of the arc dwelling in a tent, he refused to enter his house and denied himself sleep until he could build a suitable dwelling place for the Lord God of Jacob. Even though Solomon built the temple, yet God should take note that the building of such a divine dwelling initially came to the mind of his servant David—he first swore to find an earthly dwelling place for God. The historical context for Stephen's remarks is as follows.

David tells the prophet Nathan, "See now, I dwell in a house of cedar but the ark of God dwells in a tent" (2 Sm 7:2). Nathan at first confirms David's desire to build a dwelling place for the ark. However, God tells Nathan what he is to say to David. "Thus says the Lord: Would you build me a house to dwell in? I have not dwelt in a house since the day I brought up the people of Israel from Egypt to this day, but I have been moving about in a tent for my dwelling" (2 Sm 7:5-6). Moreover, God never asked that a house be built for him. Furthermore, although God favored David and made him great, he will not be the one who will build God a dwelling place, but his son, Solomon. "He shall build a house in my name, and I will establish the throne of his kingdom forever."[32]

Although a suitable house was built for the God of Jacob, Stephen now, somewhat surprisingly states,

> Yet, the Most High does not dwell in houses made with human hands, as the prophet says, "Heaven is my throne, and earth is my footstool. What house will you build for me, says the Lord, or what is the place of my rest? Did not my hand make all these things?"[33]

Stephen is contrasting what is made with human hands with what is made by the hand of God. God may dwell in the temple that was made by the hands of men, yet, because God is "the Most High," and so the Creator of all, he encompasses and exceeds the entire cosmos. Heaven is his throne, and the earth is his footstool, and, therefore, no house can contain him.[34] Moreover,

32. 2 Sm 7:13. See also 2 Sm 7:4-17.

33. Stephen is quoting Is 66:1-2.

34. Solomon himself recognized that the temple he built could not contain God. "But will God indeed dwell on the earth? Behold, heaven and the highest heaven cannot contain thee; how much less this house which I have built" (1 Kgs 8:27).

in contrasting the hands of men with the hand of God, Stephen is also noting, within the biblical context, that what is humanly made is idolatrous. Earlier, he recounted how the Israelites told Aaron to make them a god, and when the golden calf was made, they "offered a sacrifice to the idol and rejoiced in the works of their hands" (Acts 7:39–41). Also, for example, the Wisdom of Solomon declares, "But the idol made with hands is accursed and so is he who made it because he did the work, and the perishable thing was named a god" (Wis 14:8). Or again, "Cursed be the man who makes a graven or molten image, an abomination to the Lord, a thing made by the hands of a craftsman, and sets it up in secret."[35] Even the temple itself may become an idol, as if it were Israel's savior. Jeremiah, standing at the gate of the temple and speaking on God's behalf, warns the men of Judah, "Do not trust in these deceptive words: 'This is the temple of the Lord, the temple of the Lord, the temple of the Lord'" (Jer 7:4). Only if the Jews live holy lives and keep God's commandments will they find salvation.[36] These are the truths concerning God's presence in the temple, and above the heavens and on earth that Stephen wants

35. Dt 27:15. For further examples, see Ex 20:4 and 20:23, and Lv 19:4 and 26:1. Earlier, in Acts 6, when Stephen was arrested, he was accused of saying "that this Jesus of Nazareth will destroy this place [the temple]" (Acts 6:14). In the light of this accusation, I investigated the evidence of what Jesus said and did not say. Below is an abridged version of that enquiry.

All the Synoptic Gospels narrate that Jesus cleansed the temple (see Mt 21:12–13, Mk 11:15–17, and Lk 19:45–46). However, none of them recount that Jesus said anything about the destruction of the temple and that he would rebuild it in three days. After Jesus was arrested, the council sought false witnesses. According to Matthew, two came forward. They claimed, "This fellow said, 'I am able to destroy the temple of God, and to build it in three days'" (Mt 26:61). In Mark's Gospel, "some" claim to have heard Jesus say "I will destroy this temple that is made with hands, and in three days I will build another, not made with human hands" (Mk 14:58). Similarly, onlookers beneath his cross mocked Jesus. "You who would destroy the temple and build it in three days, save yourself!" (Mt 27:40; see also Mk 15:29). Since the Synoptic Gospels do not narrate an occasion where Jesus may have made such declarations, even if falsely interpreted, from where did they arise? The only source available is that found in John's Gospel.

John, in greater detail than found in the Synoptics, tells of Jesus cleansing the temple. The Jews ask, "What sign have you to show us for doing this?" By what authority has Jesus cleansed the temple? In reply, Jesus answered, "Destroy this temple, and in three days I will raise it up." To which the Jews said, "It has taken forty-six years to build this temple, and will you raise it up in three days?" The Evangelist, then, added an interpretive editorial comment. "But he spoke of the temple of his body. When therefore he was raised from the dead, his disciples remembered that he had said this" (Jn 2:13–22). In the light of this Johannine account, we see that Jesus never said that he would destroy the temple. Nonetheless, Jesus, as the Spirit-filled, incarnate Son of God, lovingly offered himself to the Father as the perfect sacrifice, the Passover sacrifice of the new and everlasting covenant. In so doing, Jesus has become, in rising from the dead on the third day, the living, everlasting temple, not made by human hands.

36. See Jer 7:5–15.

the members of the Sanhedrin to grasp, lest they refuse to live holy lives after the manner of their idolatrous and disobedient ancestors.

## Resisting the Holy Spirit (Acts 7:51-53)

Having narrated the history of God's saving actions, and the Israelites' infidelity, particularly their rejection of Moses, Stephen abruptly asserts his scathing condemnation of the Sanhedrin.

> You stiff-necked people, uncircumcised in heart and ears, you always resist the Holy Spirit. As your fathers did, so do you. Which of the prophets did not your fathers persecute? And they killed those who announced before the coming of the Righteous One, whom you have now betrayed and murdered, you who received the law as delivered by angels and did not keep it.[37]

The present members of the Sanhedrin act in the same manner as their ancestors. They too are "stiff-necked." Because their fathers made and worshiped the golden calf, the Lord in his anger told Moses, "Say to the people of Israel, 'You are a stiff-necked people; if I for a single moment I should go among you, I would consume you.'"[38] Jeremiah, speaking on God's behalf, laments. "From the day that your fathers came out of the land of Egypt to this day, I have persistently sent all my servants the prophets; yet they did not listen to me, or incline their ear, but stiffened their neck. They did worse than their fathers."[39] King Hezekiah exhorted the people to come to Jerusalem to celebrate the Passover. "Do not now be stiff-necked as your fathers were, but come to his sanctuary, which he has sanctified forever" (2 Chr 30:8). Nehemiah rehearses God's saving acts within the whole of Israel's history, yet the people are unfaithful, for they "turned a stubborn shoulder and stiffened their neck and would not obey."[40]

Not only are Stephen's Jewish brethren stiff-necked, but they are also, like their ancestors, "uncircumcised in heart and ears." Because God loved his chosen people, Moses exhorts them to "circumcise, therefore the foreskin of your heart, and no longer be stubborn" (Dt 10:15-16). Likewise, again through Jeremiah, God urges the people to "circumcise yourselves to the Lord, remove the foreskin of your hearts" (Jer 4:4). God states that the people cannot hear and obey his words because "their ears are uncircumcised."[41] Circumcision was a

37. Unless otherwise noted, all Scripture passages in this section are taken from Acts 7:51-53.
38. Ex 33:5. See also Ex 32:9 and 33:3.
39. Jer 7:25-26. See also Jer 19:14-15.
40. Neh 9:29. See also Neh 9:16-18.
41. Jer 6:10. God also declares that "all the house of Israel is uncircumcised in heart" (Jer 9:26).

sign of God's covenant with his people. God instructed Abraham, "You shall be circumcised in the flesh of your foreskins, and it shall be a sign of the covenant between me and you" (Gn 17:11). Thus, to be circumcised in the flesh signified that the Jews had a special and unique relationship to God as his chosen people. They were his people, and he was their God. Because they were so conjoined to God, his people were to be as holy as he was holy, and they, therefore, were to be always faithful to his covenant and commands.[42] "The Lord your God will circumcise your heart and the heart of your offspring, so that you will love the Lord your God with all of your heart and with all of your soul, that you may live" (Dt 30:6). However, as seen in the above scriptural quotations, while the Israelites bore the physical sign of the covenant, they had not cut themselves off from sin.[43] Their hearts were still sinful, and, because of their corrupt hearts, their ears could no longer hear and obey God's word. To Stephen's mind, this is not only the morally depraved condition of their Jewish forefathers, but also that of his Jewish listeners as well. Ultimately, they, as did their ancestors, always resisted the Holy Spirit. "They made their hearts adamant lest they should hear the law and the words which the Lord of hosts had sent by his Spirit through the former prophets."[44] "As your fathers did, so do you."[45]

Stephen proceeds with a rhetorical question, "Which of the prophets did not your fathers persecute?" Jesus himself made this same accusation against his contemporary Jewish brethren, some of whom may be Stephen's present listeners.

> Woe to you, scribes and Pharisees, hypocrites! For you build the tombs of the prophets and adorn the monuments of the righteous, saying, "If we had lived in the days of our fathers, we would not have taken part with them in shedding the blood of the prophets." Thus, you witness against yourselves, that you are sons of those who murdered the prophets. Fill up, then, the measure of your fathers.[46]

42. Lv 19:1. See also 1 Pt 1:16.

43. See Lv 26:41.

44. Zec 7:12. Isaiah avers that the stubborn Israelites "rebelled and grieved his Holy Spirit" (Is 63:10). Nonetheless, God promises, "I will give them a new heart and put a new spirit within them; I will take the stony heart out of their flesh and give them a heart of flesh, that they may walk in my statutes and keep my ordinances and obey them; and they shall be my people, and I will be their God" (Ez 11:19-20).

45. As we will see later within the Acts of the Apostles, the issue of circumcision became a heated controversy. Do male Gentile converts to Christianity need to be circumcised? This debate was resolved at the Council of Jerusalem. See Acts 15:1-29. I will more fully examine this dispute within the apostolic church at that juncture.

46. Mt 23:29-32. See also Lk 11:47-48.

The present Jews admit that their fathers killed the prophets but boast that they would not have done so had they lived at the time of the prophets. However, being "sons" of those that shed the blood of the prophets, they too, like their ancestors, will put to death the prophet whom God has now sent to them—the Spirit-filled, incarnate Son of God. In so doing, they will "fill up," bring to full measure, what their fathers had begun. What Jesus had anticipated has now come to pass, and it has been fulfilled by the very members of the Sanhedrin. "And they killed those who announced beforehand the coming of the Righteous One, whom you have now betrayed and murdered, you who received the law as delivered by angels and did not keep it."

Although the Sanhedrin's forebearers persecuted and even killed the prophets who heralded the future messiah, Stephen vehemently condemns them for an even greater crime. "You have now betrayed and murdered" "the Righteous One."[47] They did so, even though of all things, they "received the law as delivered by angels."[48] Despite the fact that the sacred law was conveyed by heavenly angels, they "did not keep it."

By referring to Jesus as the Righteous One, Stephen is alluding to the Suffering Servant Songs in Isaiah. Even though God's servant will bear our griefs, and be afflicted and wounded for humankind's transgressions, "he shall see the fruit of the travail of his soul and be satisfied; / by his knowledge shall the righteous one, my servant, make many to be accounted righteous."[49] Though the Jewish leaders "betrayed and murdered him," Jesus, as the Father's Spirit-filled, righteous, incarnate Son, offered himself as the perfect, loving sacrifice for the forgiveness of sins. In so doing, he makes all who believe in him holy and righteous before God as their risen Savior and Lord. Thus, through his sacrificial death Jesus becomes Jesus, YHWH-Saves. Now that he is risen, Jesus is being Jesus—YHWH-Saves.

Moreover, if the members of the Sanhedrin kept the angel-delivered law, they would not have condemned Jesus. Jesus declared to the unbelieving Jews in John's Gospel, "Do not think that I shall accuse you to my Father; it is Moses

47. Earlier, Peter, in Solomon's Portico, made the same condemnation. "The God of Abraham and of Isaac and of Jacob, the God of our fathers, glorified his servant Jesus, whom you delivered up and denied in the presence of Pilate, when he had decided to release him. But you denied the Holy and Righteous One, and asked for a murderer to be granted you, and killed the Author of life, whom God raised from the dead" (Acts 3:13–15).

48. Jewish tradition, in the light of the Greek version of Dt 33:2, held that angels gave the law to Moses on Mount Sinai. Paul reflects this tradition. He held that angels were intermediaries sent by God to deliver the law (see Gal 3:19).

49. Is 53:11. See the whole of Is 53.

who accuses you, on whom you have set your hope. If you believed Moses, you would believe me. But if you do not believe his writings, how will you believe my words?" (Jn 5:45-47). Once again, we have returned to "this Moses." If Stephen's brethren believed Moses and what he wrote about Jesus, the law delivered by angels, they would now believe in Jesus. However, like their forefathers, they have rejected Moses, and in rejecting him, they have rejected the one of whom he wrote. On this condemnatory note, Stephen concludes his discourse.

## The Stoning of Stephen (Acts 7:54-60)

To say that the members of the Sanhedrin were not pleased with Stephen's lengthy discourse would be an understatement. "Now when they heard these things they were enraged, and they ground their teeth against him."[50] Upon hearing what Stephen said against them, the men of the Sanhedrin physically expressed their rage by grinding their teeth against him. To grind one's teeth is to express one's displeasure or anger at what was said. However, within the biblical context it is always evildoers who gnash their teeth. Those who rejoiced at King David's "stumbling" "impiously mocked more and more, gnashing at me with their teeth" (Ps 35:15-16). Likewise, "the wicked plots against the righteous, and gnashes his teeth at him" (Ps 37:12). Again, "the wicked man sees and is angry; he gnashes his teeth and melts away; the desire of the wicked man comes to nought" (Ps 112:10). In the book of Lamentations, the Lord's enemies are the ones who "rail against you; they hiss, they gnash their teeth" (Lam 2:16). Ironically, by gnashing their teeth at Stephen, the members of the Sanhedrin have condemned themselves. They have aligned themselves with the enraged wicked who gnash their teeth at what is righteous and true. Thus, by gnashing their teeth at Stephen, they confirmed the validity of his condemnation of them.

In Matthew's Gospel, Jesus praised the faith of the Gentile centurion whose servant he healed. In contrast, Jesus has not found such faith in Israel. Thus, "many will come from east and west and sit at the table of Abraham, Isaac, and Jacob in the kingdom of heaven, while the sons of the kingdom will be thrown into the outer darkness; there men will weep and gnash their teeth."[51] At the

50. Unless otherwise noted, all Scripture passages in this section are taken from Acts 7:54-60. However, because of the length of this present narrative, it would be of no benefit to provide the entire text at the onset. Further texts will be incorporated in due course.

51. Mt 8:5-13. See also Lk 13:28-29.

conclusion of the parable of the weeds, Jesus states that at the end of time he will send his angels to gather the weeds, "sinners and evildoers" will be thrown into "the furnace of fire, where there will be weeping and gnashing of teeth" (Mt 13:41-42). Moreover, when the king finds a wedding guest present without a wedding garment, he commanded the attendant, "Bind him hand and foot, and cast him into the outer darkness, where there will be weeping and gnashing of teeth" (Mt 22:11-13). Likewise, Jesus warns that all must be ready for the coming of the Son of man, for he will come at an hour least expected. In the following illustrative parable, Jesus speaks of the wicked servant who is found mistreating the other servants and eating and getting drunk. That master will "put him with the hypocrites; there men will weep and gnash their teeth" (Mt 24:44-51). Lastly, in the parable of the talents, the servant who hid his talent, and so gained no interest, is to be "cast into inner darkness, where there will be wailing and gnashing of teeth" (Mt 25:26-30). Thus, those who gnash their teeth at what is good here on earth, as found in the Psalms and Lamentations, they will weep and gnash their teeth upon Jesus's return at the end of time, for they will be thrown into the pit of everlasting fiery darkness. The members of the Sanhedrin do not realize the precariousness of their situation. Because of their earthly, enraged teeth-gnashing at Stephen, they may ultimately eschatologically weep and gnash their teeth forever.

In contrast to the enraged teeth-grinding of the Sanhedrin, Luke informs us what Stephen is experiencing. "But he, full of the Holy Spirit, gazed into heaven and saw the glory of God, and Jesus standing at the right hand of God; and he said, 'Behold, I see the heavens opened, and the Son of man standing at the right hand of God." Here we have both Luke's depiction of what was taking place, as well as what Stephen beheld. Because Stephen was filled with the Holy Spirit, he was able to gaze into heaven, and what he saw was God's glory and Jesus standing at God's right hand. The event that is described somewhat resembles Jesus's own baptism. Upon being baptized by John, the heavens were opened, and the Holy Spirit descended upon him in the form of a dove. Within this descent of the Holy Spirit from the opened heavens, the Father declared that Jesus is his beloved Son in whom he is well pleased.[52] Now, Stephen, having been filled with the Holy Spirit, presumably since he was baptized, is able to gaze into the opened heaven. He saw the glory of God, the same God who declared Jesus to be his beloved Son. He also saw the risen, glorified Jesus standing at his Father's right hand.

52. See Mt 3:1617, Mk 1:10-11, and Lk 3:21-22. Luke narrates that the Spirit descended upon Jesus after he was baptized and while he was praying.

Normally, the risen and glorified Jesus is depicted as sitting at God's right hand. In his Letter to the Ephesians, Paul declares that when Christ accomplished his Father's work, "he raised him from the dead and made him sit at his right hand in the heavenly places," making him "head over all things for the Church, which is his body, the fullness of him who fills all in all" (Eph 1:20–22). Again, in the Letter to the Hebrews, when Jesus, the Father's Son, "made purification for sins, he sat down at the right hand of the Majesty on high, having become as much superior to angels as the name he has obtained is more excellent than theirs" (Heb 1:3–4). Likewise, "when Christ had offered for all time the single sacrifice for sins, he sat down at the right hand of God" (Heb 10:12). Moreover, like Jesus, Christians are to run the race, "looking to Jesus the pioneer and perfecter of our faith, who for the joy that was set before him endured the cross, despising its shame, and is seated at the right hand of the throne of God."[53] If the risen Jesus is seated at God's right hand, why is he now standing at God's right hand? Stephen himself states that he beholds God's glory, and "the Son of man standing at the right hand of God."

Stephen's vision is a replication of Daniel's vision. Daniel also beheld, "with the clouds of heaven there came one like a son of man, and he came before the Ancient of Days, and was presented before him. And to him was given dominion and glory and kingdom, that all peoples, nations, and languages should serve him," for his is an everlasting kingdom that will not pass away (Dn 7:13–14). He who is the Son of man is the incarnate Son of God, Jesus; and the eternal Father, the Ancient of Days, has given to him, by raising him gloriously from the dead, an everlasting kingdom. This heavenly Son of Man, the risen Jesus, has now lifted himself up from his seat at God's right hand, and he is presently standing before Stephen in order eagerly to receive him. Jesus, the risen Son of man, by his embracing stance, is already anticipating Stephen's imminent death, a death wherein he will join the heavenly Jesus and be seated, with Jesus, at the Father's right hand.

Although Stephen desires that the men of the Sanhedrin "behold" his vision, they found it and his declaration utterly intolerable. "But they cried out with a loud voice and stopped their ears and rushed together upon him." With their loud cries, they attempted to drown out Stephen's words, and by cupping their ears with their hands, they endeavored to become deaf to what he said.

53. Heb 12:2. See also 1 Pt 3:22. In Psalm 110, David prays, "The Lord says to my Lord: / 'Sit at my right hand, / till I make your enemies your footstool'" (Ps 110:1). The Lord (YHWH), who is God, says to David's Lord (YHWH) who is also God, "sit at my right hand." Jesus (YHWH-Saves), as God's risen, incarnate Son, now sits at his Father's right hand in glory.

These enraged bodily actions resulted in their violent rushing upon him. "Then they cast him out of the city and stoned him; and the witnesses laid their garments at the feet of a young man named Saul." Stoning was the punishment for seriously violating the Mosaic law. It was done outside the camp or the city in order not to pollute the camp or city.[54] Moreover, the witnesses who testified to the evil done were the first to enact the punishment. "The hand of the witnesses shall be the first against him to put him to death, and afterward the hand of all the people" (Dt 17:7). Thus, "the witnesses," that is, the members of the Sanhedrin, placed their cloaks at Saul's feet prior to casting the first stones upon Stephen.[55]

Once again, there is a contrast between what is happening to Stephen, his being stoned, and what he is doing. "And as they were stoning Stephen, he prayed, 'Lord Jesus, receive my spirit.' And he knelt down and cried with a loud voice, 'Lord, do not hold this sin against them.' And when he had said this, he fell asleep." As Jesus gave up his spirit, his last breath, to his Father, so Stephen is giving up his life to his Lord, Jesus.[56] Likewise, although his persecutors are stoning him, he is transforming his life, like Jesus, into a loving sacrifice on their behalf. He even enacts his sacrificial prayer by kneeling down. As a kneeling supplicant, he loudly cries out, "Lord, do not hold this against them." In so doing he is echoing the words of the crucified Jesus, "Father, forgive them; for they know not what they do" (Lk 23:34). Thus, as members of the Sanhedrin loudly cry out in rage as they stone him to death, Stephen loudly cries out for their salvation. Having completed what he wanted to say, "he fell asleep." In one sense, "to fall asleep" is a euphemism for death. However, a sleeping person, at the dawn of a new day, also awakes from sleep. When he is told that his friend Lazarus has died, Jesus states, "Our friend Lazarus has fallen asleep, but I will go to awake him out of sleep."[57] Jesus, as the Son of God (He Who Is) incarnate, is able to awake the dead Lazarus because he is the resurrection and the life. Jesus declares to Martha, "I am the resurrection and the

54. See Nm 15:35.

55. Here we find the first appearance of Saul. Luke is alerting the reader that this young man will become important as Paul, the apostle to the Gentiles. Saul's prominence will become evident later in the Acts of the Apostles.

56. See Mt 27:50, Mk 15:37, Lk 23:46, and Jn 19:30. The Synoptic Gospels narrated that Jesus "cried out with a loud voice" in the act of dying.

57. Jn 11:11. Later, Jesus plainly acknowledges that "Lazarus is dead." See Jn 11:14. Paul wants to assure the Christians in Thessalonica that they should not be distressed over those "who are asleep." When Jesus returns, "God will bring with him those who have fallen asleep." Those who have died will rise first and, only then, will those still living be "caught up together with them in the clouds to meet the Lord in the air" (1 Thes 4:13–18).

life; he who believes in me, though he die, yet he shall live, and whoever lives and believes in me shall never die" (Jn 11:25–26). Because Stephen fell asleep in him who is the resurrection and the life, he is assured that the risen Jesus, his Savior and Lord, will raise him up on the last day when he comes again in glory.

Luke concludes chapter seven with a final aside. "And Saul was consenting to his death." Saul, the youthful, garment-watching bystander, was not an innocent onlooker. Rather, in heart and mind, he too, with his forefathers and the Sanhedrin, was resisting "the Holy Spirit." Little did Saul know that that would soon change when the risen Lord Jesus would gloriously appear to him.

## Conclusion

By way of conclusion, I will highlight three points. First, throughout Stephen's lengthy discourse, we perceive the theological importance of Israel's history as found in the Old Testament. This is particularly found in the book of Exodus, and within that context, the singular significance of "this Moses." Although God continually worked mighty deeds at the hand of Moses, the stubborn and faithless Israelites rejected him. Likewise, they immediately broke God's covenant with them by offering sacrifice to a golden calf that they made with their own hands, they rejoiced in their idolatry. This was Israel's primordial sin, a sin that continued throughout their entire history—they were ever disloyal to God and to his covenant. As the ancient fathers rejected God and Moses, so too members of the Sanhedrin now are also stiff-necked. They have rejected God by disbelieving in the one whom he sent as Moses's promised prophet—the risen Jesus Christ, the Father's only begotten Son. While Luke is narrating what happened between Stephen and his contemporary Jewish brethren, I believe that he also has an eye on future Jewish generations. As long as they continue to reject Jesus and refuse to believe in him as their Savior and Lord, they will continue to be God's faithless and stiff-necked people, though they are his chosen and beloved nation.

Second, although he is narrating Stephen's arrest, his lengthy discourse in response to his detention, and his martyrdom, Luke has also woven within this historical narrative Stephen's imitation of Jesus. False accusations are made against him (see Acts 6:11–14 and Mt 26:60 and parallels). He has visions of the heavenly Son of man (see Acts 7:56 and Lk 22:69). Stephen commends his spirit to his Lord, Jesus (see Acts 7:59 and Lk 23:56). Lastly, he asks the sin committed against him be forgiven (see Acts 7:60 and Lk 23:34). Stephen, through his martyrdom, by bearing witness to the gospel, has conformed himself into the likeness of Christ. As the protomartyr, Stephen's martyrdom gives rise to a theology of martyrdom—all subsequent martyrs, by bearing witness to the gospel, will conform themselves to the likeness of Jesus, he who shed his blood for the salvation of the world.[58]

Lastly, through the ministry of the deacon Stephen, we perceive Jesus being Jesus. Stephen was arrested precisely because he preached that Jesus is risen. Because Jesus is gloriously risen, he can now enact his name—YHWH-Saves. Stephen preaches with the assurance that all who believe in the name of the risen Jesus, through the transforming power of the Holy Spirit, will be purified of sin and obtain eternal life. Stephen, with the conviction of faith, knows that Jesus, now until the end of time, is being Jesus—YHWH-Saves. His frustration, borne out of love, is that his Jewish brothers and sisters refuse to believe in Jesus as their divine Savior and Lord.

58. As the first martyr, it is appropriate that the church celebrates his feast on the day after Christmas.

*Chapter 8*

# THE PREACHING OF PHILIP

## The Growing Church Is Persecuted (Acts 8:1–3)

Chapter eight begins, "And on that day a great persecution arose against the Church in Jerusalem; and they were all scattered throughout the region of Judea and Samaria, except the apostles."[1] On the very day on which Stephen was stoned to death, the Jerusalem church braved a harsh persecution. Stephen's martyrdom was the catalyst of this ensuing oppression. One can surmise from the fierce opposition of the members of the Sanhedrin that the unbelieving Jews were becoming anxious over the dramatic growth of the church (*èkklesían*), and the threatening impact that it was having on the local population. This disquiet was apt to explode at the first provocation, and Stephen's stoning was the spark that lit the fuse.

Although Luke states that it was the church that was persecuted, he immediately says that "*they* were all scattered throughout Judea and Samaria." The "they" would be the members of the church. This dispersing of the church's membership is, obviously, disheartening. However, as will soon become evident, it provided the opportunity for evangelizing those who lived in Judea and Samaria.[2] So, while the Jerusalem Jews sought to suppress the church, they became the initiatory cause for its further growth beyond Jerusalem's walls. The Jewish persecutors were not following Gamaliel's earlier wise counsel.

1. Unless otherwise noted, all Scripture passages in this introduction are taken from Acts 8:1–3. However, because of the length of this present narrative, it would be of no benefit to provide the entire text at the onset. Further texts will be incorporated in due course.

2. The proclamation fulfills Jesus's prophetic mandate. The apostles will receive the Holy Spirit, "and you shall be my witnesses in Jerusalem and in Judea and Samaria and to the end of the earth" (Acts 1:8).

If what the Christians are preaching "is of God, you will not be able to overthrow them. You might even be found opposing God."[3] Significantly, Luke notes, that although "all scattered," the apostles did not. They remained in Jerusalem. The apostles remained because Jesus founded the apostolic church in Jerusalem when he poured out his Holy Spirit upon the Twelve on Pentecost. Jerusalem is, in a sense, the primatial apostolic see, and as such, the apostles could not abandon it. They had to remain loyal and steadfast to the place where they received their ecclesial apostolic mandate.[4]

Having spoken of the persecution in Jerusalem that followed upon Stephen's death, Luke states, "Devout men buried Stephen, and made great lamentation over him." In the midst of persecution, holy and dedicated men properly buried Stephen. They did so with "great lamentation." Such weeping and mourning testified to their Christian brotherly affection and respect for Stephen, for he was the first to die out of love for Jesus and faithfulness to the gospel.

In contrast, Luke declares, "But Saul laid waste the Church, and entering house after house, he dragged off men and women and committed them to prison." So, the consenting, garment-watching Saul has now become the chief marauding foe of the church. The Greek word for "laid waste" (*lymainō*) means to "ravage" or to "bring to ruin," and it is only employed here in the entire New Testament. The Psalmist laments that "the boar of the forest ravages" the vineyard (Ps 80:13). This ravaging also refers to the excessive cruelty of conquering rulers.[5] Thus, Paul ravages the church, the ecclesial community, by "entering house after house." He did not knock on door after door. Rather, he violently, with the help of his thugs, methodically, burst into people's homes—one after another. In so doing, he forcefully lugged them out, one after another—not just the men, but women as well. Saul was consumed with rage and with that rage he laid waste the church.[6] With this dire and frightful description of

3. Acts 5:38–39. In contrast to my above interpretation, it could be argued that the Jews did follow Gamaliel's counsel, and so, while they intimidated "ordinary" believers, they did not persecute the apostles—they were exempted. I do not think that this interpretation is in accord with the text.

4. Because Peter and Paul preached the gospel in Rome and were ultimately martyred in Rome, Rome became the premier apostolic see within the Roman Catholic Church. However, Jerusalem never lost its historical and ecclesial prominence as being the city in which the gospel was first proclaimed and from which the gospel was spread to all nations and peoples. See Acts 1:8.

5. See 2 Chr 16:10.

6. Immediately prior to his conversion, Luke states, "But Saul, still breathing threat and murder against the disciples of the Lord, went to the high priest and asked for letters to the

Saul, Luke has dramatically set the stage for what would be the surprisingly great marvel—Saul's conversion to Jesus Christ and his becoming a member of the church.

## Philip Preaches in Samaria (Acts 8:4–8)

Although all the scattered became evangelists, Luke now focuses on the evangelistic exploits of the second named deacon after Stephen, Philip.[7]

> Now those who were scattered went about preaching the word. Philip went down to a city of Samaria and proclaimed the Christ. And the multitudes with one accord gave heed to him and saw the signs which he did. For unclean spirits came out of many who were possessed, crying out in a loud voice; and many who were paralyzed or lame were healed. So, there was much joy in that city.[8]

That Philip went down to a town in Samaria may seem innocent enough. If one is going to evangelize people who have never heard the gospel, Samaria is as good of a place to start as any. So, Philip went to Samaria and proclaimed Jesus to be the Christ, that is, the Spirit-anointed Savior. However, the animosity between Jews and Samaritans went back centuries.[9] In Luke's Gospel,

---

synagogues at Damascus, so that if he found any belonging to the Way, men and women, he might bring them bound to Jerusalem" (Acts 9:1–2). Paul's rage knew no geographical bounds. Later, Paul, with remorse, candidly acknowledges that he did all the above. See Acts 22:4–5 and 26:9–11. Because of what he did against the church, Paul says "I am the least of the apostles, unfit to be called an apostle, because I persecuted the Church of God" (1 Cor 15:9).

Although Paul regrets his previous behavior, he immediately declares that "by the grace of God I am what I am, and his grace toward me was not in vain. On the contrary, I worked harder than any of them [the other apostles], though it was not I, but the grace of God which is with me" (1 Cor 15:10). His passionate zeal to righteously serve the God of Israel by violently suppressing the gospel is now transformed by divine grace into a dynamic, no-holds-barred effort to preach that same gospel. In this effort he surpassed even the other apostles. Here we learn something of his emotional and psychological makeup. Whether as Saul or as Paul, he could do nothing by half measures.

7. See Acts 6:5.

8. Unless otherwise noted, all Scripture passages in this section are taken from Acts 8:4–8.

Interestingly, in Luke's Gospel, when Jesus was making his way to Jerusalem and passed through Samaria, "the people would not receive him" (Lk 9:51–56). They rejected Jesus not only because he was a Jew, but also because he was going to Jerusalem, which the Jews, unlike the Samaritans, maintained was the proper place to worship God. See Jn 4:19–20.

9. Although the Samaritans were originally descendants of the northern tribes of Jacob, they intermarried with foreigners and worshipped foreign gods. The Jews, therefore, considered them contaminated. "The king of Assyria brought people from Babylon, Cuthah, Avva, Hammath, and Sepharvaim, and placed them in the cities of Samaria" (2 Kgs 17:24). By intermarrying with these people, the Samaritans were no longer fully Jewish, but now a mixed race.

when Jesus healed the ten lepers, only one came back to thank him. "Now he was a Samaritan," one whom even Jesus called "this foreigner" (Lk 17:15-19). Nonetheless, even though he was a foreign Samaritan, he was the one who was grateful. In John's Gospel, at Jacob's well, Jesus asks a Samaritan for a drink of water. She replied by asking, "How is it that you, a Jew, ask a drink of me, a woman of Samaria?" John adds an aside: "For Jews have no dealings with Samaritans" (Jn 4:7-9). Later, after Jesus spoke of the living water that he could give, that of the Holy Spirit received in Baptism, the woman, recognizing Jesus to be a prophet, notes, "Our fathers worshipped on this mountain; and you say that in Jerusalem is the place where men ought to worship." Jesus responds by informing her that in the future one will neither worship on this mountain nor in Jerusalem. "But the hour is coming and now is, when true worshippers will worship the Father in spirit and truth, for such the Father seeks to worship him. God is spirit, and those who worship him must worship him in spirit and truth." The Samaritan woman then states, "I know that the Messiah is coming (he who is called Christ); when he comes, he will show us all things," to which Jesus declares, "I who speak to you am he."[10] Significantly, as the Samaritan woman came to believe that Jesus is the messianic Christ, so Philip now goes to Samaria "and proclaimed to them the Christ." By going to Samaria, Philip will now fulfill Jesus's prophecy and assume, and so continue, Jesus's own ministry to the Samaritans. By coming to faith in Jesus as the Christ and by being baptized into him by the power of the Holy Spirit, they will become worshippers of the Father in spirit and in truth.

Given the acrimonious history between the Jews and the Samaritans, it is somewhat surprising what Luke says next. "And the multitudes with one accord gave heed to what was said by Philip, when they heard him and saw the signs which he did." Huge numbers of Samaritans paid heed to Philip's declaration that Jesus was the Christ, and they did so without causing discord among themselves. They were of "one accord" that what Philip professed should be believed.[11]

10. Jn 4:19-27. By informing the Samaritan woman that he is the Christ by saying that he who speaks to her "am he" (*ego eimi*), Jesus is also declaring that he is God—He Who Is. Jesus is the Spirit-filled, incarnate Son of God. Thus, for Philip to proclaim that Jesus is the Christ necessitates that he is, therefore, the Father's eternal, Spirit-filled Son. To be the Christ is to be God's Son.

11. That the Samaritans accepted the gospel from a Jewish evangelist manifests that the gospel reconciles those who were once enemies—the gathering of all peoples and nations into one in Christ Jesus. Although Paul was speaking of the division between Gentiles and Jews, what he says could equally apply to the divisions found between all nations. "For he [Jesus] is our peace, who has made us both one, and has broken down the dividing wall of hostility" (Eph 2:14).

The truth of what Philip proclaimed concerning the Christ was confirmed by "the signs that he did." "For unclean spirits came out of many who were possessed, crying with a loud voice; and many who were paralyzed or lame were healed." As Jesus performed exorcisms and miraculous healings within the context of his proclamation of the good news, so Philip does the same in proclaiming the Christ.[12] The working of signs always attracts people to the gospel, as well as validating the truth of the gospel. They cannot be separated. Moreover, exorcisms and healings are signs of the inbreaking of the new creation. Sickness, the power of Satan, and the curse of death entered God's good creation because of sin. The expelling of demons and the healing of the sick testify that through Jesus, ultimately through his death and resurrection, a new earth is coming into existence, where there will be everlasting life, with no more sickness and death. John, in his vision of the new Jerusalem where God will abide with his people, says, "He will wipe away every tear from their eyes, and death shall be no more, neither shall there be mourning nor crying nor pain any more, for former things have passed away" (Rv 21:4). In this evangelistic context wherein the Christ is proclaimed and exorcisms and healing are enacted, Luke concludes, "So there was much joy in that city." Philip himself would have been joyful. Moreover, what we perceive here through Philip's preaching the gospel and his working of miracles, healings, and exorcisms in Jesus's name is Jesus being Jesus—YHWH-Saves. He is continuing to act through the ecclesial and apostolic ministry of Philip.

## Simon the Magician (Acts 8:9-25)

However, things in that city take a strange turn.

> But there was a man named Simon who had previously practiced magic in the city and amazed the nation of Samaria, saying that he himself was somebody great. They all listened to him, from the least to the greatest, saying, "This man is that power of God which is called Great." And they listened to him, because for a long time he had amazed them with his magic.[13]

12. Mark, in his Gospel, describes Jesus casting out a mute spirit from a boy in this manner: "And after crying out and convulsing him terribly, it came out" (Mk 9:25-26). Demons violently attempt to resist Jesus's power, but ultimately, they come out with fearsome loud cries, for they cannot withstand his authority over them. Thus, as demonstrated by Philip, the demons remain fearful of Jesus as they continue to come out with terrified "loud voices" when exorcised in his name.

13. Unless otherwise noted, all Scripture passages in this section are taken from Acts 8:9-25. However, because of the length of this present narrative, it would be of no benefit to provide the entire text at the onset. Further texts will be incorporated in due course.

The magician, Simon, mesmerized the whole of Samaria with his magic.[14] He even prided himself as "somebody great." Because of his magical feats, everyone in the town listened to him and concluded that he possessed the "power of God which is called Great." Because God, as He Who Is, exists in a singular manner, he is great in a singular manner. His greatness differs in kind, and not in degree, from all other finite forms of greatness.[15] Therefore, the people, the least no less than the great, for a long time believed that Simon shared in this great divine power, and so they paid him great respect, for they were enthralled by his magical prowess.

> But when they believed Philip as he preached good news about the kingdom of God and in the name of Jesus Christ, they were baptized, both men and women. Even Simon himself believed, and after being baptized he continued with Philip. And seeing signs and great miracles performed he was amazed.

With the arrival of Philip, with his preaching of the good news, things began to change in the city. The people came to believe that Jesus is the Christ, and that he established the kingdom of God, where all who abide in him will enter into God's heavenly presence. Believing in these truths, both men and women were baptized, for it is through that transforming power of the Holy Spirit that one comes to abide in the risen Jesus Christ and thus becomes a child of the heavenly Father. So taken was Simon that he himself believed and was baptized. Having been baptized, Luke tells the reader that he "continued with Philip." In what manner he "continued" is ambiguous. However, one can surmise that he followed Philip around the city because he continued to work miracles. "And seeing signs and great miracles performed he was amazed." Simon was now mesmerized by Philip's power, and he may have thought that, since he had been baptized, he could now work miracles just like Philip. As will be seen shortly, he ever more ardently and jealously wanted to possess that power for himself. His motives for continuing with Philip were, then, far from being pure. He had little interest in bringing his fellow Samaritans to conversion and faith in Jesus. It was "divine" power that he craved.

14. Luke does not provide examples of Simon's magical capability. Did he pull rabbits out of a hat? Hardly. His magical power was not that of a tricky entertainer. Rather, he possessed spiritual power that was more ominous.

15. God's greatness is often professed in the Old Testament. Jeremiah declared, "There is none like you, O Lord; you are great, and your name is great in might" (Jer 10:6). "For great is the Lord, and greatly to be praised, and he is held in awe above all gods" (1 Chr 16:25, see also 1 Chr 29:11). "For great is the Lord, and greatly to be praised; he is to be feared above all gods" (Ps 96:4). See also Neh 1:5 and Is 12:6.

Luke next informs the reader of two new arrivals into the Samaritan city. Because of their actions, Simon's craving for power will reach fever pitch.

> Now when the apostles at Jerusalem heard that Samaria had received the word of God, they sent to them Peter and John, who came down and prayed for them that they might receive the Holy Spirit; for the Spirit had not yet fallen on any of them, but they had only been baptized in the name of the Lord Jesus. Then they laid hands on them, and they received the Holy Spirit.

This passage raises multiple significant theological issues. The apostles in Jerusalem became aware that the Samaritans, through the preaching of Philip, had "received the word of God," that is, that the risen Jesus was the Spirit-anointed Christ. Because of this exciting news, the apostles sent Peter and John to them.[16] They were sent for the explicit purpose that they pray over those who had come to faith. The point of praying over them was so that "they might receive the Holy Spirit; for the Spirit had not yet fallen on them, but they had only been baptized in the name of the Lord Jesus."

There is no simple interpretation that easily explains Luke's above statement. If one receives the Holy Spirit when one is baptized, why then is there the further need of praying over a baptized person so that the Holy Spirit would fall upon them? Prior to his ascension, Jesus informs the apostles that, while John baptized with water, they will shortly "be baptized with the Holy Spirit" (Acts 1:5). At the conclusion of his Pentecost sermon, subsequent to the apostles having been "filled with the Holy Spirit," Peter declared to his listeners, "Repent, and be baptized every one of you in the name of Jesus Christ for the forgiveness of your sins; and you shall receive the gift of the Holy Spirit."[17]

16. As previously seen in Acts, Peter and John work together, though Peter, as the head of the apostles, is invariably the spokesman. However, this passage contains the last time in Acts that John is mentioned as an active participant in an event. Narratives concerning Peter's activity will continue.

17. Acts 2:4 and 2:38. What Luke narrates in Acts is in accord with what Jesus teaches in John's Gospel. Jesus emphatically tells Nicodemus, "Truly, truly, I say to you, unless one is born of water and the Spirit, he cannot enter the kingdom of God" (Jn 3:5). Baptism, the means by which one receives the Holy Spirit, allows one to enter God's kingdom. Similarly, Jesus informs the Samaritan woman that he will give water that will become "a spring of water welling up to eternal life" (Jn 4:14). That Jesus's teaching here concerns the receiving of the Holy Spirit is confirmed in John 7. Jesus proclaims that if anyone is thirsty, they should come to him and drink, for "Out of his heart shall flow rivers of living water." John then adds an interpretative aside. "Now this he said about the Spirit, which those who believed in him were to receive; for as yet the Spirit had not been given, because Jesus was not yet glorified" (Jn 7:38–39). Only after Jesus is gloriously risen from the dead is he empowered to pour out the Holy Spirit upon the church, and is the church then empowered to baptize with the Holy Spirit. Paul tells

Undisputedly, the Holy Spirit is given within the act of being baptized. If such is an established fact, how are we to understand Luke's statement that having been baptized, the Samaritans need to receive the Holy Spirit? This need arises from another fact: "the Spirit had not yet fallen on them," since they "had only been baptized in the name of the Lord Jesus." Luke simply concludes, "Then they (Peter and John) laid their hands on them, and they received the Holy Spirit." Does not Luke's historical account of what took place in Samaria contain an inherent theological contradiction? What theological reasoning lay within the action of the apostles, particularly Peter and John? How would they have answered the question "If the Samaritans received the Holy Spirit at Baptism, in what manner is the Spirit coming upon them when you pray over them and impose your hands?" Unfortunately, we do not possess an apostolic answer.

Traditionally, both within the Western and Eastern ecclesial traditions, this passage has been interpreted as distinguishing the Sacrament of Baptism from that of the Sacrament of Confirmation. One receives the Holy Spirit when one is baptized, and then one also further receives the Holy Spirit when one is confirmed—a strengthening of the Spirit whereby one is empowered to defend and profess the faith. This difference is no doubt true, and the text may have given rise to the above sacramental distinction between Baptism and Confirmation.[18] Nonetheless, I believe it is an unhistorical interpretation, that is, it is an interpretation that is not faithful to what the text historically portrays in the Acts of the Apostles. The passage is not attempting to make a sacramental distinction between Baptism and Confirmation.

---

the Corinthians that Christians form one body. "For by one Spirit we were all baptized into one body—Jews or Greeks, slaves or free—and all made to drink of one Spirit" (1 Cor 12:12–13). The drinking of the one Spirit through the waters of Baptism initiates one into the one body of Christ, the church. See also Ti 3:5.

The Acts of the Apostles often refers to Baptism "in the name of the Lord Jesus Christ," or some similar formula (see Acts 2:38, 8:16, 10:48, 19:5, and 22:16). Is being baptized "in the name of the Lord Jesus" different from being baptized "in the name of the Father, and of the Son, and of the Holy Spirit"? (Mt 28:19). Given that Jesus, as the risen Lord, is the one who baptizes through the sacramental ministry of his church, by means of a bishop, priest, deacon, or even lay person, all Baptisms are enacted in his "name." To be baptized in the name of Jesus is for the Lord to immerse those whom he baptizes into the divine life that he himself shares with the Father and the Holy Spirit. So, the two different expressions emphasize two inter-related aspects of the Sacrament of Baptism. One, all are baptized in the name of Jesus, in that he baptizes through the instrumentality of his church. Two, the efficacious effect of being baptized in the name of Jesus is that one comes to participate in the inter-relational divine life of the Father, the Son, and the Holy Spirit.

18. In the light of this interpretation, Philip, then, could be seen as the deacon who baptizes, and Peter and John as "bishops" who enact the Sacrament of Confirmation.

For a proper understanding of what took place in Samaria when Peter and John prayed over and laid hands upon those baptized, wherein they received the Holy Spirit, one needs to revisit what took place at Pentecost. In that event the apostles "were all filled with the Holy Spirit and began to speak in other tongues, as the Spirit gave them utterance" (Acts 2:4). Nowhere is it said that the apostles were baptized in what today would be termed the sacramental sense. They could not possibly be baptized in a "normal" manner because there was no prior baptized person to baptize them. Thus, when the Spirit came upon them on Pentecost, they were "baptized," in that, they were interiorly cleansed of sin and transformed into the likeness of the risen Christ such that they became adopted sons of the Father. In this apostolic Pentecost baptism, the apostles were thus empowered to sacramentally baptize others. In baptizing the apostles on Pentecost, Jesus was enacting his name, that is, he was being YHWH-Saves, for through baptism the apostles reaped the salvific benefits that Jesus merited through his death on the cross and in his glorious resurrection.

Moreover, through this outpouring of the Holy Spirit, Jesus also further empowered them "to speak in other tongues, as the Spirit gave them utterance." Thus, within this Pentecostal event there resides both the institution of the Sacrament of Baptism as well as what came to be called the charismatic or spiritual gifts of the Spirit, such as speaking in other tongues. For Paul, all Christians, having been baptized in the one Spirit, become one body in Christ. Within that body, God has appointed "first apostles, second prophets, third teachers, then workers of miracles, then healers, helpers, administrators, speakers in various tongues" (1 Cor 27-28). All of these gifts, whether they be ecclesial offices, such as apostles, prophets, or teachers, or spiritual gifts that are freely given to others, such as the ability to enact miracles or to heal, etc., are all for the upbuilding of the body. On Pentecost, the apostles, in the outpouring of the Holy Spirit, were both baptized and the beneficiaries of the charismatic or spiritual gifts, such as the ability to work miracles, heal, and to speak in other tongues.[19] In giving these charismatic gifts to his apostles, Jesus empowered them to more fully enact his name, YHWH-Saves, for now they could fully replicate Jesus's own earthly ministry. Again, through the apostles, Jesus continues to fully enact his name, YHWH-Saves, not only through the Sacrament of Baptism, but also through the Spirit's charismatic gifts. Thus, when Peter and John came to Samaria and prayed over and laid hands upon those who were baptized so that the Holy Spirit might fall upon them, they

19. In Acts, we have already seen that the apostles worked miracles and healed people in the name of Jesus Christ.

did so that they might receive their share in the spiritual or charismatic gifts of the Holy Spirit. The apostles, in the persons of Peter and John, wanted to ensure that the Samaritans acquired the full benefits of Pentecost—the receiving of the Holy Spirit through Baptism and the Spirit-filled, charismatic gifts as well. The apostolic experience of Pentecost is to be the same Pentecostal experience for all who come to faith in Jesus as their Lord and Savior. What was one unified Pentecostal experience for the apostles, that of being baptized and of receiving the spiritual gifts, became two distinct, though related, experiences or events for subsequent Christians.[20]

20. The above interpretation is later confirmed, but in a reversed order. Cornelius, who was a devout man, received a vision of an angel. The angel told him to send men to Joppa, and they were to bring Peter to him. Peter, in turn, had a vision of all kinds of animals which he was to kill and eat. Peter responds that he has never eaten what was unclean. A voice told Peter that what God has cleansed is no longer unclean. Although Peter was perplexed, the men sent by Cornelius came and requested that he come with them to Caesarea where Cornelius lived. Peter went with them, and he preached the gospel to Cornelius and his entire household. "While Peter was still saying this, the Holy Spirit fell on all who heard the word. And the believers from among the circumcised who came with Peter were amazed, because the gift of the Holy Spirit had been poured out even on the Gentiles. For they heard them speaking in tongues and extolling God. Then Peter declared, 'Can anyone forbid water for baptizing these people who have received the Holy Spirit just as we have?' And he commanded them to be baptized in the name of Jesus Christ" (Acts 10:44-48). See the whole of chapter ten.

The most theologically significant thing that Peter declared in the above is that Cornelius and his household "have received the Holy Spirit just as we have." The experience that the apostles had on Pentecost is the exact same experience that they now had. As the Holy Spirit was poured out on the apostles, so now it fell upon them (Observe that Peter and John prayed over and laid hands upon the Samaritans, "for the Spirit had not yet fallen on them"). Moreover, as the apostles spoke in tongues, so now Cornelius and his household spoke in tongues. Because of this pouring out and falling upon of the Holy Spirit, Peter declares that there is no reason why all these people cannot be baptized with water in the name of Jesus Christ. Thus, with the Holy Spirit falling upon them, accompanied by their speaking in tongues, and with their being sacramentally baptized, Cornelius and his household have been subsumed into and so share in the entire apostolic Pentecostal experience.

This same Pentecostal pattern is found later in Acts. When Paul came to Ephesus and found that some of the people only received "John's baptism," and so did not receive the Holy Spirit, he had them baptized. "They were baptized in the name of the Lord Jesus. And when Paul had laid hands upon them, the Holy Spirit came on them; and they spoke with tongues and prophesied" (Acts 19:1-6). As with the apostles on Pentecost, the Ephesians attained the complete Pentecostal experience. They were sacramentally baptized, and so received the Holy Spirit. Moreover, with the laying on of hands, the Holy Spirit fell upon them whereupon they received the spiritual or charismatic gifts—that of speaking in tongues and prophesying. For Jesus to be Jesus, YHWH-Saves, he must bestow the full benefits of the Holy Spirit—those contained in Baptism and those attained through the laying on of hands—the spiritual gifts. In so doing Jesus, is being Jesus.

As an aside, it strikes me that the contemporary Charismatic or Pentecostal Renewal within all the Christian communities presently exemplifies what took place among the Samaritans

Now, there must have been some visible manifestation of these various charismatic gifts when Peter and John prayed over and laid hands upon the baptized Samaritans because Simon became wildly animated. Ever keen to possess magical power, Simon, as we will immediately see, was anxious to purchase this ability to impart these spiritual gifts himself.

> Now when Simon saw that the Spirit was given through the laying on of the apostles' hands, he offered them money, saying "Give me also this power, that any one on whom I lay my hands may receive the Holy Spirit."

Simon failed to recognize that Jesus, as the head of the church, freely bestows spiritual gifts and powers for the upbuilding of his body. Jesus is hardly enticed by the offer of money, and the leaders of his church cannot be bribed into selling spiritual powers and benefices—though historically that may have, at times, become the case.[21]

Peter responds with a stunning rebuke and a call to repentance.

> But Peter said to him, "Your silver can perish with you, because you thought you could obtain the gift of God with money! You have neither part nor lot in this matter, for your heart is not right with God. Repent therefore of this wickedness of yours, and pray to the Lord that, if possible, the intent of your heart may be forgiven you. For I see that you are in the gall of bitterness and in the bond of iniquity."

Peter has no regard for money, though Simon devotes his magical ability to acquire wealth. Thus, Peter declares that Simon, with his silver in hand, can perish. "Perish" could mean simply that when Simon dies his money will perish with him. However, given what Peter will say shortly, "perish" acquires a more ominous and dreadful meaning—that of perishing in hell. Such everlasting

---

and within the apostolic church as a whole. Significantly, just as Pentecost was not of human origin, but a sovereign work of God, so there is no human initiator of the present Charismatic or Pentecostal revival. It, too, is of divine origin. Within the charismatic context, Christians who have been baptized and confirmed, and so have received the Holy Spirit, are now prayed over and hands are laid upon them so that the Holy Spirit might "fall upon" them. The effect is that Jesus comes vibrantly alive within them. They now possess a personal relationship with Jesus as their Lord and Savior. Moreover, they receive and manifest, as God determines for each, the various charismatic or spiritual gifts of the Spirit. Thus, they also have now shared in the entire apostolic Pentecostal experience. Furthermore, they also become some of the most effective Christian evangelists, for often, as in the apostolic church, their preaching of the word is accompanied by miracles, healings, and exorcisms.

Interestingly as well, most of the saints, if not all of them, manifested the spiritual gifts—performing miracles, healings, and exorcisms.

21. "Simony" came to be designated as the sin of selling and buying ecclesial privileges or benefices.

condemnatory perishing is due to the fact that Simon thought he could purchase God's gift. Because of this malevolent attitude, Peter emphatically states, "You have neither part nor lot in this matter, for your heart is not right before God." Simon, unlike the deacon Philip, has no part, or even a small portion, in the church's ministry, such as praying over and laying hands on others so that the Spirit may fall upon them. He will not share in the apostolic mystery wherein Jesus is being Jesus. He is utterly excluded. The reason is simply that his heart is not in conformity with God.[22] Peter advises him as to what he needs to do. "Repent therefore of this wickedness of yours, and pray to the Lord that, if possible, the intent of your heart may be forgiven you."[23] Although Simon ought to repent of his sin, and although he ought to supplicate the Lord for forgiveness, it may not be possible that such pardon will be given. The problem is not that God would deny his clemency or that the sin was so wicked that it could not be forgiven. No, the difficulty resides within Simon himself. Forgiveness may be impossible, because of what Peter perceives. "For I see that you are in the gall of bitterness and in the bond of iniquity." The phrase "gall of bitterness" sounds dreadful, but what does it mean? To be in a state where one is in a "gall of bitterness" is to be so filled with rancor and duplicitousness that one is pungent and putrid with evil. If that is not bad enough, Simon is also "in the bond of iniquity," that is, he is enslaved to the authority of Satan himself. Simon recognizes the hopelessness of his situation, and he cries in despair to Peter. "Pray for me to the Lord, that nothing of what you have said may come upon me." On that note, Luke abruptly concludes his narrative concerning Simon the magician.[24]

Almost as an afterthought, as if he perceived the need to bring to a proper end to this entire segment, Luke says, "Now when they had testified and spoken the word of the Lord, they returned to Jerusalem, preaching the gospel to many villages of the Samaritans." So, as they made their way back to Jerusalem, Peter and John visited many Samaritan villages all the while preaching the gospel and testifying to Jesus's resurrection and his lordship. They had accomplished their mission, that of praying over and laying their hands upon all who were baptized in order that the Spirit might fall upon them.

22. See Ps 78:37. The hearts of the Israelites were not steadfast toward God.

23. There are other instances in Acts where the power of the risen Lord Jesus triumphs over magical and superstitious practices. See Acts 13:6–12, 16:16–18, and 19:18–19.

24. What happened to Simon? Well, we do not know. Though it may be improbable, hopefully, because of Peter's prayers on his behalf, he was freed from the curse of his sins and obtained God's forgiveness, and so lived a holy life as a baptized Christian.

## Philip and the Ethiopian Eunuch (Acts 8:26–40)

While Peter and John were making their way back to Jerusalem, Philip left Samaria and continued his evangelistic journey.

> But an angel of the Lord said to Philip, "Rise and go toward the south to the road that goes down from Jerusalem to Gaza." This is a desert road. And he rose and went. And behold, an Ethiopian, a eunuch, a minister of Candace the queen of the Ethiopians, in charge of all her treasure, had come to Jerusalem to worship and was returning; seated on his chariot, he was reading the prophet Isaiah.[25]

So, an angel of the Lord directs Philip where he is to go next. Philip is now under the providential guidance God himself. He is to rise up, that is, he should immediately make himself alert and ready, and being prepared, he should take the desert road that goes south from Jerusalem to Gaza, a city that sits on the coast of the Mediterranean Sea. Being obedient to the angel's divine command, Philip rises up and sets off. Given that an angel has given Philip such detailed instructions, it is not surprising what Luke declares next: "Behold," he comes across an Ethiopian. The "behold" not only alerts the reader that something wholly unanticipated has just occurred, but also that something very significant will now take place. Central to this surprising providential occurrence is the person that Philip meets, so much so that Luke describes him in detail. This Ethiopian was a eunuch, and as such, he was "a minister of Candace the queen of the Ethiopians." It was not unusual in the ancient world for royal courts to have castrated men, and even young boys, as servants and ministers. "Candace" could be the proper name or the title of the queen of Nubia, which was also called Ethiopia by the Greeks. As a royal minister, this Ethiopian was "in charge of all her treasures," which indicates that he was extremely trustworthy. What was this Ethiopian eunuch doing traveling along a desert road? Well, he was returning home after he had been to Jerusalem where he worshipped. Historically non-Jews came to Jerusalem to worship. However, because he was castrated, he could not enter the temple itself. The Mosaic law decrees "He whose testicles are crushed or whose male member is cut off shall not enter the assembly of the Lord."[26] Although the eunuch could not join the

25. Unless otherwise noted, all Scripture passages in this section are taken from Acts 8:26–40. However, because of the length of this present narrative, it would be of no benefit to provide the entire text at the onset. Further texts will be incorporated in due course.

26. Dt 23:1. Importantly, God, through the prophet Isaiah, foretells that such restrictions will no longer apply in the messianic age. The foreigner will not be separated from the Jews, nor the eunuch say, "I am a dry tree." "For thus says the Lord: 'To the eunuchs who keep my

Jewish assembly, he, nonetheless, had gone to Jerusalem to worship the one, true God of Israel.

Seated in his horse-drawn chariot as he was journeying home, the eunuch was reading from the book of the prophet Isaiah.[27] Presumably, this was a rather large chariot with a driver, and one in which passengers could be seated inside, for Philip would soon join hm. Now, "the Spirit said to Philip, 'Go up and join this chariot.' So, Philip ran to him, and heard him reading Isaiah the prophet, and asked, 'Do you understand what you are reading?'" Philip's youthful athleticism is seen in his ability to run after and catch up with the chariot. Upon arrival, he hears the eunuch reading a passage from Isaiah, and inquires, to the probably surprised eunuch, whether he understands what he is reading.[28] In response, the eunuch rhetorically asks, "How can I, unless someone guides me?" Intuiting that Philip could "guide" him in his ignorance, "he invited Philip to come and sit with him."

Having climbed into the chariot and taken a seat aside the eunuch, Luke informs us which scripture the eunuch was reading.

> Now the passage of Scripture which he was reading was this: "As a sheep led to the slaughter or a lamb before its shearer is silent, so he opens not his mouth. In his humiliation justice was denied him. Who can describe his generation? For his life is taken up from the earth."[29]

This Isaian passage is taken from the fourth of what are termed the Suffering Servant Songs.[30] These passages foretell of God's messianic servant who

---

sabbaths, who choose the things that please me and hold fast to my covenant, I will give in my house and within my walls a monument and a name better than sons and daughters; I will give them an everlasting name which shall not be cut off'" (Is 56:3–5).

To those eunuchs who are faithful to his covenant and his laws, God, within the temple's precincts, will place a "monument," that is, something by which they are remembered. Normally, men are remembered through their progeny—their "sons and daughters," and subsequent descendants. However, even though the means of their begetting children has been "cut off," yet their name will be remembered. God will give these faithful eunuchs a name that is even "better" than children, and one that will last forever.

27. The Greek word indicates that this was a traveling chariot and not a war chariot.

28. In antiquity, reading out loud to oneself was the norm, but silent reading was not unknown. St. Augustine, in his *Confessions*, tells of St. Ambrose reading silently to himself. See, *Confessions*, 6, 3, 3. During the seventeenth century in Western societies, individuals began reading silently to themselves.

29. Is 53:7–8. In the English Revised Standard Version, this passage is translated as follows. "He was oppressed, and he was afflicted, yet he opened not his mouth, and like a sheep that before its shearers is dumb, so he opened not his mouth. By oppression and judgment he was taken away; and as for this generation, who considered that he was cut off out of the land of the living, stricken for the transgressions of my people?"

30. Is 52:13–53:12. The other three Suffering Servant Songs are Is 42:1–9, 49:1–13, and 50:4–11.

would unjustly be rejected, chastised, and killed by this sinful generation. However, he will freely take upon himself humankind's sins and punishment, and offer himself, as the pure and innocent lamb of sacrifice, on behalf of humankind's salvation. Isaiah is describing the means by which Jesus would become Jesus, YHWH-Saves.

With this passage in hand, the eunuch said to Philip, "Please, about whom does the prophet say this, about himself or about someone else?" Then Philip "opened his mouth, and beginning with this Scripture, he told him the good news of Jesus."[31] Philip, in giving a Christological interpretation to this Isaian passage concerning God's future suffering servant, explained to the Ethiopian the entire good news that Jesus is the Son of God incarnate, who through his sacrificial death and glorious resurrection, has brought salvation to all nations. Again, in other words, Philip is informing the eunuch about the way in which Jesus became Jesus.

Philip must have concluded his catechetical instruction by referring to the Sacrament of Baptism, for Luke says,

> And as they went along the road, they came across some water, and the eunuch said, "See, here is water! What is to prevent me being baptized?" And he commanded the chariot to stop, and they both went down into the water, Philip and the eunuch, and he baptized him.

So, the faith-filled and thrilled eunuch quickly points out the presence of water, water that Philip himself must have also seen. Water being present, there was no apparent reason that he could not be baptized on the spot, and so he immediately halted the chariot. That Luke notes that both Philip and the eunuch went down into the water together infers that Philip was amenable to baptizing him, and so he did. Had Philip not gotten out of the chariot with the eager eunuch, it would have meant that he was not disposed to performing the Baptism.[32] Moreover, although the eunuch was not permitted to join fully in Jewish worship because of his castration, he is fully able to become an

31. It seems somewhat odd that Luke should note that Philip "opened his mouth," before he began to explain the Scripture passage to the eunuch. One, obviously, must open one's mouth to speak. In his Gospel, prior to Jesus's sermon on the mount, Matthew states, "And he opened his mouth and taught them" (Mt 5:2). Thus, this is not a normal opening of one's mouth, but the opening of one's mouth to give divine instruction. Philip, in opening his mouth, is about to provide the correct, Spirit-filled interpretation of how Jesus has fulfilled this Isaian passage.

32. What is designated as verse 37 is absent from the body of the text. It reads, "And Philip said, 'If you believe with your heart, you may.' And he replied, 'I believe that Jesus Christ is the Son of God.'" It is omitted because this verse is not in the best ancient manuscripts but is only found in a Western text. It was more than likely added because it contains the eunuch's explicit act of faith in Jesus as the Christ and God's incarnate Son.

accepted member among the Christian community. No physical impairment can keep one from faith and Baptism, and, therefore, from salvation and eternal life. For Jesus to be truly and fully Jesus, he must be capable of saving everyone who comes to faith in him and so be baptized in his name.

After Philip baptizes the Ethiopian eunuch, Luke informs the reader what immediately took place. "And when they had come up out of the water, the Spirit of the Lord caught up Philip; and the eunuch saw him no more, and went on his way rejoicing." At the conclusion of coming out of the water, God's very Spirit lifted up Philip and carried him off.[33] That he is carried off by the Spirit indicates that Philip is being taken to a divinely designated new location where he will continue his evangelistic mission. Because of Philip's sudden departure, "the eunuch saw him no more." Nonetheless, he "went his way rejoicing." The eunuch must have been surprised, if not startled, by Philip's sudden disappearance. However, Philip's departure did not dampen the eunuch's joy. He simply continued his journey back to Ethiopia—filled with delight and gratitude in knowing that the Holy Spirit now dwelt within him. He had become a new creation in Christ.[34]

As for Philip, Luke informs the reader that he "was found in Azotus, and passing on he preached the gospel to all the towns till he reached Caesarea." Normally, one does not speak of "finding" someone, unless one is looking for that person. However, since Philip disappeared and was carried off by the Spirit, the next place he was seen, and so found, was the city of Azotus. Starting with Azotus, he proceeded north and went from town to town until he arrived at Caesarea, all the while continuing to preach the gospel as he went.[35] At this juncture Luke ends his narrative concerning Philip.

33. In the Old Testament, Elijah the prophet, on two occasions, is carried off by the Spirit (see 1 Kgs 18:2 and 2 Kgs 2:16).

34. One cannot but admire the Ethiopian eunuch. The entire story manifests his faith in worshiping the one true God in Jerusalem, his intense desire to learn in reading the prophet Isaiah, his docility in wanting to be taught by Philip, his eagerness in wanting to be baptized immediately upon seeing the water, and his pleasant and gracious joyfulness throughout. It is not surprising, then, that the early theologian Irenaeus (ca. 120–ca. 200) writes that he was the first person to evangelize Ethiopia. He also says that his name was Simeon Bachos. Also, historically, the eunuch is thought to have been dark skinned, which would make sense, since he was from Ethiopia.

35. Azotus, also called Ashdod, is about fifty miles south of Caesarea. Other coastal cities along the way would have been Jamnia, Joppa, and Antipatris. In describing his journey to Jerusalem, Paul states that when he and his companions came to Caesarea, "we entered the house of Philip the evangelist, who was one of the seven, and stayed with him" (Acts 21:8). Thus, we see that Philip remained in Caesarea for some time. Interestingly, Paul, rightly, terms him "the evangelist."

## Conclusion

In chapter eight of the Acts of the Apostles, Luke highlights three points in his historical narrative. First, with the onset of the persecution in Jerusalem, the preaching of the gospel spread. This is primarily witnessed in Philip evangelizing the towns in Samaria. Moreover, because of the eunuch's conversion, the gospel also made its way to Ethiopia. Theologically, these two events are significant.

Jesus told the Canaanite woman, who asked him to free her daughter from a demon, "I was sent only to the lost sheep of the house of Israel" (Mt 15:21-28). Moreover, when Jesus sent out his twelve apostles to proclaim that the kingdom of God was at hand, he said, "Go nowhere among the Gentiles, and enter no town of the Samaritans, but go rather to the lost sheep of the house of Israel" (Mt 10:5-6). With Philip's preaching to the towns of Samaritans and converting the Ethiopian eunuch, these restrictions have now been abrogated. Here we perceive that, through Jesus's saving death and lifegiving resurrection, salvation is now extended to all peoples and nations. As we noted above, Peter was very dramatically made aware of this when the Holy Spirit came upon the Gentile Cornelius and his household.

Second, the gospel triumphs over all forms of superstition and magic, specifically as found in Simon the magician. Moreover, by the laying of their hands upon the baptized Samaritans, Peter and John brought to completion the Pentecost event—the receiving of the spiritual or charismatic gifts.

Lastly, chapter eight began with Saul laying waste the Christians in Jerusalem. Chapter nine takes up Saul's continuing rage against the Christian community. Moreover, he is not simply satisfied with persecuting the church in Jerusalem, but with zeal he wishes to harass the Christians in other cities as well. However, as we will now see in chapter nine, God had other plans for Saul.

In all the above, we find Jesus being Jesus. Through the ministry of the church, specifically through the apostolic preaching and sacramental actions of Philip, Peter, and John, Jesus's work of salvation continues to flourish—now in regions outside of Jerusalem among the Samaritans and the Gentiles. As Luke's historical narrative proceeds, we will hear of the geographical extension of the gospel, and so the expansion of the apostolic church.

*Chapter 9*

# PAUL'S CONVERSION AND PETER'S HEALINGS

## Saul Continues His Persecution (Acts 8:1-2)

Chapter eight of the Acts of the Apostles began with the outbreak of persecution against the church in Jerusalem. This harassment resulted in many of the Christians scattering to Judea and Samaria, though the apostles remained in Jerusalem. The leading henchman of this maltreatment appears to have been Saul, for he was said to have "laid waste" to the church, entered "house after house" and "dragged off men and women and committed them to prison" (Acts 8:1-3). Having narrated Philip's evangelistic ministry in Samaria and the conversion of the Ethiopian eunuch, chapter nine resumes with Saul's continuing endeavors to persecute the church, now outside of Jerusalem.

> But Saul, still breathing threats and murder against the disciples of the Lord, went to the high priest and asked him for letters to the synagogues at Damascus, so that if he found any belonging to the Way, men and women, he might bring them bound to Jerusalem.[1]

So, Saul is still laying waste to the Jerusalem church, even to the point of committing "murder." Luke, here is employing a "biased" word. Saul would have admitted that he was killing Christians because of their heretical belief that Jesus was the Christ. He would not agree that he was committing "murder," that is, a criminal offense for which he ought to be arrested, prosecuted, and condemned, and thus himself be sentenced to death. Saul was convinced that, in killing Christians, he was performing a holy act—the cleansing of Jerusalem of an outbreak of evil, the plague of Christianity.

1. Unless otherwise noted, all Scripture passages in this Introduction are taken from Acts 9:1-2.

Moreover, Luke speaks of Saul threatening and murdering "the disciples of the Lord." Again, for Luke, Saul is not simply killing those who believe that Jesus is the expected messiah, the Spirit-anointed Christ, he is murdering those who profess that Jesus is the risen, incarnate Lord. Luke is, once more, accentuating the divine identity of Jesus. As Lord, Jesus is He Who Is, YHWH, and, therefore, he is, as his name affirms, the risen YHWH-Saves. Thus, Saul, as he will soon learn, ultimately is not simply persecuting "the disciples of the Lord," but the Lord himself.

To expand his persecution of the church, Saul "went to the high priest and asked him for letters to the synagogues at Damascus." The Jerusalem high priest, as the one who administered the temple, exercised authority over the synagogues outside of Jerusalem. Thus, by obtaining letters from him, Paul would have the proper credentials for his actions: "if he found any belonging to the Way, men and women, he might bring them bound to Jerusalem." As he "dragged off men and women and committed them to prison" in Jerusalem, so now, having "bound" them, he could bring "men and women" back to Jerusalem for prosecution. By emphasizing men and *women*, Luke is highlighting Saul's callousness—even against defenseless womenfolk.

Luke, for the first time, designates the church as "the Way."[2] By employing this title, Luke is alluding to Isaiah. "A voice cries: 'In the wilderness prepare the way of the Lord, make straight in the desert a highway for our God'" (Is 40:3). This passage from Isaiah, in turn, recalling a passage from the Book of Exodus: "And the Lord went before them by day in a pillar of cloud to lead them along the way, and by night in a pillar of fire to give them light that they might travel by day and by night" (Ex 13:21). Likewise, in the messianic age, "a highway shall be there, and it shall be called a Holy Way; the unclean shall not pass over it, and fools shall not err therein."[3] As the Lord led his people from the slavery of Egypt into the promised land, a Holy Way, so the nascent apostolic church recognized that the risen Jesus, their divine Lord, has made a Way for them into God's holy kingdom. Jesus himself proclaimed, "I am the way, and the truth, and the life; no one comes to the Father, but by me" (Jn 14:6). As *ego eimi*, Jesus is the incarnate way to the Father, for he literally embodies, as God's divine Word, the fullness of the Father's truth as well as the fullness of the Father's life. To abide in the now-risen Jesus is, then, to abide in the Father. Thus, Jesus is himself the only way to the Father. Because the church abides

2. See also Acts 18:26, 19:9 and 23, 22:4, and 24:14 and 22.

3. Is 35:8. See also Is 43:19, 48:17, and 62:10–12. All these passages speak of God making a way for his people into a newness of life.

in Jesus the Way, the church itself is "the Way" that leads to the Father, for to abide in Jesus the Way is to abide in the Father.

## The Conversion of Saul (Acts 9:3-19a)

> Now as he journeyed, he approached Damascus, and suddenly a light from heaven flashed about him. And he fell to the ground and heard a voice saying to him, "Saul, Saul, why do you persecute me?" And he said, "Who are you Lord?" and he said, "I am Jesus, whom you are persecuting; but rise and enter the city, and you will be told what you are to do."[4]

Saul had almost reached his destination, Damascus, where he was to bring any Christians he found back to Jerusalem, when "suddenly a light from heaven flashed about him." That the light was from heaven denotes that it is of divine origin. That it flashed about him specifies that it did not simply flare up around him, but actively embraced him. He was subsumed into the heavenly light. Moreover, this heavenly light had such a divine force that it caused Saul to fall to the ground. He could not withstand its effect upon him. Rather, he was under its all-embracing power.

From within the heavenly light, Saul heard a voice. Luke here does not identify whose voice it is. Who is speaking will be revealed only when Saul himself inquires who it is who is speaking to him. The voice first calls out, "Saul, Saul."[5] The voice, by declaring his name twice, is not just attempting to get Saul's attention. Rather, this is a divine calling wherein revelation and instruction will now be given. When Abraham was about to kill his son, Isaac, God cried out, "Abraham, Abraham!" To which Abraham responded, "Here am I." Then God said, "Do not lay your hand on the lad or do anything to

4. Unless otherwise noted, all Scripture passages in this section are taken from Acts 9:3-19a. However, because of the length of this narrative, it would be of no benefit to provide the entire text at the onset. Further texts will be incorporated in due course.

Luke, here, is presenting his third person account of Saul's conversion. Later in Acts, Saul will twice give his own personal account of his conversion (see Acts 22:1-16 and 26:12-18).

5. "Saul" is the Hebrew name of the Greek name "Paul." Thus, Jesus spoke to him in Hebrew. Later, when Saul recounts his conversion experience, he says, "And when we had all fallen to the ground, I heard a voice saying to me in the Hebrew language, 'Saul, Saul, why do you persecute me?'" (Acts 26:24). It is possible that, being from the tribe of Benjamin, Saul was named after Israel's first king, the Benjamite Saul (see Rom 11:1 and 1 Sm 9:1-2). Interestingly, later in Acts, he is referred to as "Paul" (see Acts 13:9). From that point on he is consistently called "Paul." This change is more than likely due to the fact that he begins his missionary journeys to the Gentiles who spoke Greek. In his letters, which were written in Greek, he always refers to himself as "Paul." See, for example, 1 Cor 1:12-13, 16:21; Eph 3:1; Col 4:18; 1 Thes 2:18; 2 Thes 3:17; and Phlm 9.

him" (Gn 22:11-12). Similarly, God spoke to Jacob when he was hesitant to go to Egypt at the time of the famine: "Jacob, Jacob." As did Abraham, Jacob declares, "Here am I." Then, God states, "I am God, the God of your father; do not be afraid to go to Egypt; for I will make you a great nation."[6] So, the voice doubly calls out Saul's name, and first asks, "Why do you persecute me?" The voice's question is of immense theological significance as will become immediately evident. Saul replies, "Who are you, Lord?" Saul knows that he is in the presence of the "Lord," that is, someone who rightly can be addressed as God, He Who Is. The problem is that of discovering the identity of the divine "Lord" who is now calling out Saul's name.[7] In response to Saul's query, the voice declares, "I am Jesus, whom you are persecuting." So, the voice that spoke to Saul out of the all-encompassing light that engulfed the prostrated Saul is none other than the risen Jesus. He is the Lord.

Now, in revealing to Saul that he is the Lord, Jesus also revealed to him the living unity between himself and those who believe in him. So intimately are they conjoined that to persecute his followers is to persecute Jesus himself. They are one. Thus, Saul's conversion experience would become the basis of his theology of the body of Christ, the church, wherein Jesus is Lord and head and all the faithful are members—through the indwelling of the Holy Spirit, they are one living reality with him and with one another. In revealing the reality of the body of Christ, Jesus did not simply employ a metaphor, as if Jesus's unity with his members is *like* a human body. Rather, as the human body is ontologically composed of the head and members, being one living reality, so Christ and those who abide in him are one living reality as well.[8]

6. Gn 46:2-3. The same pattern can be found when God appears to Moses at the burning bush and summons him doubly by name, and Moses responds by affirming that he is here (see Ex 3:4). Likewise, God addresses the young Samuel doubly when calling him as he was sleeping (1 Sm 3:4).

7. As we have seen on numerous occasions, the term "Lord" (*kurie*) can be employed as a divine title designating Jesus's divine sonship as well as his risen status as the divine Savior. It can also be used as a reverential title for a man, and thus can be translated as "sir." Some English translations of the Bible, such as the New American Bible, translate Saul's question as "Who are you, sir?" This is an erroneous translation. Saul knew that he was not addressing a mere man, a "sir," but that he was addressing someone who is divine (as evidenced by the all-encompassing light), someone who rightly bears the title "Lord." It is the identity of this "Lord" that Saul is seeking.

8. For Saul's theological exposition of the body of Christ, see Rom 12:4, 1 Cor 12:12-13, Eph 4:15-16, and Col 1:18. Although within a human body all the organs compose one "person," in Christ's body Jesus as head and those who abide in him maintain their individual distinct identities. Thus, the Roman Catholic theological and magisterial tradition speaks of the mystical body of Christ. Moreover, it is the indwelling of the Holy Spirit in Jesus and the members of

After he identifies himself as the one whom Saul is persecuting, Jesus instructs the prostrate Saul as to what he is to do: "but rise and enter the city, and you will be told what you are to do." So, Saul is to complete his journey to Damascus, and once there, he will be informed as to what he will subsequently do. Now, amid Saul's conversion experience, the men "who were traveling with him stood speechless, hearing the voice but seeing no one." Saul's companions were dumbfounded by what was taking place. Though they heard the voice, they saw no one—for there was no one to see. Saul did not see Jesus himself but the heavenly, divine light that flashed about him. This radiated heavenly light manifested that it was Jesus who spoke to Saul.[9]

Nonetheless, "Saul arose from the ground; and when his eyes were opened, he could see nothing; so, they took him by the hand and brought him to Damascus. And for three days he was without sight, and neither ate nor drank." Having been instructed by Jesus to go to Damascus, Saul got up. The text then reads that Saul's "eyes were opened" as if he was not the one who opened them, and when they were opened, Saul discovered that he was blind. Saul was blinded by the heavenly light of Jesus just as one is blinded by looking directly at the sun.[10] Thus, Saul had lost control of his eyes. They had to be opened for him as implied above, but only Jesus could open his eyes so that he could see once again. Here, we perceive a paradoxical parable. Saul was

---

his body that effects their oneness, making them one living reality. See *Catechism of the Catholic Church*, nos. 787–795; and Vatican Council II, *Lumen gentium*, no. 7.

9. Here Luke states that his fellow travelers heard "the voice." In his first account of his conversion experience, Saul states, "Now those who were with me saw the light but did not hear the voice of the one who was speaking to me" (Acts 22:9). Thus, we have a contradiction as to whether his fellow companions heard the voice or not. There is no way of discerning which is historically true. I would tend to favor Saul's version, since Luke was not present and is writing in the third person. In his third account Saul states again that he and his companions saw the light, and that "when we had all fallen to the ground, I heard a voice saying to me . . ." (Acts 26:14). Here, while everyone falls to the ground, Saul states that he heard the voice and does not comment on whether the others heard the voice as well.

10. In his third account of conversion, Saul tells King Agrippa that "at about midday, O king, I saw on the way a light from heaven, brighter than the sun, shining around me and those who journeyed with me." Moreover, Saul relates that Jesus told him that he was sending him "to open their eyes, that they may turn from the darkness to light and from the power of Satan to God, that they may receive forgiveness of sins and a place among those who are sanctified by faith in me" (Acts 26:16–18). Saul was sent by God to preach so that the conversion experience that he himself had undergone might become the same experience for those who come to faith in the risen Lord Jesus and are sanctified through baptism—the opening of their eyes, their going from darkness to light, their being freed from the power of the devil to the power of God, their obtaining the forgiveness of sins and their entering into ecclesial fellowship of the apostolic church.

going to Damascus to persecute the church. He "saw" clearly what he must do, but he was blind, for he did not have the eyes of faith to see that Jesus was the risen Lord. Saul now possesses the spiritual eyes of faith because he beheld the heavenly light of the Lord Jesus, but that light has presently physically blinded him.

As we will see shortly, when Paul does arrive at Damascus, he will be healed of his physical blindness, but more importantly, he will, then, be immediately baptized. Through the divine light of the Holy Spirit, Saul will be able to see Jesus clearly, for he will have been born anew into God's kingdom. Saul's physical blindness attests to his spiritual blindness, and the regaining of his physical sight testifies to his newborn spiritual illumination effected through the Sacrament of Baptism. He was baptized in the name of the Lord Jesus, and in that name, he was cured of his disbelief and enlightened by faith. In the meantime, Saul was led to Damascus by the hands of his companions. Ironically, Saul wanted to lead Christians back to Jerusalem to be prosecuted, but now he is being led to Damascus to be baptized into the church that he was persecuting. Upon his arrival, Luke informs us, "And for three days he was without sight, and neither ate nor drank." As Jesus was buried for three days, so Saul is now entombed in darkness for three days, and being so interred, he, as if dead, neither ate nor drank.

What we perceive in Saul's conversion is Jesus being Jesus, YHWH-Saves. By appearing to Saul in his resurrected glory, he saves him from sin and ushers him into the light of eternal life. Moreover, in being baptized in the name of Jesus, Saul is transformed, by the power of the Holy Spirit, into the risen likeness of Jesus himself, and so he becomes a beloved son of the Father. Jesus will now use Saul to be his apostolic means through whom the gospel will be preached to the Gentiles. In so doing they too will experience Jesus being Jesus in their lives—the one who saves them from the curse of sin and death and bestows upon them the new life of the Holy Spirit.

> Now there was a disciple at Damascus named Ananias. The Lord said to him in a vision, "Ananias." And he said, "Here I am, Lord." And the Lord said to him, "Rise and go to the street called Straight, and inquire in the house of Judas for a man of Tarsus named Saul; for behold, he is praying, and he has seen a man named Ananias come in and lay hands on him that he might regain his sight."

Ananias is identified as a "disciple," that is, he believes in Jesus, and so he is a member of "the Way"—the apostolic church. In a vision, the Lord, that is, the risen Jesus, speaks to him. This "vision" does not appear to be a visual apparition, but rather an auditory locution, for he speaks to Ananias. The Lord only calls out his name once. Normally, as was noted above, when God speaks to someone to assign a particular mandate, he addresses that person doubly. Nonetheless, Ananias responds in the traditional biblical fashion, "Here I am, Lord." Ananias is present and alert, attentively waiting to hear the Lord's words. The Lord instructs him to "rise and go to the street called Straight and to inquire at the house of Judas for a man from Tarsus named Saul; for behold he is praying." As the Lord Jesus instructed Saul to rise and go, so now he commands Ananias to rise and go. Ananias is to get himself ready to set out on the mission that Jesus is about to entrust to him. He is to proceed to Straight Street, and once there, he is to inquire at Judas's house "for a man from Tarsus named Saul." The nature of the Lord's instructions gives the impression that while he may know where Straight Street is, Ananias may not have known Judas and so where exactly he lives. Nonetheless, when he finds it, he is to ask about the presence of "a man from Tarsus named Saul." Again, it appears that Ananias is not personally acquainted with Saul since he notes that he is from Tarsus, thus imparting repute to Saul, for Tarsus was a prestigious city.[11]

The Lord also alerts Ananias as to what is taking place with regards to Saul. "Behold, he is praying, and he has seen a man named Ananias come in and lay hands so that he might regain his sight." What Ananias is to note is that Saul is praying, and within his prayer he sees a man, and that man is none other than Ananias himself. He is coming to him and, by laying his hands upon him, he will be healed of his blindness. If the Lord Jesus thought that such an affirmative description of the praying Saul would easily persuade Ananias to rise and go immediately to Judas's house, he was sorely mistaken. "But [and this is an impassioned 'but'] Ananias answered, 'Lord, I have heard from many about this man, how much evil he has done to your saints at Jerusalem; and here he has authority from the chief priests to bind all who call upon

11. Tarsus was the capital of the ancient Roman province of Cilicia in Turkey. It was located near the eastern Mediterranean coast of Turkey and was a port city since it was located on the Cydnus River. Moreover, it was a center of learning, and, from the second century BC, had a large Jewish population. Having been arrested by the Jews, Saul tells the centurion who was guarding him at his trial, "I am a Jew, from Tarsus in Cilicia, a citizen of no mean city" (Acts 21:39). We see here that Saul was proud of his hometown and saw it as enhancing his intellectual and cultural prestige. Likewise, it was here that Saul became an ardent Jew. Again, at his trial, he informs his Jewish prosecutors, "I am a Jew, born at Tarsus in Cilicia, but brought up in this city at the feet of Gamaliel, educated according to the strict manner of the law of our fathers, being zealous for God as you all are this day" (Acts 22:3). Gamaliel was a prominent Jewish rabbi noted for his learning. Thus, having studied under Gamaliel also added to Saul's eminence as a scholarly Jew.

your name.'" It is almost as if Ananias is saying to the Lord, "Are you out of your mind?!" Ananias has heard from many, not a few, about this notorious man. He reminds the Lord what Saul has done to "*your* saints," *your* very holy ones, in Jerusalem. The very reason he is in Damascus is because he has the authority, from the temple chief priests no less, to arrest "all who call upon *your* name." Although Ananias obviously is not thrilled, to say the least, with the idea that he go to Saul, his arguments focus on what he considers to be the Lord's best interests and those of the church. Let us stay clear of this troublemaker, lest we give him the opportunity to wreak more havoc. Ananias is so fearfully obsessed with Saul's reputation that he disregards the reason why the Lord is sending him to Saul. The prayerful Saul is waiting for his arrival so that Ananias can "lay his hands on him so that he might regain his sight." The Lord pays no mind to Ananias's rebuttal, but simply says, "Go, for he is a chosen instrument of mine to carry my name before the Gentiles and kings and the sons of Israel; for I will show him how he must suffer for the sake of my name." The discussion is over, Ananias is to "go." The Lord provides the reason for this mandate. Saul is the Lord's designated means to bring his salvific name to the Gentiles, to kings, and to his Jewish brethren. Moreover, the Lord will reveal to Saul all that he will endure for the sake of his name.[12]

Luke quickly resumes the narrative.

> So, Ananias departed and entered the house. And laying his hands on him he said, "Brother Saul, the Lord Jesus who appeared to you on the road by which you came, has sent me that you may regain your sight and be filled with the Holy Spirit." And immediately something like scales fell from his eyes and he regained his sight. Then he rose and was baptized and took food and was strengthened.

Immediately upon entering Judas's house, Ananias addresses Saul as "brother" and lays hands upon him. The person whom he formerly feared and deprecated, he now acknowledges to be his brother, for Saul is about to enter into ecclesial fellowship with him. He too will be a disciple of the Lord Jesus. With the laying on of hands, Ananias first informs Saul that the Lord Jesus who appeared to him on the road had now sent him.[13] He, then, tells him why the

12. What the Lord Jesus prophetically foretells here will be fulfilled in the remainder of Acts. Saul will preach the gospel to the Gentiles, to kings, and to the Jews, and in so doing, he will undergo many hardships. Also see 2 Cor 11:21–29.

13. Interestingly, while Ananias knew that Saul was in Damascus, and while the Lord told him that Saul was praying and expecting him, he did not previously express any knowledge that the risen Lord Jesus had appeared to him. Nonetheless, at some point, he must have been told of Saul's conversion experience.

Lord sent him—"that you might regain your sight and be filled with the Holy Spirit." Thus, the laying on of Ananias's hands will have a twofold effect, the restoring of Saul's sight and his being filled with the Holy Spirit. In being filled with the Spirit of truth, Saul will not only receive his physical sight, but he will also receive the light of faith by which he will see Jesus clearly as his Lord and Savior. This Holy Spirit will be, then, the same blazing, Spirit-filled light that enveloped him when the Lord Jesus spoke to him along the road. Immediately upon Ananias saying the above, "something like scales fell from his eyes and he gained his sight." As the dazzling light of the Holy Spirit blinded Saul, so now the healing light of the Spirit restored his sight. The scales of darkness gave way to the light of faith.[14]

Having regained his sight, Saul "rose and was baptized, and he took food and was strengthened." Although Saul received the Holy Spirit when Ananias laid hands on him, it was still necessary for him to receive the Sacrament of Baptism.[15] Through the Spirit-filled waters of Baptism he was cleansed of sin and incorporated into the ecclesial apostolic body of the church. As Saul himself would later declare, "There is one body, one Spirit, just as you were called to one hope that belongs to your call, one Lord, one faith, one baptism, one God and Father of all, who is above all and through all, and in all" (Eph 4:4–6). The Sacrament of Baptism, through the indwelling of the Holy Spirit, initiates and continually furthers this ecclesial oneness of faith and hope, and establishes this communion with the heavenly Father through Jesus Christ his incarnate risen Son. Moreover, when Saul was without his sight for three days, he neither ate nor drank, but now that he has regained his sight and was baptized, he "took food and was strengthened." Entombed for three days in physical and spiritual darkness, Saul is incapable of eating. Now that he has arisen from his tomb through the life-giving light of Baptism, having died and risen

14. The scales that fell from Saul's eyes may have been something like cataracts. Although Saul was healed of his blindness, nonetheless, he had poor eyesight later in his life, some form of an eye disease. He writes to the Galatians "it was because of a bodily ailment that I preached the gospel to you at first; and though my condition was a trial to you, you did not scorn or despise me, but received me as an angel of God, as Christ Jesus.... For I bear witness that, if possible, you would have plucked out your eyes and given them to me" (Gal 4:13–15). This visual impediment may also be the reason that he states at the conclusion of his Letter to the Galatians, "See with what large letters I am writing to you with my own hand" (Gal 6:11). Saul wrote with big letters so that he himself could see what he had written.

15. This sequence of the Holy Spirit coming upon Saul followed by his being baptized is similar to Peter and John coming to Samaria, though in reverse. Philip had baptized the Samaritans, but then Peter and John laid hands on those baptized so they might receive the Holy Spirit (see Acts 8:14–17).

*with* Christ, he has become a new creation *in* Christ; and so he newly partakes of food so as to be strengthened to embark on his ministry as an apostle of Jesus Christ.

## Saul's Initial Preaching (Acts 9:19b–22)

> For several days he was with the disciples at Damascus. And in the synagogues immediately he proclaimed Jesus, saying, "He is the Son of God." And all who heard him were amazed, and said, "Is not this the man who made havoc in Jerusalem of those who called on this name? And he has come here for this purpose, to bring them bound before the chief priests." But Paul increased all the more in strength, and confounded the Jews who lived in Damascus by proving that Jesus was the Christ.[16]

So having regained his physical strength, Saul remained, "for several days," in Damascus with Jesus's disciples—though now as one of them. Saul, always zealous in whatever he does, "immediately" began to evangelize in the local synagogues. He proclaimed that Jesus was "he who is the Son of God."[17] From Luke's brief declaration, Saul does not appear to be hesitant to profess that Jesus is the Son of God. Judaism was singular, within a pagan environment, in believing in one God. Thus, for Saul to declare that Jesus is the Son of God implies that he did not consider such a truth to undermine God's ontological oneness. Inherent, then, within his affirmation is a trinitarian understanding of the one God, though the belief that the Holy Spirit is truly divine as the Father and the Son is yet to be fully articulated.[18]

Not surprisingly, "all who heard him were amazed." They recall, among themselves, that he had wreaked havoc among the Christians in Jerusalem—those who called upon the name of Jesus as their risen Lord. Moreover, he purposely came to Damascus to bring back bound Christians to the chief priests in Jerusalem. However, Luke notes that Saul "increased all the more in strength." Having regained his physical strength, Saul went from strength to strength in his ardent preaching, so much so that he "confounded" the Jews

16. Unless otherwise noted, all Scripture passages in this section are taken from Acts 9:19b–22.

17. During the course of his later missionary journeys, he would invariably begin his preaching in the cities' synagogues. See for example, Acts 13:5, 14:1, and 17:1–3 and 10.

18. This is the only time Jesus is called the Son of God in Acts. However, in Paul's sermon at Antioch, he quotes Psalm 2:7, "You are my Son, today I have begotten you." In the Old Testament, the phrase "sons of God" appears in Gn 6:1–4; Jb 1:6, 2:1, and 38:7. The phrase is used to describe lesser heavenly beings, such as angels, who serve the Most High.

in Damascus "by proving that Jesus was the Christ," that is, the long-awaited, Spirit-filled Messiah. Such proselytizing behavior, in the end, could not be tolerated.

## Saul's Escape from Damascus (Acts 9:23-25)

> When many days had passed, the Jews plotted to kill him, but their plot became known to Saul. They were watching the gates day and night, to kill him; but his disciples took him by night and let him down over the wall, lowering him in a basket.[19]

After spending "several days" with the disciples in Damascus, and now "after many days had passed, the Jews plotted to kill him" (Acts 9:19). It is somewhat difficult to sort out Saul's itinerary. In his Letter to the Galatians, he says that he "went away into Arabia; and again I returned to Damascus, and then, after three years I went up to Jerusalem."[20] The "many days that had passed" could be the three years he spent upon returning to Damascus prior to his going to Jerusalem. Or, it could mean that he spent three years in Arabia, and then returned to Damascus prior to going to Jerusalem.[21] However this is interpreted, upon his return the Jews conspired to kill him. So intent were they that they kept watch at all the gates "day and night." Their attempt was foiled when some of those who became Saul's disciples got wind of the plot. Ingeniously, at night they lowered him down in a basket over the wall. While he may have been somewhat afraid of being caught, he probably was also grinning to himself at the thrill of being lowered down in a basket.[22]

19. Unless otherwise noted, all Scripture passages in this section are taken from Acts 9:23-25.

20. See Gal 1:17-18.

21. What was Saul doing in Arabia, which is southeast of Palestine? Presumably, he was praying in order to strengthen himself spiritually prior to undertaking his apostolic ministry.

22. In 2 Corinthians he states that he must boast in his weaknesses. As his first example, Saul declares, "At Damascus, the governor under King Aretas guarded the city of Damascus in order to seize me, but I was let down in a basket through a window in the wall and escaped his hands" (2 Cor 11:30-33). Once again, because of his firsthand personal knowledge, unlike Luke, Saul provides greater detail. He was not simply lowered down the wall in a basket, but "through a window in the wall." Moreover, the governor of Damascus himself was involved in the attempt to kill Saul. In the Old Testament there are examples of others escaping by being lowered from a city wall. The prostitute in Jericho let the Jewish spies "down by a rope through the window, for her house was built into the city wall, so that she dwelt in the wall" (Jos 2:15). Young David's wife, Michal, helped him to escape from Saul's attempt to kill him by letting him "down through a window" (1 Sm 19:11-12).

## Saul in Jerusalem (Acts 9:26–31)

Having safely escaped the clutches of Jews, Luke next narrates Saul's experiences in Jerusalem.

> And when he had come to Jerusalem, he attempted to join the disciples; and they were all afraid of him, for they did not believe that he was a disciple. But Barnabas took him, and brought him to the apostles, and declared to them how on the road he had seen the Lord, who spoke to him, and how in Damascus he had preached boldly in the name of Jesus.[23]

When he came to Jerusalem, Saul did not receive a warm welcome initially. Out of fear, his fellow disciples did not believe that he was truly one of them. His notorious reputation preceded him. However, Barnabas befriended him, and introduced him to the apostles.[24] Moreover, he informed the apostles of Saul's conversion experience and "how on the road he had seen the Lord, who spoke to him, and how in Damascus he had preached boldly in the name of Jesus." Luke does not inform the reader how Barnabas obtained this information pertaining to Saul's conversion. Nonetheless, his testimony convinced the apostles that Saul could be trusted as an authentic disciple of the Lord Jesus.[25] Having gained the apostles' trust, Saul "went in and out among them in Jerusalem," that is, he was free to go about Jerusalem without any hindrance from the apostles, for he was now one of them. Not surprisingly, he preached "boldly in the name of the Lord." Specifically, "he spoke and disputed against the Hellenists; but they were seeking to kill him." As Stephen disputed with the Jewish Hellenists, so now Saul is debating with them; and as they stoned Stephen, so they now seek to kill Saul. However, "when the brethren knew it, they brought him down to Caesarea, and sent him off to Tarsus." Saul's Christian brothers, having got wind of the plot to kill him, hastily took him to Caesarea, and from there they dispatched him to his hometown of Tarsus,

23. Unless otherwise noted, all Scripture passages in this section are taken from Acts 9:26–31. However, because of the length of this narrative, it would be of no benefit to provide the entire text at the onset. Further texts will be incorporated in due course.

24. As we have seen in chapter four of Acts, Barnabas, "whose name means, Son of encouragement" was a Levite from Cyprus (Acts 4:36). By assisting Saul and introducing him to the apostles, he lived up to his name.

25. In his Letter to the Galatians, Saul states that "after three years I went up to Jerusalem to visit Cephas, and remained with him fifteen days. But I saw none of the other apostles except James the Lord's brother. (In what I am writing to you, before God, I do not lie!)" (Gal 1:18–20). Again, Luke's account gives the impression that Saul met with all twelve apostles, whereas Saul provides firsthand exact details—and he does not lie. He was in Jerusalem one day more than a fortnight, and only visited with Peter and James the Lord's brother.

where presumably he would be safe and cared for. In all the above, from what took place in Damascus and now in Jerusalem, we perceive the great love the nascent apostolic church had for Saul. While there initially may have been distrust and fear, the disciples and apostles ultimately watched over and protected him from harm—ensuring that he would not be captured and killed.

As was expressed earlier, we now see it as a reality. Once Saul became a member of the apostolic church, he became an evangelistic instrument of the risen Jesus. Through Saul, Jesus was able to be Jesus, for through his preaching many were already being converted. In this pattern, as will be evident later, Jesus will continue to be Jesus, for throughout Saul's missionary journeys Jesus will save many through him.

Luke, abruptly and amazingly, concludes his narrative on Saul in a very buoyant manner.

> So, the Church throughout Judea and Galilee and Samaria had peace and was built up; and walking in the fear of the Lord and in the comfort of the Holy Spirit it was multiplied.

Is Luke implying that with the conversion of Saul, and with his return to Tarsus, things settled down throughout the whole of Palestine? I do not think so, but he offers no explanation of why the persecution and harassment of the church subsided. Nonetheless, peace reigned, and within that calm, the church was strengthened and grew in numbers.[26] Moreover, the members of the church "walked in the fear of the Lord," that is, they lived lives of devoted honor and respect for the risen Jesus. In so doing, they experienced the life-giving and love-giving wellbeing of the Holy Spirit, the Spirit that fosters love of and faithfulness to Jesus.

## Peter's Miracles in Lydda and Joppa (Acts 9:32–43)

> Now as Peter went here and there among them all, he came down also to the saints that lived at Lydda. There he found a man named Aeneas, who had been bedridden for eight years and was paralyzed. And Peter said to him, "Aeneas, Jesus Christ heals you; rise and make your bed." And immediately he rose. And all the residents of Lydda and Sharon saw him, and they turned to the Lord.[27]

26. As we have seen, Luke has spoken previously of the ever-increasing growth of the church. See Acts 2:41 and 6:7.

27. Unless otherwise noted, all Scripture passages in this section are taken from Acts 9:32–43. However, because of the length of this narrative, it would be of no benefit to provide the entire text at the onset. Further texts will be incorporated in due course.

Luke's narrative here now turns once more to the ministry of Peter. He visits "the saints" in various towns "here and there," one of which was Lydda.[28] Upon his arrival, he learns of a paralyzed man by the name of Aeneas, who had been bedridden for eight years. He said to him, "Jesus Christ heals you; rise and make your bed." Here we find an excellent example of Jesus being Jesus. Peter does not say to Aeneas, "In the name of Jesus, I say to you arise." Rather, it is Jesus Christ himself who is performing the miraculous healing, without, in a sense, the mediation of Peter. Because Jesus Christ has healed Aeneas, Peter declares, "rise and make your bed." Although he is confirming Jesus's healing of Aeneas by telling him to arise and make his bed, he almost sounds like an irate father telling his slothful teenage son to get up and make his bed. Unlike the lethargic teenage boy, Aeneas "immediately" rose. As many came to believe in Jesus when he was on earth because of the healings he performed, so now "all the residents of Lydda and Sharon," upon seeing the healed Aeneas, "turned to the Lord." Because of Jesus's act of healing, the people came to believe in him as their saving Lord—YHWH-Saves.

From Lydda, Peter journeys to Joppa.

> Now there was at Joppa a disciple named Tabitha, which means Dorcas or Gazelle. She was full of good works and acts of charity. In those days she fell sick and died; and when they had washed her, they laid her in an upper room. Since Lydda was near Joppa, the disciples, hearing that Peter was there, sent two men to him without delay entreating him, "Please come to us without delay." So, Peter rose and went with them.[29]

Tabitha was an exemplary disciple of Jesus, for she "was full of good works and acts of charity." However, she died, and upon her death, the disciples in Joppa, having heard that Peter was in Lydda, sent for him. Peter immediately "rose" and went with the two men who came for him.

> And when he had come, they took him to the upper room. All the widows stood beside him weeping, and showing coats and garments which Dorcas made while she was with them. But Peter put them all outside and knelt down and prayed; then turning to the body he said, "Tabitha, rise." She opened her eyes, and when she saw Peter, she sat up. And he gave her his hand and lifted her up. Then calling the saints and widows he presented her alive. And it

28. Lydda is in Judea twelve miles from the Mediterranean Sea. It was north of the road that led from Jerusalem to the port city of Joppa. Both Lydda and Joppa are at the southern edge of the Plains of Sharon along the Mediterranean coast.

29. "Tabitha" and "dorcas" are the Hebrew and Greek words respectively for "gazelle." It would appear, then, that Joppa had both a Jewish and Greek population. This may be due to its being a port city where Greek-speaking traders resided.

> became known throughout all Joppa, and many believed in the Lord. And he stayed in Joppa many days with one Simon, a tanner.

Immediately upon arrival, Peter was taken to the upper room where Dorcas's body was laid out. Although Luke is seriously writing about a sad event, I find some humor in the opening scene. The distraught elderly widows stood beside him, though I think they were probably jostling around him attempting to be the one who was the closest to the great Peter, the prince of the apostles. They, more than likely, interrupted one another as each endeavored to point out Dorcas's exquisite needlework, the beauty of the patterns, and the quality of the cloth of which the coats and garments were made. Little did they grasp that Peter was not really interested in the widows' present admiration for and love of the deceased Dorcas. Peter had his own more immediate and important agenda. So, as he patiently, in a gentlemanly fashion, ushered the chattering widows out of the room, he may have raised his eyebrows and rolled his eyes, relieved to get down to the business at hand. As the text states, "*But* Peter put them *all* outside." Although Peter is now going to bring Dorcas back to life, he is going to do so after the manner of Jesus himself, for he is but an instrument of the risen Jesus. Peter's words and actions replicate what Jesus previously had done. Thus, through Peter, Jesus is being Jesus, YHWH-Saves.

In Mark's Gospel, when Jairus, a ruler of the synagogue, besought Jesus to come and heal his dying daughter and who had died prior to his arrival, Jesus "saw a tumult, and people weeping and wailing loudly." Jesus reprimanded their unwarranted lamenting. Upon entering the room where the dead daughter lay, Jesus "took her by the hand" and said, "'Talitha cumi,' which means, 'Little girl, I say to you arise.' And immediately the girl got up and walked" (Mk 5:35–42). So, presently Peter, having put the weeping and wailing widows out of the room, knelt to pray, for he knew that only by the power of the risen Jesus could he raise Dorcas back to life. He, then, approached the body and, employing similar words to Jesus, he said in Hebrew, "Tabitha, rise." Whereupon "she opened her eyes, and when she saw Peter she sat up." And, as Jesus took the hand of the Jairus's daughter, so Peter "gave her his hand and lifted her up." Peter's words and actions were, in a sense, Jesus's own words and actions, for they effected what Jesus himself previously had done. Having raised Dorcas to life, Peter called "the saints and widows" and "presented her alive. And it became known throughout all Joppa, and many believed in the Lord." Jesus's holy disciples obviously were thrilled to see the living Dorcas, and the widows, assuredly, must have been the ones who spread the word "throughout all Joppa," enthusiastically noting that they, yes, they themselves, were present at this momentous and unparalleled event. Significantly, though, then it would have been the widows' testimony that brought many to believe "in the Lord," for which they would have also been rightly proud.

Luke notes, at the end of chapter nine, that Peter "stayed in Joppa many days with one Simon, a tanner." Chapter ten will narrate what took place at Joppa during the remainder of Peter's stay. While there, he resided with a man named Simon, who was a tanner. The description of Simon as "a tanner" is theologically significant. As a tanner, Simon would have been unclean because he worked with dead animals. Anyone who "touches an unclean thing, whether the carcass of an unclean beast or a carcass of unclean cattle" himself becomes unclean (Lv 5:2). Thus, by staying with Simon, Peter is himself associating with what is unclean. However, as will be seen in chapter ten, it is revealed to Peter that, in the light of the gospel, no animal is to be considered unclean.[30]

## Conclusion

What we have found in chapter nine of the Acts of the Apostles is Jesus being Jesus. This is seen in the risen Jesus appearing to Paul, which brings about his conversion—he comes to believe that Jesus is his risen Lord. Moreover, Paul's subsequent preaching of the gospel both in Damascus and in Jerusalem manifests Jesus being Jesus in that many come to believe in him through Paul, the apostle. Likewise, we perceived Jesus being Jesus through Peter's healing of Aeneas at Lydda, and particularly in his raising Dorcas from the dead. Although Peter is the efficacious instrument, it is Jesus, as YHWH-Saves, who is the healer and the restorer of life. All of which is a prefigurement of the ultimate healing and restoration. At the end of time, when he returns in glory, with the same glory that he revealed to Paul, Jesus will raise from the dead all who abided with him on earth so that they may forever abide gloriously with him in heaven. This heavenly resurrection-abiding in Jesus will effect the fully abiding with the Father in the communion of the Holy Spirit. Whereupon, Jesus will have fully enacted his name, YHWH-Saves, for all will be fully transformed into his risen likeness.

30. See Acts 10:13–16.

*Chapter 10*

# PETER AND THE CONVERSION OF THE GENTILES

Chapter nine of the Acts of the Apostles concluded with Peter coming from Joppa, where he was staying, to Lydda. The reason for his journey was that a disciple of Jesus, Tabitha or Dorcas, had died, and her fellow Christians sent for him. Upon his arrival, he raised her from the dead. Chapter ten continues to narrate events surrounding Peter's ministry, particularly the conversion of Cornelius, the first Gentile Christian. Cornelius's conversion took place in Caesarea, a port about thirty miles north of Joppa.[1] What we perceive here is somewhat ironic. On Pentecost, Peter preached to "Jews, devout men from every nation under heaven"—"Parthians and Medes and Elamites and residents of Mesopotamia, Judea and Cappadocia, Pontus and Asia, Phrygia and Pamphylia, Egypt and the parts of Libya belonging to Cyrene, and visitors from Rome, both Jews and proselytes, Cretans and Arabians" (Acts 2:5-11). Because of Peter's preaching, "about three thousand souls" came to faith in Jesus Christ (Acts 2:41). However, when Peter was arrested and later preached to the Sanhedrin, the scribes and priests refused to believe in Jesus.[2] In light of the Jewish leaders' rejection of the gospel, it is not so surprising that Peter, as will Paul, proceeds to evangelize the Gentiles. With this brief historical setting, we can proceed with our theological interpretation of chapter ten.

1. Herod the Great expanded the port of Caesarea, making it the Roman capital of Judea.

2. See Acts 4:5-22 and 5:27-33. Similarly, when Stephen preached the gospel to the Jewish council, they rejected his words concerning Jesus as the anticipated Messiah just as their ancestors had rejected the words of Moses (see Acts 7:1-54).

## Cornelius's Vision (Acts 10:1-8)

> At Caesarea there was a man named Cornelius, a centurion of what is known as the Italian Cohort, a devout man who feared God with all his household, gave alms liberally to the people, and prayed constantly to God. About the ninth hour of the day, he saw clearly in a vision an angel of God coming in and saying to him, "Cornelius." And he stared at him in terror, and said, "What is it, Lord?" And he said to him, "Your prayers and your alms have ascended as a memorial before God. And now send men to Joppa, and bring one Simon who is called Peter; he is lodging with Simon, a tanner; whose house is by the seaside." When the angel who spoke to him had departed, he called two of his servants and a devout soldier from among those that waited on him, and having related everything to them, he sent them to Joppa.[3]

Luke provides a remarkable amount of detail in the above verses, thus manifesting the historicity of his account—much of which is theologically significant. Luke first informs the reader that in Caesarea there was a centurion belonging to the Italian Cohort.[4] Immediately, the reader is aware that this Roman soldier is not a Jew but a Gentile. Though not a Jew, Cornelius is "a devout man who feared God with all of his household." Cornelius's devoutness is seen in his reverential fear of the one true God of the Jews, that is, YHWH; and the same was true of his entire Gentile household. Traditionally such Gentiles who believed in YHWH were termed "God-fearers," for they participated in Jewish worship in synagogues and obeyed the ethical and religious teachings contained in the Torah. However, because these Gentile believers were not circumcised, they were not deemed fully Jewish. Such would be the case even if they were circumcised since Jewishness pertains not simply to a religion but to a specific race, one that is distinct from all Gentile races. Nonetheless, in conformity to Jewish practice, Cornelius "gave alms liberally to the people and prayed constantly to God." As found in the book of Tobit, "Prayer is good when accompanied by fasting, almsgiving, and righteousness" (Tb 12:8). Thus, the Gentile, Cornelius, lived as a fervent Jew both by way of praying to the one true God and in his generosity toward all—thereby fulfilling the two greatest commandments, love of God and love of neighbor. "Hear, O Israel: The Lord our God is one Lord; and you shall love the Lord your God with all your heart, with all of your soul, and with all of your might" (Dt 6:4-5). Likewise, "You shall love your neighbor as yourself: I am the Lord."[5]

3. Unless otherwise noted, all Scripture passages in this section are taken from Acts 10:1-8.

4. This "Italian Cohort" is thought to be a battalion of archers which originally resided in Italy but was reassigned to Syria around AD 69.

5. Lv 19:18. Jesus declares that "on these two commandments depend all the law and the

Having provided a synopsis of his devout Jewish character, Luke immediately recounts Cornelius's vision. "About the ninth hour of the day," that is, about 3:00 PM, Cornelius "saw clearly in a vision an angel of God coming in." This mid-afternoon hour is the same hour when prayers and sacrifices were offered in the temple.[6] So at this sanctified hour, Cornilius clearly saw, by means of a vision, an angel sent by God. By specifying that the angel is "of God," Luke wants the reader to recognize that the angel's appearance manifested a divine purpose. Although Cornelius "clearly saw" the angel, this "seeing" was by means of "vision," which seems to imply that the "vision" was something he perceived in his mind. He did not observe the angel as someone "standing" before him. However, within this mental "vision," he did see an angel "coming in," which gives the impression that the angel came into the physical room where Cornelius was. Thus, there is both a spiritual and a material aspect to this angelic vision, both of which accentuate the reality of the vision. Although the angel, as a non-material being, was not ocularly observed, yet he was unmistakably "seen" within Cornelius's mind as truly present to him. Thus, this "vision" is not some ethereal other-worldly event, but one that took place at a specific time, in a particular place, to a real human being.

Within the vision, Cornelius heard the angel say to him, "Cornelius." What Cornelius interiorly heard may have been a "word" spoken by an angel, but the "voice" was that of God, for the angel was "an angel of God." God was calling out his name—"Cornelius." Although "he stared at him [the angel] in terror," nonetheless, Cornelius immediately desires to know what the Lord wishes of him.[7] "What is it, Lord?" God, speaking through the angel, proceeds to inform Cornelius what he wishes him to do. This initiatory exchange follows the biblical pattern of a divine calling. For example, when Moses approached the burning bush, "God called out of the burning bush, 'Moses, Moses!' And he said, 'Here am I'" (Ex 3:4). God proceeded to appoint Moses to be the instrument through whom God would free his people from the slavery of Egypt. As with

prophets" (Mt 22:38-40). In Mark's Gospel, a scribe asks Jesus which commandments are the greatest. Jesus states that love of God and love of neighbor are the greatest, to which the scribe confirms Jesus's response. Jesus then declares, "You are not far from the kingdom of God" (Mk 12:28-34). By keeping these two great commandments, Cornelius is, then, not far from God's kingdom—he is well prepared. Thus, when Peter proclaims to him the good news of Jesus Christ, Cornelius immediately believes as the Holy Spirit comes down upon him and his household (see Acts 10:44).

6. Earlier Luke tells the reader that "Peter and John were going up to the temple at the hour of prayer, the ninth hour" (Acts 3:1). Similarly, an angel came to Daniel while he was praying during the time of the evening sacrifice (see Dn 9:20-21).

7. Cornelius's "terror" was a reverential fear at being in God's presence.

Moses, the angel now says to Cornelius, "Your prayers and your alms have ascended as a memorial before God. And now send men to Joppa, and bring one Simon who is called Peter; he is lodging with Simon, the tanner, whose house is by the seaside." There is present here a simultaneity that is theologically significant. As prayers and sacrifices were being offered in the temple at the ninth hour, so at the same time, Cornelius's prayers and alms have arrived "as a memorial before God." By referring to Cornelius's "prayers and alms" as a "memorial," the angel is alluding to the memorial offerings noted in the book of Leviticus. When someone brings "a cereal offering" mixed with oil and frankincense to the priest, "the priest shall burn this as a memorial portion upon the altar, an offering by fire, a pleasing odor to the Lord."[8] Thus, Cornelius's prayers and alms are his devotional sacrificial offerings to the Lord, and these, like the fragrant odor of burning incense, "have ascended before the Lord." Within the context of Cornelius's sacrificial prayers to God and his generosity to others, God commands him to "send men to Joppa" to fetch "Simon who is called Peter." God proceeds to give Cornelius specific directions as to where he can be found—he "is lodging with Simon, a tanner, whose house is by the seaside." Providing the details of where Simon is lodging, again, bears witness to the historicity of this event. More importantly, God is informing Cornelius that the "Simon" he is to bring back is also called "Peter," and so God is apprising him (and Luke, and the reader) that he is the "Rock" upon whose faith the apostolic church is built. Cornelius, the Gentile, must come to believe what Peter, the Jew, proclaimed—that the historical Jesus is none other than the Christ, the Son of the living God.

The angel, having delivered his divine message, "departed." Again, although Cornelius had "seen a vision" of an angel, that "vision," as noted above, possessed a component other than simply being mental, so here too the angel is said to have "departed" as if he were leaving a real place, a room, wherein he had appeared. Upon the angel's departure, Cornelius sprang into action, for he immediately fulfilled God's command. "He called two of his servants and a devout soldier from among those who waited on him, and having related everything to them, he sent them to Joppa." Cornelius was a "devout" solder who "feared God," so he sent to Peter at Joppa not only two of his servants, but also "a devout soldier." By sending a soldier who was spiritually devout, along with the others, Cornilius felt assured that what was related to them concerning his divine vision would be properly communicated to Simon Peter. Cornelius was not just some fanatical Gentile visionary.

8. Lv 2:1–2. See also Lv 2:9 and 16, and Sir 38:11.

As God had instructed Cornelius what to do, so God would now prepare Peter as to what he was to do upon the arrival of Cornelius's messengers.

## Peter's Vision (Acts 10:9-16)

> The next day, as they were on their journey and coming near the city, Peter went up on the housetop to pray, about the sixth hour. And he became hungry and desired something to eat; but while they were preparing it, he fell into a trance and saw the heaven opened, and something descending, like a great sheet, let down by four corners upon the earth. In it were all kinds of animals and reptiles and birds of the air. And there came a voice to him, "Rise, Peter; kill and eat." But Peter said, "No, Lord; for I have never eaten anything that is common or unclean." And the voice came to him again a second time, "What God has cleansed, you must not call common." This happened three times, and the thing was taken up at once to heaven.[9]

So, as Cornelius's messengers were journeying to Joppa and approaching the city, Peter, at about noon, "went up on the housetop to pray."[10] However, he "became hungry and desired something to eat."[11] While "they were preparing it, he fell into a trance."[12] Here "trance" is used in the biblical sense wherein divine communication is given. Thus, within this state, Peter "saw the heaven opened, and something descending, like a great sheet, let down by four corners upon earth." Like an upside-down parachute hung by its cords, a huge blanket came down from the open heaven to earth. In this divine vision from heaven, there "were all kinds of animals and reptiles and birds of the air," all of which represented living creatures of God's original good creation. A voice instructed Peter, "Rise, Peter, kill and eat," to which Peter adamantly responded, "No, Lord; for I have never eaten anything that is common or unclean."[13] Peter's refusal is based upon what is written in the book of Leviticus, chapter 11. Here God informs Moses which beasts the Israelites are permitted or forbidden to eat. "The voice came to him a second time, 'What God

9. Unless otherwise noted, all Scripture passages in this section are taken from Acts 10:9-16.

10. Palestinian homes at the time frequently had an exterior staircase that led to a flat roof.

11. I find here a bit of humor. Peter had the best of intentions. He went to the quiet of his rooftop to pray. However, once there, he became hungry and wanted something to eat. His desire for food exceeded his wish to pray. Nonetheless, Peter's desire for food is, by providential design, the needed ingredient for what immediately transpires next.

12. Luke does not state who the "they" are—presumably members of Simon's household where Peter was lodging.

13. Within the narrative of this trance, Luke speaks of "a voice" speaking to Peter. Peter, since what he is seeing is from heaven, takes it as the voice of the "Lord."

has cleansed, you must not call common.' This happened three times, and the thing was taken up at once to heaven."

The divine content of this vision is both to be taken literally and by way of an allegory founded upon the literal. Through the saving death and lifegiving resurrection of Jesus, the Messiah, God has made a new covenant not only with the Jews but also with the whole of humankind—the Gentiles. Therefore, the dietary laws that pertained to the old covenant are now obsolete, and so are no longer obligatory.[14] Peter was, then, permitted to eat what was formerly common and unclean. This understanding, in turn, allegorically applies to the distinction between Jews (those who were ritually clean) and the Gentiles (those who were ritually unclean). In the light of the new covenant wrought in Jesus Christ, both Jews and Gentiles were truly made clean, for they were cleansed of sin and made interiorly righteous in the Holy Spirit.[15] Luke concludes by informing the reader that this vision "happened three times," after which "the thing [the sheet filled with animals] was taken up at once to heaven." Why Peter's vision was repeated three times is left unexplained—presumably to emphasize its divine origin and significance. What it all meant Peter will eventually come to realize.

## The Arrival of Cornelius's Messengers (Acts 10:17–23a)

> Now, while Peter was inwardly perplexed as to what the vision which he had seen might mean, behold, the men that were sent by Cornelius, having made inquiry for Simon's house, stood before the gate and called out to ask whether Simon who was called Peter was lodging there. And while Peter was pondering the vision, the Spirit said to him, "Behold, three men are looking for

14. In Mark's Gospel, Jesus rhetorically asks the Jews who thought that what entered a man made him unclean. "Do you not see that whatever goes into a man from outside cannot defile him, since it enters, not the heart, but his stomach, and so passes on?" Mark, then, adds an aside, "(Thus he declared all foods clean)" (Mk 7:18–19).

This teaching was reiterated by Paul. "I know and am persuaded in the Lord Jesus that nothing is unclean in itself" (Rom 14:14). Likewise, while the unconverted Jews still forbid the eating of some foods, "everything created by God is good, and nothing is to be rejected if it is received with thanksgiving; for then it is consecrated by the word of God and prayer" (1 Tm 4:3–5). This passage is the theological basis for Christians blessing their food before meals.

15. In his Letter to the Ephesians, Paul declares that the Gentiles were "separated from Christ, alienated from the commonwealth of Israel, and strangers to the covenants of promise, having no hope and without God in the world. But now in Christ Jesus you who were once far off have been brought near in the blood of Christ." Jews and Gentiles have, in Christ, become "one new man in place of two," having "broken down the dividing wall of hostility" (Eph 2:12–15). See Eph 2:11–22.

> you. Rise and go down, and accompany them without hesitation; for I have sent them." And Peter went down to the men and said, "I am the one you are looking for, what is the reason for your coming?" And they said, "Cornelius, a centurion, an upright and God-fearing man, who is well spoken of by the whole Jewish nation, was directed by a holy angel to send for you to come to his house, and to hear what you have to say." So, he called them in to be his guests.[16]

First, we must take note of the details contained in the above narrative. Again, this specificity testifies to the historicity of Luke's account. How Luke obtained the specifics of this entire story of Cornelius's conversion is unknown, but he could have acquired it from conversations with either Cornelius or Peter or both—someone who experienced it firsthand.

While Peter was pondering the meaning of his vision, unsure of what to make of it, Cornelius's three messengers made inquiries as to the whereabouts of Simon's house. Having found it, they "stood before the gate and called out to ask whether Simon who was called Peter was lodging there." This is what Luke wants the reader to behold—the calling out for Simon, for it is he, the apostolic Rock, who now becomes the principal actor in this narrative. The three men are not simply "calling out" for Peter, the man, they are rightly "calling out" for the faith that Peter proclaims, that Jesus Christ is the Son of the living God.

As the three men were attempting to rouse someone's attention to find out if Peter is in the house, and as Peter was musing over the meaning of his vision, "the Spirit said to him, 'Behold, three men are looking for you. Rise and go down and accompany them without hesitation; for I have sent them.'" Interestingly, and of theological significance, at the onset of this sequence of events, it was an angel whom Cornelius saw in a vision. Nonetheless, when the angel called out Cornelius's name, he addressed the angel as "Lord" as if he were divine. This divinely sent angel instructed Cornelius to send messengers to Peter in Joppa requesting him to come to Caesarea. However, the Holy Spirit presently informed Peter that he was the one who sent the messengers to him. So, the narrative speaks of an angel, the Lord, and the Spirit. By way of theologically reconciling these historical appellations, one could acknowledge that the Holy Spirit inspired the angel with the content of what he was to relay to Cornelius. Cornelius, for his part, recognized that the angelic message was of Spirit-filled divine origin, and so addressed the angel as Lord. Thus, when

16. Unless otherwise noted, all Scripture passages in this section are taken from Acts 10:17–23a.

the Spirit told Peter that he sent messengers to him, he spoke correctly, for he, as "Lord," along with the Father and the Son, is as truly divine as they are divine. Moreover, this account reveals something important: by "speaking" to Peter, the Spirit reveals himself to be a personal divine subject, a "who," in communion with the persons of the Father and the Son. The Spirit is not some impersonal divine power.

While Luke wants the reader to behold the messengers calling out to Peter, what the Spirit wants Peter to "behold" is "the three men" who are seeking him. The Spirit commands him, "Rise and go down and accompany them without hesitancy; for I have sent them." Peter is to rise from his meal and proceed down from the rooftop and follow them, and he is to do so "without hesitation." Why would Peter be hesitant? They are unclean Gentiles! Peter has never associated with what is "unclean and common." The "perplexed" Peter was now to enact the vision that he found so baffling. Nonetheless, at the Spirit's insistence, he "went down to the men and said, 'I am the one you are looking for; what is the reason for your coming?'" Having identified himself, Peter wants to know the purpose of their presence—why would Gentiles want to speak to a Jew, and a Jewish Christian at that?

In response, the three messengers inform Peter of the divine origin and purpose of the mission. "Cornelius, a centurion, an upright and God-fearing man, who is well spoken of by the whole Jewish nation, was directed by a holy angel to send for you to come to his house, and to hear what you have to say." The men effusively want to make a good impression before Peter—both as to who Cornelius is and to the divinely inspired nature of their mission. If they make a muddle of their charge, Peter might refuse their request. Thus, Peter must pay close attention to what they have to say. They are coming on behalf of Cornelius, who is not only a Roman centurion, but more importantly he is an upright man and, above all, God-fearing. Thus, although he is uncircumcised, Cornelius practices the liturgical and ethical codes of the Jewish people. Moreover, he is respected not just by some Jews but by "the whole Jewish nation." Upon hearing this claim, Peter may have wondered how anyone could be admired by an entire nation, especially a Roman Gentile living within the sizeable geographical confines of Israel. Nonetheless, Peter must have realized that they made such an exaggerated assertion with the best of intentions—emphatically wanting him to know that Cornelius was especially loved by the Jewish people who knew him. Moreover, not only was Cornelius someone of remarkable importance, but also he was directed, not just by any "ordinary" angel, but by "a holy angel" to send for Peter and to request that he come to his house so as to hear him speak. Who could refuse a request that was prompted by a "holy" angel? Peter was convinced by their account, even if it was somewhat embellished. "So he called them in to be his guests." His inviting the three men to be his guests in the home of Simon, who was a tanner, further illustrates that Peter recognized that he could associate with those who were unclean without being contaminated himself. This recognition finds its culmination in what transpires next.

## Peter's Arrival at Cornelius's House (Acts 10:23b–29)

> The next day he rose and went off with them, and some of the brethren from Joppa accompanied him. And on the following day they entered Caesarea. Cornelius was expecting them and had called together his kinsmen and close friends. When Peter arrived, Cornelius met him and fell down at his feet and worshipped him. But Peter lifted him up, saying, "Stand up; I too am a man." And as he talked with him, he went in and found many persons gathered; and he said to them, "You yourselves know how unlawful it is for a Jew to associate with or to visit any one of another nation; but God has shown that I should not call any man common and unclean. So when I was sent for, I came without objection. I ask then why you sent for me."[17]

Having set off from Joppa the following day with some of his Jewish-Christian brethren, Peter arrived at Caesarea the next day. Anticipating his coming, Cornelius was not alone when Peter arrived. He not only gathered "his kinsmen" but also his "close friends." Cornelius generously and graciously desired that his entire family and all his acquaintances would hear what Peter would have to tell them. Now, at Peter's appearance, "Cornelius met him."[18] Upon meeting Peter, Cornelius did something that is somewhat surprising. "He fell at his feet and worshipped him." One would think that Cornelius would have known better. However, Cornelius could have been so overwhelmed at coming into the presence of the prince of the apostles, that he did what he considered proper. However, Peter knew that such actions were not only inappropriate but also blasphemous. Thus, Peter's rebuke. "Stand up; I too am a man." One is not permitted to fall on one's knees and adore a mere man, even if that man does possess some divinely appointed ecclesial status.

17. Unless otherwise noted, all Scripture passages in this section are taken from Acts 10:23b–29.

18. Here, there is a bit of ambiguity. The text states, "When Peter entered." Shortly, the text states that "when he [Peter] went in," that is, entered into Cornelius's house. Does the first "entering" refer to Caesarea or to Cornelius's house? It would appear that Cornelius first met Peter when he entered the city, prior to his going into his house.

After this somewhat awkward and embarrassing moment, Peter talked with Cornelius as "he went in and found many persons gathered." Luke gives the impression that Peter was taken aback at the number of gathered people. Despite his amazement, Peter began to address them. He reminds them of what they already know. "It is unlawful for a Jew to associate with or to visit any one of another nation." However, "God has shown me that I should not call any man common or unclean." Obviously, Peter is here recalling, though not in detail, his previous vision and the words spoken to him—"What God has cleansed, you must not call common" (Acts 10:15). Because of this revelatory vision, Peter concludes his introductory remarks, "So when I was sent for, I came without objection." Nothing now stood in the way of Peter's associating with Gentiles. What Peter does want to know is why they sent for him. Peter is still perplexed. He still has not grasped the full significance of his revelatory vision of all the unclean animals, all of which he is no longer to consider common. He does not perceive that the reason Cornelius sent for him and why he has gathered everyone together is to hear what Peter has to say—the proclamation of the gospel. Given his somewhat surprising ignorance, Cornelius must now reiterate to Peter the vision that he had.

## Why Cornelius Sent for Peter (Acts 10:30-33)

> And Cornelius said, "Four days ago, about this hour, I was keeping the ninth hour of prayer in my house; and behold, a man stood before me in bright apparel, saying, 'Cornelius, your prayer has been heard and your alms have been remembered before God. Send therefore to Joppa and ask for Simon who is called Peter; he is lodging in the house of Simon, a tanner, by the seaside.' So, I sent to you at once, and you have been kind enough to come. Now therefore we are all present in the sight of God, to hear all that you have been commanded by the Lord."[19]

Cornelius first sets the historical background of the present meeting between himself and Peter. Four days previously, Cornelius was praying at about 3:00 PM, that is, at the hour when the evening sacrificial liturgy was being offered in the temple. What Peter must "behold" is that "a man stood before" Cornelius, and he was dressed "in bright apparel." Here again, we find another version of Cornelius's vision, though this time it does not appear to be a spiritual or mental vision, but a real ocular event. Moreover, Cornelius specifies

19. Unless otherwise noted, all Scripture passages in this section are taken from Acts 10:30-33.

that it was "a man" who stood before him, whereas previously Luke spoke of Cornelius having a vision of an angel, though, as we saw, he also seemed to be able to see that angel as well. Although he now declares that he saw "a man" standing before him, Cornelius does accentuate that he wore "bright apparel," which implies that this visible "man" was clothed with the radiance of a heavenly angel, and so was an angelic divine messenger. Thus, amid Cornelius's various accountings of his experience, one can reconcile the differences among them.

Cornelius next recounts to Peter what this angelic man told him, which is almost verbatim Luke's original account.[20] The angel's command to Cornelius has now been achieved, for Peter has now "been kind enough to come."[21] Because of Peter's gracious presence, all those assembled are "here present in the sight of God," that is, they have gathered in his name "to hear all" that Peter has "been commanded by the Lord." Thus, both those present and what Peter is about to say are in accordance with the will of the Lord God—the hearing of the gospel of Jesus Christ.

## Peter's Proclamation of the Good News (Acts 10:34-43)

> And Peter opened his mouth and said: "Truly I perceive that God shows no partiality, but in every nation anyone who fears him and does what is right is acceptable to him. You know the word which he sent to the sons of Israel, preaching good news of peace by Jesus Christ (he is Lord of all), the word which was proclaimed throughout all Judea, beginning in Galilee after the baptism which John preached: how God anointed Jesus of Nazareth with the Holy Spirit and with power; how he went about doing good and healing all that were oppressed by the devil, for God was with him. And we are witnesses to all that he did both in the country of the Jews and in Jerusalem."[22]

Luke prefaces Peter's proclamation by denoting that he "opened his mouth." He employed this same phrase previously with regard to Philip when

20. See Acts 10:3-5. As noted previously, since Luke's account of this event almost exactly parallels Cornelius's account, one can assume that Luke received it from Cornelius himself.

21. There appears to be an incomplete thought in the present Luken text. Cornelius says that "he sent to you at once." What Cornelius sent at once to Peter were "messengers."

22. Unless otherwise noted, all Scripture passages in this section are taken from Acts 10:34-43. However, because of the length of Peter's proclamation, the remainder of this passage will be inserted later.

Peter's present proclamation is an abbreviated form of Mark's Gospel, which has been traditionally recognized as an account of Peter's preaching. The church, from the beginning, held that Mark was Peter's disciple.

he began to preach the gospel to the Ethiopian eunuch.[23] By means of this specification, Luke is accentuating that what will now come forth from Peter's mouth, as was the case with Philip, will be God's truth as to who Jesus Christ is. One only truly lives by what comes forth from the mouth of God.[24]

Peter begins by once more alluding to what he had previously learned through his vision of the unclean animals being lowered on a sheet from heaven—what God has cleansed is not common or unclean. In this light, Peter can rightly say, "Truly I perceive that God shows no partiality, but in every nation anyone who fears him and does what is right is acceptable to him." To God, one's nationality, whether Jew or Gentile, is not what makes one pleasing. Rather, what delights him is the reverential fear and righteous obedience shown to him.

With this introduction, Peter proceeds to recall what God has revealed, something his listeners already acknowledge. "You know the word which he sent to the sons of Israel, preaching good news of peace by Jesus Christ (he is Lord of all)." Although Peter is preaching to Gentiles, he first speaks of God's word that was revealed to the Jews, that is, that peace with God is achieved through Jesus Christ through whom sins are forgiven and holiness of life is obtained.[25] Moreover, Jesus Christ "is the Lord of all," and so this salvific peace with God is available to the Gentiles as well. This saving word "was proclaimed throughout all of Judea, beginning in Galilee after the baptism which John preached: how God anointed Jesus of Nazareth with the Holy Spirit and with power." John the Baptist's call to repentance, accompanied by his baptism of repentance, prepared the way for the coming of the Messiah. God revealed that this Messiah was none other than "Jesus of Nazareth," for "God anointed him with the Holy Spirit and with power."[26] In so doing, God the Father declared that Jesus was his Spirit-filled Son in whom he was well pleased. In the power of the Holy Spirit, Jesus "went about doing good and healing all that were oppressed by the devil, for God was with him." The good that Jesus did can be seen in the miracles that he enacted and in the exorcisms that he performed, and so he demonstrated that God's kingdom was now at hand.

23. See Acts 8:35.

24. See Dt 8:3.

25. By first referencing the Jews, Peter is implicitly acknowledging that they hold pride of place as God's chosen people, a people to whom he first revealed himself and with whom he made a covenant.

26. By specifying that Jesus was from Nazareth, Peter is heightening the historical reality of Jesus. The Messiah was an identifiable man from a particular earthly city and not some ethereal heavenly being.

Peter emphatically declares, "We are witnesses to all that he did both in the country of the Jews and in Jerusalem." By speaking of "we," Peter is referring to all the apostles, for, from the beginning, throughout the entire country of Israel and in the sacred city of Jerusalem, they saw all that Jesus did and heard all that he had said. To all of which, Peter and the apostles now bear truthful testimony.

At this juncture, Peter proceeds to declare the central saving mysteries of the gospel.

> They put him to death by hanging him on a tree; but God raised him on the third day and made him manifest; not to all the people but to us who were chosen by God as witnesses, who ate and drank with him after he rose from the dead. And he commanded us to preach to the people, and to testify that he is the one ordained by God to be judge of the living and the dead. To him all the prophets bear witness that everyone who believes in him receives forgiveness of sins through his name.

Although he did many good things throughout the whole of Israel, the Jews killed Jesus "by hanging him on a tree." By speaking of Jesus's crucifixion as his being hung "on a tree," Peter is referring to what is declared in the book of Deuteronomy. "And if a man has committed a crime punishable by death and he is put to death, and you hang him on a tree, his body shall not remain all night upon the tree, for a hanged man is accursed by God; you shall not defile your land which the Lord God gives you for an inheritance." (Dt 21:22–23).

The Jews condemned Jesus for blasphemy by making himself out to be God's Son, and such a crime was punishable by death.[27] That he was hung on a tree verified that he was indeed cursed by God. Moreover, by specifying that Jesus was hung on a tree, Peter is also recalling the Suffering Servant Songs in Isaiah.

> Surely he has borne our griefs and carried our sorrow; yet we esteemed him stricken, smitten by God, and afflicted. But he was wounded for our transgressions, he was bruised for our iniquities; upon him was the chastisement that made us whole, and with his stripes we were healed. All we like sheep have gone astray; we have turned every one to his own way; and the Lord has laid on him the iniquity of us all.[28]

As one cursed by God, and so hung on a tree, Jesus bore the grief and sorrow of humankind's sin. As one cursed, he was thought to be "stricken and

27. See Mt 26:63–66, Mk 14:61–64, and Lk 22:66–71. In John's Gospel, Jesus declared that he and the Father were one. Because of this declaration, the Jews attempted to stone him for blasphemy, for "you, being a man, make yourself God" (Jn 10:29–33).

28. Is 53:4–6. See also Is 42:1–4, 49:1–6, 50:4–11, and 52:13–53:12.

smitten by God." Although he was lacerated for humankind's depravity, yet, through his suffering, all were healed and made whole. In being hung upon a tree, Jesus took upon himself the curse of Adam's sin, and, in so doing, he recreated the whole of Adam's progeny. Jesus, having shouldered the curse of sin and having been hung on a tree, and so having freed humankind from sin's scourge, Peter immediately states, "But God raised him on the third day and made him manifest; not to all people but to us who were chosen by God as witnesses, who ate and drank with him after he rose from the dead." By raising Jesus gloriously from the dead on the third day, the Father both verified the efficaciousness of Jesus's death and attested to its beneficent fruit—eternal life. God chose Peter and the apostles as his witnesses to Jesus's resurrection, for to them God made him visibly manifest. Because Jesus ate and drank with them, they can now rightly attest to his bodily resurrection.[29]

Moreover, the risen Jesus "commanded" Peter and the apostles "to preach to the people, and to testify that he is the one ordained by God to be judge of the living and the dead." So, what God declared at Jesus's baptism, that he was the Father's Spirit-filled Messiah, and what was anticipated in Jesus's miracles and exorcisms, and what was salvifically accomplished in his death and resurrection, finds its culmination in the Father ordaining him to be the final judge of the living and dead. When Jesus gloriously returns at the end of time, he will judge both those who are alive on earth and those who have died, that is, he will allot to them either their eternal reward or their everlasting punishment. To this truth, the apostles presently give testimony.

What Peter declares here finds it revelational warrant in what Jesus commanded at his ascension. First, immediately prior to his ascension, Jesus tells his apostles that they will receive "power when the Holy Spirit has come upon you; and you shall be my witnesses in Jerusalem and in all Judea and Samaria and to the ends of the earth."[30] This bearing witness to the risen Jesus to the

29. Interestingly, Peter is here referring to what is only found in Luke's Gospel account of Jesus's post-resurrection appearances. In Luke 's Gospel, Jesus stresses the bodily nature of his risen humanity. "See my hands and my feet, that it is I myself; handle me, and see; for a spirit has not flesh and bones as you see that I have." Because the apostles were still befuddled in disbelief, Jesus provides the culminating proof of risen bodily existence. He asks, "Have you anything here to eat?" They gave him "a piece of broiled fish, and he took it and ate before them" (Lk 24:39–43). Thus, one might suspect that, although Peter's discourse is historically accurate, yet Luke interposes here an element from his Gospel, which would also be historically true. One further minor comment. Peter speaks of Jesus not only eating with the apostles but also drinking with them. Luke, in his Gospel, does not speak of Jesus drinking.

30. Acts 1:8. In his Gospel, Luke also narrates Jesus's last words to his apostles just prior to his ascension, though in a slightly abbreviated form. "Thus, it is written, that the Christ should suffer and on the third day rise from the dead, and that repentance and forgiveness of sins

ends of the earth is now taking place through the testimony of the apostolic church. Second, having given this evangelistic commission, Jesus ascended in a cloud out of the sight of the apostles. Within that heavenly cloud, two angels appeared and said, "Men of Galilee, why do you stand looking into heaven? This Jesus, who was taken up from you into heaven, will come in the same way as you saw him go into heaven" (Acts 1:11). The purpose of Jesus's eschatological return is to judge the living and the dead.

Having spoken of Jesus's return, Peter concludes his address by declaring that "all the prophets bear witness that everyone who believes in him receives forgiveness of sins through his name." As the fulfillment of the entire prophetic tradition, Jesus is the one in whose name believers find the forgiveness of their sins.

When Peter was making his concluding remarks, Luke next informs the reader of what suddenly and unexpectedly transpired.

## The Holy Spirit Is Poured Out upon the Gentiles (Acts 10:44–48)

> While Peter was still saying this, the Holy Spirit fell on all who heard the word. And the believers from among the circumcised who came with Peter were amazed, because the gift of Holy Spirit had been poured out even on the Gentiles. For they heard them speaking in tongues and extolling God. Then Peter declared, "Can anyone forbid water for baptizing these people who have received the Holy Spirit just as we have?" And he commanded them to be baptized in the name of Jesus Christ. Then they asked him to remain for some days.[31]

should be preached in his name to all nations, beginning from Jerusalem. You are my witnesses of these things" (Lk 24:46–48). What Luke narrates in his Gospel and in the Acts of the Apostles is in conformity with what Jesus declared to his apostles prior to his ascension as found in Matthew's Gospel. "All authority in heaven and on earth has been given to me. Go therefore and make disciples of all nations, baptizing them in the name of the Father and of the Son and of the Holy Spirit, teaching them to observe all that I have commanded you; and lo, I am with you always until the close of the age" (Mt 28:18–20). Observe that Jesus is with his apostolic church until the end of time whereupon he will come to judge the living and the dead. This apostolic mandate is also found in the Gospel of Mark. Jesus said to his apostles, "Go into the whole world and preach the gospel to the whole of creation. He who believes and is baptized will be saved; but he who does not believe will be condemned" (Mk 16:15–16; see also Mk 16:19). Inherent within Mark's account is the notion that, when Jesus returns at the end of time, those who believed and were baptized will be judged worthy of salvation, while those who did not believe will be rightly condemned.

31. Unless otherwise noted, all Scripture passages in this section are taken from Acts 10:44–48.

While Peter was completing his proclamation of the gospel, the Holy Spirit "fell" on those who heard his "word." This "falling" of the Holy Spirit implies that the Spirit's coming upon the Gentiles was not subtle or discreet, but one of dramatic power and with an immediate, visible, transforming effect. This present "falling" was not unlike, as Peter will soon confirm, what took place when the Holy Spirit came upon the one hundred twenty in the upper room on Pentecost; where there was the sound of a heavenly, rushing wind filling the house.[32] Moreover, the Holy Spirit fell upon those who "heard the word," that is, upon those who believed what Peter had been proclaiming concerning Jesus, that he is the risen Christ and the saving Lord of all. Here we perceive, in Luke's account, the intrinsic connection between faith and the reception of the Holy Spirit. Faith is the catalyst for the Spirit's descent.

Now, the circumcised Jewish Christians who came with Peter "were amazed," for "the Holy Spirit had been poured out even on the Gentiles." That Luke notes that the Spirit came upon those who were not circumcised to the astonishment of the circumcised implies that circumcision has now become salvifically obsolete. One is not made a member of God's elect through circumcision, nor is it any longer a sign of being a member of God's chosen people. Circumcision has been replaced by the transforming divine life of the Holy Spirit—he who makes one interiorly holy, and so a true son of the Father in Christ Jesus.[33] The sign that verified that the Holy Spirit had fallen upon the Gentiles is that the circumcised Christians "heard them speaking in tongues and extolling God." In response to this phenomenon, Peter declared, "Can any

32. See Acts 2:1–2.

33. Although the circumcised, in the above, were amazed that the Holy Spirit was poured out upon the uncircumcised Gentiles, they acknowledged that such did indeed take place. However, Paul will later, among the Galatians, be confronted by Jewish Christians who demand that convert Gentiles must not only be baptized, but that they must also be circumcised. They were known as "the circumcision party" (Gal 2:12). (As we will see in chapter eleven of Acts, Peter will be challenged by this same party.) Paul refuted such an erroneous claim. Paul declares, "Now I, Paul, say to you that if you receive circumcision, Christ will be no advantage to you.... For in Christ Jesus neither circumcision nor uncircumcision is of any avail, but faith working through love" (Gal 5:2–7). Paul, himself, boasts in nothing but the cross of Jesus Christ, "for neither circumcision counts for anything, nor uncircumcision, but a new creation" (Gal 6:14–16). One is made a new creation in Christ through the indwelling of the Holy Spirit. Thus, being circumcised is of no saving value. In his First Letter to the Corinthians, Paul provides this pastoral principle, "This is my rule in all the churches. Was anyone at the time of his call already circumcised? Let him not seek to remove the marks of circumcision. Was anyone at the time of his call uncircumcised? Let him not seek circumcision. For neither circumcision counts for anything nor uncircumcision, but keeping the commandments of God. Everyone should remain in the state in which he was called" (1 Cor 7:17–21). See also Rom 2:25–29.

one forbid water for baptizing these people who have received the Holy Spirit just as we have?" For Peter, the event that took place on Pentecost has now been replicated in their midst. The Holy Spirit had fallen upon all who were in the upper room, whereupon they spoke in multiple languages and told of "the mighty works of God" (Acts 2:5–11). Because of this same Pentecostal experience, Peter concludes that there is no valid reason why these Gentiles can be denied the water of baptism.[34] This being the case, Peter "commanded them to be baptized in the name of Jesus Christ."

As we discussed earlier when treating Philip's missionary journey to Samaria, there is, in light of the above, a theological anomaly here. Although Philip baptized the Samaritans "in the name of the Lord Jesus," Peter and John were sent in order that they might lay their hands on the previously baptized, "for the Holy Spirit had not yet fallen on any of them" (Acts 8:14–17). Presently, the Holy Spirit "fell on all who heard the word," and, given that the Holy Spirit had been poured upon them, Peter commands that they "be baptized in the name of Jesus Christ." Theologically, what is one to make of these conjoined and yet reversed events? Peter recognized that, although the Holy Spirit had fallen upon the Gentiles, they still needed to be sacramentally incorporated into the church, the ecclesial apostolic community. That sacramental incorporation can only be achieved through water baptism. Thus, he commanded that they "be baptized in the name of Jesus Christ." This sequence of events is in keeping with what took place after Peter's Pentecost discourse. Having completed his proclamation of the gospel, Peter declared that those who believe must repent "and be baptized in the name of Jesus Christ for the forgiveness of sins," so that they might "receive the gift of the Holy Spirit" (Acts 2:37–38). Having been baptized, "there were added that day about three thousand souls" (Acts 2:41). The present Gentiles are to be baptized that they might sacramentally obtain the definitive and transforming gift of the Spirit, whereby they are numbered among the members of the apostolic community.

Luke concludes his narrative of the conversion of Cornelius and his fellow Gentiles by saying that "they asked him [Peter] to remain for some days." Presumably, Peter graciously and happily complied with this request.

34. By conjoining water with baptism, Peter is acting in accord with what Jesus told Nicodemus in John's Gospel. "Truly, truly, I say to you, unless one is born of water and the Spirit, he cannot enter the kingdom of God" (Jn 3:5).

## Conclusion

In concluding chapter ten of the Acts of the Apostles, I want to make three points. First, we once more perceive in this chapter Jesus being Jesus, that is, Jesus enacting his name as YHWH-Saves. Here he did so through the conversion of Cornelius and his Gentile household. With the Gentiles becoming Christian, the ecclesial apostolic community, the church, is radically transformed. It is no longer simply composed of circumcised Jewish Christians.

Second, the conversion of the Gentiles, however, subsequently brought strife within the nascent church precisely over the issue of circumcision. As we will see in chapter eleven of the Acts of the Apostles, Peter is confronted over why he did not have the Gentiles circumcised. Peter will have to defend his actions. Moreover, as will become evident, the growth of Gentile converts will continue to increase, while Jewish converts will, in comparison, dwindle.

Third, this lack of Jewish converts sadly continues to this day. I have argued that because of this lack of Jewish Christians within the Church, the body of Christ lacks what is vital to it—a full complement of Jewish Christians.[35] The body of Christ can only be robust and vibrant when both Jews and Gentiles are among its living members, together bearing witness to Jesus as the definitive Lord and universal Savior. Only when Christian Jews and Christian Gentiles are conjoined in the oneness of faith will the risen Jesus return in glory at the end of time (Rom 11:11–15).

35. See T. G. Weinandy, "The Jews and the Body of Christ: An Essay in Hope," *Pro Ecclesia* 27, no. 4 (2018): 412–24.

*Chapter 11*

# PETER'S DEFENSE OF HIS ACTIONS AND THE CHURCH IN ANTIOCH

In chapter ten of the Acts of the Apostles, Luke narrated the vision of the Gentile Roman centurion, Cornelius, wherein an angel instructs him to send for Simon who is called Peter and is residing in Joppa. Peter, likewise, had a vision. Peter saw all kinds of animals being lowered down from heaven on a sheet, whereupon the Lord told him that he should not consider them common or unclean. Peter came to understand that the Lord was referring to the Gentiles. They are not to be considered common or unclean. Rather, even though they did not belong to God's chosen people, the Jews, they could, nonetheless, become believers in Jesus Christ and, thus, be baptized in his name—becoming thereby members of the church. Thus, when messengers from Cornelius arrived, Peter, without any hesitation, went with them to Caesarea. Upon his arrival, he proclaimed the gospel to the Gentile Cornelius and his household and friends. The Holy Spirit fell upon them and, at Peter's command, they were sacramentally baptized. Although these events took place in Caesarea, word of the conversion of the Gentiles reached the other apostles, and so we will now find, at the onset of chapter eleven, Peter proceeding to Jerusalem to give an account of what took place and to defend his actions.

## Peter's Report to the Jerusalem Church (Acts 11:1–18)

Now the apostles and the brethren who were in Judea heard that the Gentiles also had received the word of God. So, when Peter went up to Jerusalem, the circumcision party criticized him, saying, "Why did you go to uncircumcised men and eat with them?" But Peter began and explained to them in order.[1]

While in Judea, the apostles and other Christian brethren heard that the Gentiles "also had received the word of God."[2] The word "also" is theologically significant, for that "also" denotes that not only did the Jews come to believe in Jesus, which would have been expected, but "also" the Gentiles, which would have been surprising and unanticipated. They, after all, were considered common and unclean. Nonetheless, they "also received the word of God," that is, they "received" in faith Peter's proclamation of the gospel, and, the Spirit having fallen upon them, they were baptized in the name of Jesus Christ. Thus, they became members of the nascent ecclesial community, which, up to this point, was entirely composed of Jewish converts. With the conversion of the Gentiles, the complexion of the Church radically changed—a change that continues to be evident today. So revolutionary was this ecclesial transformation that not everyone was pleased.

In this contested context, when Peter went to Jerusalem, "the circumcision party" immediately confronted him. "Why did you go to uncircumcised men and eat with them?" Peter was already aware that some would see his actions as problematic. Upon entering Cornelius's home, he stated, "You yourselves know how unlawful it is for a Jew to associate with or visit anyone of another nation." However, God had shown him that he "should not call any man common or unclean" (Acts 10:27–28). Now, although the Jews of the circumcision party expressed their condemnation of Peter for entering the home of a Gentile and eating with such men, one wonders if that was their real theological concern. Yes, what Peter did was contrary to the Jewish law, and so something for which he could be rightly reprimanded. Nonetheless, were members of the circumcision party merely harping on a legality whereby the real "depravity" could be censored while appearing to remain hidden? If the circumcision party is rightly named, then their primary concern would not be Peter's entering a Gentile home and eating with Gentile men. Rather, their disquiet would be that Peter did not circumcise these men prior to their baptism. Thus, the

1. Unless otherwise noted, all Scripture passages in this section are taken from Acts 11:1–18. Because this section contains many verses, I will provide the remainder of them in due course.

2. Luke states that the apostles were in Judea, and so present when Peter came to Jerusalem. Thus, the apostles were present when the circumcision party criticized Peter for associating with the uncircumcised Gentiles. How they reacted to such a reproach is not stated. However, at the Council of Jerusalem, he will again recall that he, by divine authority, preached the gospel to the Gentiles (see Acts 15:6–9).

critical question within the early church now comes clearly into the light—are both circumcision and baptism necessary for salvation?[3] Peter responds to the pushback coming from the circumcision party by relating the propriety of his divinely authorized actions.[4]

In describing the vision that he had when in a trance, Peter states what he saw when the sheet was lowered from heaven. "Looking at it closely I observed animals and beasts of prey and reptiles and birds of the air." Peter wants the members of the circumcision party to know that he "looked closely" at what he saw, for what he clearly observed is of the utmost revelational importance. He beheld unclean animals. Moreover, the Lord commanded that he kill and eat them, to which demand, Peter adamantly refused to obey, for he had never eaten what is unclean and common. Nonetheless, God told him that what he had cleansed, he should not call common. Peter states that this happened three times—thus emphasizing to members of the circumcision party the same threefold emphasis that God revealed to him. For Peter, what was divinely revealed to him in his vision is no small matter.

Moreover, Peter tells of the men who arrived from Caesarea, and what they communicated to him pertaining to Cornelius's angelic vision wherein

3. Here I am doing something rather unusual. I am going to footnote much of what I noted in chapter ten. I do so because I believe that it is important to grasp this fundamental issue within the early church as well as to appreciate the way the apostolic church responded to it. Its response would become a defined doctrine, and so become the church's magisterial teaching henceforth. Although this issue will be fully resolved later at the council in Jerusalem (see Acts 15:1–29), where it will be theologically interpreted, below is again Paul's response to it as found in his Letter to the Galatians.

In Galatia, Paul was confronted by Jewish Christians who demanded that convert Gentiles must not only be baptized, but that they must also be circumcised. They were known as "the circumcision party" (Gal 2:12), the same designation as given above. Paul refuted such an erroneous claim. Paul declares, "Now I, Paul, say to you that if you receive circumcision, Christ will be no advantage to you.... For in Christ Jesus neither circumcision nor uncircumcision is of any avail, but faith working through love" (Gal 5:2–7). Paul, himself, boasts in nothing but the cross of Jesus Christ, "for neither circumcision counts for anything, nor uncircumcision, but a new creation" (Gal 6:14–16). One is made a new creation in Christ through the indwelling of the Holy Spirit. Thus, being circumcised is of no saving value. In his First Letter to the Corinthians, Paul provides this pastoral principle, "This is my rule in all the churches. Was anyone at the time of his call already circumcised? Let him not seek to remove the marks of circumcision. Was anyone at the time of his call uncircumcised? Let him not seek circumcision. For neither circumcision counts for anything nor uncircumcision, but keeping the commandments of God. Everyone should remain in the state in which he was called" (1 Cor 7:17–21). See also Rom 2:25–29.

4. As was noted previously, when theologically interpreting chapter ten of Acts, what Peter will now recount is, almost verbatim, what Luke narrated in Acts 10:9–16. Because of this repetition, I will not copy the entire text here. Nonetheless, Peter does accentuate some aspects of his vision, upon which I will comment theologically.

he was to send for him. Now, in Luke's prior account, Cornelius's messengers came to Peter and told him that a holy angel had instructed Cornelius to request that Peter "come to his house," so that he might "hear what you have to say" (Acts 10:22). Presently, Peter states that the angel gave the following instructions, "Send to Joppa and bring Simon called Peter; he will declare to you a message by which you will be saved, you and all of your household." Peter previously wanted the members of the circumcision party to know that he looked "closely" at all the animals in the sheet. Now he embellishes upon what Cornelius and his household were to hear him say. Peter here provides the content of what was previously undisclosed. Peter is to declare to them "a message" wherein all of them "will be saved." Again, Peter wants the members of the circumcision party to understand, in no uncertain terms, that he was divinely commissioned to preach the good news—a message that is salvific not only for the Jews but also for the Gentiles. Peter is attempting to expand the very narrow and restrictive mindset of those of the circumcision party.

Having presented to the members of the circumcision party the divinely revealed reasons as to why he entered the house of uncircumcised men and ate with them, Peter relates what immediately transpired upon his proclaiming the gospel of salvation. "As I began to speak, the Holy Spirit fell on them just as on us at the beginning." What Peter narrates here is, again, in conformity with Luke's previous account. "While Peter was still saying this, the Holy Spirit fell on all who heard the word. And the believers from among the circumcised who came with Peter were amazed, because the gift of the Holy Spirit had been poured out even on the Gentiles. For they heard them speaking in tongues and extolling God" (Acts 10:44-46).

Thus, what Peter presently states in his defense could simply be put in this manner, "It is not my fault. Do not blame me. The Holy Spirit fell upon the uncircumcised Gentiles on his own authority. I had nothing to do with it. I merely, in preaching the saving gospel to them, provided the occasion wherein the Holy Spirit was poured out upon them." What the members of the circumcision party also needed to grasp is that the Spirit "fell on them just as on us at the beginning."[5] What Peter and the other apostles experienced at Pentecost, at

5. Again, later, at the Council of Jerusalem, Peter makes, in similar words, the same point. "Brethren, you know that in the early days God made choice among you, that by my mouth the Gentiles should hear the word of the gospel and believe. And God who knows the heart bore witness to them, giving them the Holy Spirit *just as he did to us*; and he made no distinction between us and them, but cleansed their hearts by faith" (Acts 15:7-9, emphasis added). Also, it was noted that, at the onset of chapter eleven, Luke said that "the apostles" were present during Peter's ensuing defense of his actions. Peter now speaks in terms of "us," which implies that he is referring to himself and to the apostles who were also present at this Jerusalem gathering.

"the beginning," is the same Pentecostal event that the uncircumcised Gentiles have now experienced. This same occurrence, as Luke noted earlier, included the Gentiles "speaking in tongues and extolling God." This Spirit-anointed gift further confirmed the outpouring of the Holy Spirit. Moreover, then, as the circumcised believers were initially amazed, so now the members of the circumcision party should also be joyfully astonished, rather than grumbling that the Gentiles were uncircumcised. What is of revelational importance is not the issue of circumcision, but the reality of the Holy Spirit coming upon the Gentiles.

Peter proceeds to relate what he recalled when the Spirit fell upon the Gentiles just as the Holy Spirit had done at the beginning. "And I remembered the word of the Lord, how he said, 'John baptized with water, but you shall be baptized with Holy Spirit.' If then God gave the same gift to them as he gave to us when we believed in the Lord Jesus Christ, who was I that I could withstand God?" What Peter recollects is what Jesus declared to the apostles immediately prior to his ascension. Jesus charged the apostles not to leave Jerusalem, but to wait for the Father's promise, that is, that John "baptized with water, but before many days you shall be baptized with the Holy Spirit."[6] Since the uncircumcised Gentiles were baptized in the Holy Spirit, "the same gift" that was given to the Jewish apostles, when they "believed in the Lord Jesus Christ," Peter rhetorically asks, "who was I that I could withstand God?"[7] No one, not ever Peter, the prince of the apostles, can prevail against or overrule the actions of the almighty and all-powerful God. The members of the circumcision party must acknowledge that, having been baptized in the Holy Spirit, the uncircumcised Gentile Christians are of equal status with the circumcised Jewish Christians. Upon Peter concluding his defense of his actions, "they heard this, they were silenced." The circumcision party had no rebuttal.

6. At the conclusion of Luke's Gospel, Jesus instructs his apostles to stay in Jerusalem, "until you are clothed with power from on high" (Lk 24:49). To be clothed with heavenly power is to be baptized in the Holy Spirit. Moreover, in Luke's Gospel, John the Baptist declared to the people, "I baptize you with water; but he who is mightier than I is coming, the thong of whose sandals I am not worthy to untie; he will baptize with the Holy Spirit and with fire" (Lk 3:16). See also Mt 3:11 and Mk 1:7–8. Likewise, Peter's recollection is in keeping with John the Baptist's declaration in the Gospel of John. "I saw the Spirit descend as a dove from heaven and remain on him. I myself did not know him; but he who sent me to baptize with water said to me, "he on whom you see the Spirit descend and remain, this is he who baptizes with the Holy Spirit." And I have seen and have borne witness that this is the Son of God" (Jn 1:32–34).As the risen, incarnate, Spirit-filled Son of God, Jesus is the one who baptizes in the Holy Spirit those who believe in him.

7. By designating the risen Jesus as "Lord," Peter is professing that he is divine, for the term "Lord" (*kurion*) is the Greek equivalent of YHWH—He Who Is. Likewise, by referring to Jesus as "Christ," he is declaring that he is the anticipated, Spirit-anointed, messianic savior.

Silence gave confirmation to Peter's defense. Peter had won the day on behalf of the Gentile converts. Moreover, Luke adds, "And they glorified God, saying, 'Then to the Gentiles also God has granted repentance unto life.'" Whether the "they" who remained "silent" were the same "they" who "glorified God," is doubtful. The circumcision party may have lost today's conflict, but upon future fields of battle they would take up arms again. Nonetheless, the Gentiles could be assured that, by repenting of their sins and by coming to faith in the Lord Jesus Christ, they, along with the Jews, held equal pride of place within the nascent ecclesial community—the church. Thus, they too were able to obtain eternal life.

## The Church in Antioch (Acts 11:19-30)

Luke abruptly moves to the evangelistic endeavors that were taking place in the city of Antioch, particularly among the Gentiles.

> Now those who were scattered because of the persecution that arose over Stephen traveled as far as Phoenicia and Cyprus and Antioch, speaking the word to none except Jews. But there were some of them, men of Cyprus and Cyrene, who on coming to Antioch spoke to the Greeks also, preaching the Lord Jesus.[8]

In the aftermath of the persecution following Stephen's martyrdom, many fled to Phoenicia, Cyprus, and Antioch, all of which had substantial Christian populations.[9] Since these fleeing refugees were predominately Jewish Christians, they proclaimed the gospel, "the word," to fellow Jews. However, "some of them," those from Cyprus and Cyrene, when they came to Antioch, also "preached the Lord Jesus" to the Greeks or the Hellenists.[10] It would appear that the evangelization was equally successful among the Hebrew-speaking Jews and the Greek-speaking Hellenists, "for the hand of the Lord was with them, and a great number that believed turned to the Lord." To speak of "the

8. Unless otherwise noted, all Scripture passages in this section are taken from Acts 11:19-30. Because this section contains many verses, I will provide the remainder of them in due course.

9. Luke is referencing what he stated earlier, "And on that day [the day of Stephen's death] a great persecution arose against the Church in Jerusalem; and they were all scattered throughout the region of Judea and Samaria, except the apostles" (Acts 8:1). Phoenicia was a region in northwest Galilee; Cyprus is an island in the Mediterranean; and Antioch was a major city in Syria.

10. Greeks or Hellenists, as briefly noted in chapter six, were Jews who were deported during the Assyrian and Babylonian conquests (ca. 597 BC and ca. 721 BC). The Jewish diaspora continued to grow with large Jewish populations in Rome and Alexandria, Egypt, and, as is now seen here in Acts, in Antioch. Cyrene was a port city in northern Africa in what would today be Libya.

hand of the Lord" denotes not only that the risen Lord Jesus was with those who spoke, but, more so, that he imbued, with the lifegiving power of the Holy Spirit, the words of those who spoke. Thus, this Spirit-filled proclamation so inflamed, in turn, the hearts and minds of those who heard that they "turned to the Lord."

Luke, next, narrates the consequence of this successful evangelization in Antioch.

> News of this came to the ears of the Church in Jerusalem, and they sent Barnabas to Antioch. When he came and saw the grace of God, he was glad; and he exhorted them all to remain faithful to the Lord with steadfast purpose; for he was a good man, full of the Holy Spirit and faith. And a large company was added to the Lord.

Upon hearing of Philip's successful missionary journey to Samaria, the apostles send Peter and John.[11] Similarly, the Jerusalem church, now upon hearing the exciting news that many in Antioch had "turned to the Lord," sends Barnabas to learn what was occurring and to foster its advance. But why would the Jerusalem church assign Barnabas to this task and not someone else? The reason is that "he was a good man, full of the Holy Spirit and of faith." Moreover, Luke previously informed his readers that the apostles themselves gave him the name Barnabas. His given name was "Joseph," but the apostles "surnamed" him Barnabas, a name that means "Son of encouragement"[12] Precisely because Barnabas was noted for being a man who exhorted and animated others, he possessed the requisite qualities needed to encourage the recent Christian converts in Antioch. Thus, it is not surprising to read what Luke immediately narrates. "When he came and saw the grace of God, he was glad, and he exhorted them all to remain faithful to the Lord with steadfast purpose." Luke concludes his summary of the evangelistic efforts in Antioch by stating, "And a large company was added to the Lord." As Luke noted the many conversions in Jerusalem, so here he records the significant conversions in Antioch.[13]

11. See Acts 8:14.

12. Acts 4:36. As was seen earlier, Barnabas, in accordance with his name, introduced the newly converted Paul to the wary apostles. "And when he [Paul] had come to Jerusalem he attempted to join the disciples; and they were afraid of him, for they did not believe that he was a disciple. But Barnabas took him, and brought him to the apostles, and declared to them how on the road he had seen the Lord, who spoke to him, and how at Damascus he had preached boldly in the name of Jesus" (Acts 9:26–27). As will become evident, Barnabas manifests a great love of and protective care for Paul, although they will ultimately go their separate ways because of a dispute over Mark (see Acts 15:3–41).

13. See Acts 2:41, 2:47, and 5:14.

Luke narrates that Barnabas, having given encouragement to the brethren in Antioch then "went to Tarsus to look for Saul, and when he found him, he brought him to Antioch, and they taught a large company of people; and in Antioch the disciples were for the first time called Christians." Here, as noted above, we find Barnabas manifesting his care for Paul. Because Paul was so successful in evangelizing in Jerusalem, having been brought there by Barnabas, he was forced to flee to Tarsus, his hometown. However, the impression is now given that Paul was alone and left to his own devices, and, because of this isolation, Barnabas presently goes to Tarsus in search of him, and having found him, he brings him back to Antioch where he could more fully participate in Christian fellowship and get proper care. While in Antioch, "for a whole year they met with the Church, and taught a large company of people." As a twosome, Barnabas and Paul not only were members of the church in Antioch, but they also continued their apostolic ministry of evangelization and teaching.

Here Luke also adds an aside. It was in Antioch that "the disciples were for the first time called Christians." As the faith-filled followers of Jesus Christ, it is only proper that they be designated Christians. Though, the question arises "Did the disciples give themselves this name, or did those who were not followers of Jesus give this name to them?" I would argue that those who were not followers of Jesus designated those who were followers of Jesus "Christians," for they identified them as a distinct group apart from themselves and the common population of Antioch.[14]

At this juncture, Luke narrates several interrelated issues.

> Now in those days prophets came down from Jerusalem to Antioch. And one of them named Agabus stood up and foretold by the Spirit that there would be a great famine over all of the world; and this took place in the days of Claudius. And the disciples determined, everyone according to his ability, to send relief to the brethren who live in Judea; and they did so, sending it to the elders by the hand of Barnabas and Saul.

By speaking of "prophets," Luke attests to the fact that such charismatic seers were common within the early church.[15] Agabus was one of the prophets within the Jerusalem church who had now come to Antioch. That he "stood up" implies that his prophesy took place within an ecclesial assembly. What

14. I have been employing the designation "Christian" throughout, for it is a simple way of referring to those who believe in Jesus Christ—the very reason that the term was coined in the first place.

15. See Rom 12:6–8, 1 Cor 12:8–10 and 12:28–30, and Eph 4:11.

he is to foretell is inspired by the Holy Spirit, for only the Spirit is the source of authentic prophesies.[16] He foretells "a great famine over all the world; and this took place in the days of Claudius." Now, Agabus speaks of a future "great famine" that would occur over the known world, and Luke adds that this famine had taken place "in the days of Claudius," who was emperor at the time.[17] In light of this famine, the disciples concluded that a collection should be taken up, and that everyone, in accordance with their means, is to contribute. This aid would be given "to the brethren who lived in Judea."[18] Having done so, they sent it to the elders in the trusted hands of Barnabas and Saul.[19]

## Conclusion

In the first part of chapter eleven of the Acts of the Apostles, we do not find Jesus being Jesus, YHWH-Saves, in that he does not perform any new saving actions. However, what we do find is Peter defending the radically new revelatory action that he did enact—that of sending the Holy Spirit upon Cornelius and the Gentiles. As I previously stated in the above theological interpretation, this salvific action revolutionized the nascent church—both Jews and Gentiles were now equal members of the Spirit-filled, ecclesial community.

We also examined, in the second part of chapter eleven, the growth of church membership in Antioch, where those who believed in Jesus were first called Christians. This noteworthy growth, again, was among both Jews and Greeks. Moreover, this significant event took place outside of Judea and Jerusalem, and so manifested the church's ever expanding evangelistic outreach.

Lastly, the Jerusalem church was so enthused by what it heard that it sent Barnabas and Saul to Antioch. Upon their arrival Barnabas and Saul rejoiced in

16. In his second letter, Peter states, "First of all you must understand this, that no prophecy of Scripture is a matter of one's own interpretation, because no prophecy ever came by the impulse of man, but men moved by the Holy Spirit spoke from God" (2 Pt 1:20–21).

17. Ancient historians, such as Tacitus, Suetonius, and Josephus, likewise speak of a famine that took place in the eastern Mediterranean. Since it was during the reign of Emperor Claudius (AD 41–54), this famine would have occurred in the 40s.

18. This is the first of two collections that Paul took up for the aid of the poor and needy in Jerusalem (see Acts 24:17). Also see Rom 15:25–28, 1 Cor 16:1–4, and 2 Cor 9:1–5.

19. "Elders" could also be translated presbyters since the Greek term used here is *presbyterous*. "The elders" would have been the Jewish Christian leaders in Judea and Jerusalem, who may have been, at this point, ordained bishops or priests. In the seven letters of Ignatius of Antioch (d. 103) we find a clear demarcation of deacons, priests, and bishops. Notice as well that Luke first names Barnabas and then Saul, which gives the impression that, while they are a twosome, Barnabas, thus far, is considered more significant than Saul, who continues to be under Barnabas's wing.

what they saw—the significant number of those who believed in the Lord Jesus Christ. Moreover, Barnabas and Saul were, themselves, instrumental in preaching the gospel, and so contributed to the growth of the church in Antioch.

In chapter twelve of Acts, Luke returns to narrating the continuing persecution of the church in Jerusalem. Peter, once more, figures prominently in this narrative, and to that story we now turn.

# *Chapter 12*

# PETER'S IMPRISONMENT AND THE DEATH OF HEROD

## Herod's Persecution of the Church (Acts 12:1–5)

Having provided Peter's defense of baptizing Cornelius and other uncircumcised Gentiles, and having described the growth of the church at Antioch, Luke, in chapter twelve of the Acts of the Apostles, proceeds to narrate Herod's persecution of the church at Jerusalem, particularly the arrest of Peter. He states:

> About that time Herod the king laid violent hands upon some who belonged to the Church. He killed James the brother of John with the sword; and when he saw that it pleased the Jews, he proceeded to arrest Peter also. This was during the days of Unleavened Bread. And when he had seized him, he put him in prison, and delivered him to four squads of soldiers to guard him, intending after the Passover to bring him out to the people. So, Peter was kept in prison; but earnest prayer for him was made to God by the Church.[1]

What Luke is about to recount is "about" the same time as Barnabas and Saul were sent to deliver relief to the famine-stricken brethren in Jerusalem. At "about that time" Herod commenced a vicious persecution upon "some who belonged to the Church."[2] That Luke states that he "laid hands" upon those

1. Unless otherwise noted, all Scripture passages in this section are taken from Acts 12:1–5.

2. King Herod was Herod Agrippa I. He ruled Palestine from AD 41 to 44. His grandfather was Herod the Great who ruled at the time of Jesus's birth (see Lk 1:5). This Herod was responsible for the killing of the Holy Innocents in the hope that he would eliminate the new "born king of the Jews" (Mt 2:1–18). Herod Antipas, the son of Herod the Great, had John the Baptist beheaded (see Mt 14:1–12, Mk 6:14–29, and Lk 9:7–9). The Herods had a long history of violence, one that continues into the apostolic age.

tyrannized accentuates that he was personally engaged—his was not a hands-off approach, letting others to do the dirty work.

Herod "killed James the brother of John with the sword." He is the first apostle, one of the Twelve, to be martyred, and, following Stephen, the second to die for the faith. His execution was carried out in a Roman manner—by decapitation.[3] Because the Jews were delighted that he had slain James, Herod "proceeded to arrest Peter also." Now, the killing of James and the arrest of Peter took place at the time "of Unleavened Bread," that is, during Passover. Since Jerusalem was overflowing with pilgrims, Herod's strategy was to keep Peter in prison until the end of Passover whereupon he would "bring him out to the people."[4] By parading Peter before the immense crowd, Herod knew that the people's admiration for him would increase.[5] In the meantime, Herod assigned "four squads of soldiers to guard him." So, Peter not only was arrested and securely ensconced in prison, but he was also guarded by an overwhelming number of soldiers. What Herod did not realize was that he was making Peter's escape even more miraculous than it would have been if he had simply put him behind bars—how could anyone abscond from such a meticulous and careful incarceration? Luke concludes his introductory narrative by stating that "Peter was kept in prison." Nonetheless, "earnest prayer for him was made to God by the Church." The church's prayers to God were answered and in a manner not anticipated by the brethren who offered them.

3. See Acts 7:54–60. James and John were sons of Zebedee. John, according to tradition, is the only apostle who was not martyred. Luke designates James as the son of Zebedee to distinguish him from others with the same name. Another apostle is also called James who is the son of Alphaeus. To distinguish them, James the son of Zebedee is often referred to as James the Greater and James the son of Alphaeus is called James the Lesser. See Mt 10:1–4; Mk 3:16–19; Lk 6:14–16; and Acts 1:13. Matthew and Mark also speak of a "James" who was a "brother" of Jesus (see Mt 13:55 and Mk 6:3). Paul also speaks of a "James" who is termed the Lord's "brother" (see Gal 1:19). This "James" is more than likely the "James" who was appointed by the apostles as the first bishop of Jerusalem. Traditionally, all who are called "brothers" of Jesus are considered to be his cousins or relatives. The author of the Letter of James is neither James the son of Zebedee, nor James the son of Alphaeus, but it could be James, who is later considered the first bishop of Jerusalem.

4. As Pilate brought out the scourged and thorn-crowned Jesus at the time of Passover for all the condemning mob to see, so Herod now wants to bring Peter out on the day following Passover for all the condemnatory crowd to see. Peter, by imitation, is following his crucified Lord. The ancient tradition is that Peter was crucified upside down at Rome.

5. In referring to "the Jews" and "the people" Luke is primarily denoting the Jewish leaders and those who were actively taking part in the persecution of the Jewish Christians, and not the entire Jewish population.

## An Angel Comes to the Rescue (Acts 12:6-11)

> The very night when Herod was about to bring him out, Peter was sleeping between two soldiers, bound with two chains, and sentries before the door were guarding the prison; and behold, an angel of the Lord appeared, and a light shone in the cell; and he struck Peter on the side and woke him, saying, "Get up quickly."[6]

On the "very night" prior to when Herod was to display him before all the people, that is, the day after Passover, Peter was sleeping. As Luke had previously stressed the extreme precautions Herod employed to assure Peter's arrest and imprisonment, so now he accentuates the extreme conditions under which Peter is now held in prison. He is not only "sleeping between two soldiers," but he is also "bound with two chains," (not just one). Moreover, there are also "sentries before the doors" who are guarding the prison. Once again, the confinement is such that there is no possible way for Peter to escape barring a miracle, and that is exactly what took place. The prayers of the church were not only heard, but they were also answered.

Amid all the security, Luke wants the reader to "behold." What is to be beheld is "an angel of the Lord" that has now appeared in Peter's cell, and in that dark enclosure "a light shone." The light of God's divine presence was manifested by the appearance of an angel. The angel "struck Peter on the side and woke him." How a spiritual being can physically poke a bodily human being is not addressed, but since it happened, it can assuredly be done. He commanded Peter to get up quickly, and simultaneously "the chains fell off his hands." Next, the angel instructed Peter to get dressed and to put on his sandals. Peter did so. Furthermore, the angel told him to wrap his cloak around him and to follow him. The angel's attention in coaching Peter to get himself ready to leave manifests the historicity of the event. Peter had to later tell his brethren what took place, although at the time he thought it more to be a dream. As Luke states, "And he went out and followed him; he did not know that what was done by the angel was real, but thought he was seeing a vision." Nonetheless, "when they had passed the first and the second guard, they came to the iron gate leading into the city. It opened to them of its own accord, and they went out and passed through one street; and immediately the angel left him." Luke, having enumerated, in great detail, all the measures taken to ensure that Peter could not escape, here narrates, again in great detail, how they were all

6. Unless otherwise noted, all Scripture passages in this section are taken from Acts 12:6-11. Because this section contains many verses, I will provide the remainder of them in due course.

overcome. They first consecutively passed two guards, then they came to the gate that led into the city which opened without the aid of anyone, whereupon they went down a street. With Peter's escape now accomplished, the angel, having accomplished the task the Lord had sent him to do, immediately disappeared. Luke states that "Peter came to himself," that is, he was assured that what he had just experienced happened and was not some illusion. Moreover, Peter declared to himself, "Now I am sure that the Lord has sent his angel and rescued me from the hand of Herod and from all that the Jewish people were expecting." Luke began chapter twelve by stating that "Herod laid violent hands upon some who belonged to the Church." Peter has now been rescued by the Lord from those violent hands. Likewise, Herod intended to display Peter to all the people with the further intent of killing Peter just as he had executed James. However, the Lord has averted Peter from that fate as well. Again, in so doing, the prayers of the church were answered.[7]

## Peter Knocks and Knocks (Acts 12:12-17)

> When he realized this, he went to the house of Mary, the mother of John whose name was Mark, where many had gathered together and were praying. And when he knocked at the door of the gateway, a maid named Rhoda came to the gateway to answer. Recognizing Peter's voice, in her joy she did not open the gate but ran in and told that Peter was standing at the gate. They said to her, "You are mad." But she insisted that it was so. They said, "It is his angel!" But Peter continued knocking; and when they opened, they saw him and were amazed. But motioning to them with his hand to be silent, he described to them how the Lord had brought him out of prison. And he said, "Tell this to James and to the brethren." Then he departed and went to another place.[8]

When he realized that an angel of God had indeed freed him from prison, Peter went to the house of Mary, who is the mother of John who is also named Mark.[9] This would have been the house where, as Luke earlier mentioned, the church had gathered to pray earnestly on Peter's behalf.[10] Thus, Peter went

7. See Acts 12:1-5.

8. Unless otherwise noted, all Scripture passages in this section are taken from Acts 12:12-17.

9. Scholars note that many Jews at the time had two names, one Roman and one Jewish. Here "John" would have been the Jewish name and "Mark" the Roman name. Mark was a missionary companion of both Peter and Paul, and he was also a cousin of Barnabas (see Acts 12:25 and 13:5, 1 Pt 5:13, Col 4:10, Phlm 24, and 2 Tm 4:11). Traditionally he is known as the author of the second Gospel, which is thought to comprise the preaching of Peter. This is the only mention in the New Testament of Mary as the mother of John Mark.

10. See Acts 12:5.

there for he knew that they would be assembled in prayer. What transpires next strikes me as a scene from one of Shakespeare's comedies, and because it reads as a comedy, it could not have been made up—it is historically accurate.

So, when he arrived, Peter "knocked at the door of the gateway," that is, the outer gate whereby one can then enter the house beyond. Now, a maid by the name of Rhoda came to the door of the gateway to see who was there. Peter must have not only been knocking but also raising his voice to get the attention of those in the house, for Rhoda recognized his voice. However, she was so overly excited with joy upon hearing Peter's voice that she did not let him in. Rather, she ran off to tell the others that Peter was at the gate. One can imagine Peter's consternation when he hears Rhoda running off into the distance, her dash becoming ever less audible. Upon telling the others that Peter was at the gate, they not only did not believe her, but also told her she was "mad." Rhoda asserted that she was not out of her mind, but that Peter was truly at the gate. Such insistence provoked a rather curious and farfetched response from the others. It was not Peter who was knocking at the door, but "his angel." Once again, we have a proposal where an immaterial angel can perform a physical act—that of knocking. However, contained in this odd response is a theological truth. Although Peter is at the gateway, he does have a guardian angel who protects him, and thus one might conclude that every human person has an angel guardian.[11] In the meantime, while all this wasted and futile bantering was taking place, the frantic Peter continued his persistent knocking on the door in the hope that someone would, finally, let him in. When "they," and not the scatterbrained Rhoda, did open the door, they were amazed to see Peter. Their astonishment must have been vocally expressed, for Peter motions to them to keep silent—probably putting his finger to his lips. He was frightfully aware that he had just been freed from prison miraculously, and he did not want such commotion to alert any pursuers as to his whereabouts. Nonetheless, Peter described to all of them "how the Lord had brought him out of the prison."[12]

11. Jesus teaches that children should not be despised, for "their angels always behold the face of my Father who is in heaven" (Mt 18:10). Within Scripture angels are often depicted as guardians and guides (see Tb 12:15; Jb 33:23-34; Ps 34:7 and 91:11; and Heb 1:14).

12. I have portrayed the above scene as a comedy—Peter's persistent knocking, scatterbrained Rhoda being mad, the improbable suggestion that it was Peter's angel at the door, etc. However, for those who were participants in this event, it would have been a very serious matter—Peter's life was at stake. Nonetheless, as time passed, I suspect they, too, and to those they later told, saw the humor in the whole affair and reminisced, "Remember the time ..." how Peter was stuck outside knocking, while they bewilderedly and ineptly attempted to sort out what was going on—all to thunderous laughter.

Having told everyone how he was freed from prison, Peter then instructs them to tell what happened "to James and to the brethren." Who is this "James"? and why should he and "the brethren" know about what occurred? It cannot be James the brother of John since he was killed by Herod. Likewise, it is improbable that it is James the son of Alphaeus, for Peter would have specified this sonship. This leaves James who was the relative or cousin of Jesus, who, as noted earlier, was appointed by the apostles to be the first bishop of Jerusalem. Moreover, he would be the James who saw the risen Jesus.[13] Thus, as bishop of Jerusalem and as one to whom the risen Lord Jesus appeared, Peter thought it proper and right that James specifically, and the brethren in general, knew of his escape from prison. Luke concludes this present narrative by stating that Peter "departed and went to another place."[14]

## The Demise of the Soldiers (Acts 12:18–19)

> Now when day came, there was no small stir among the soldiers over what had become of Peter. And when Herod had sought for him and could not find him, he examined the sentries and ordered that they should be put to death. Then he went down from Judea to Caesarea, and remained there.[15]

Peter miraculously escaped at night, so as the sun rose the next day, the soldiers that were guarding him were in a dither—What happened to Peter? He was here last night but he is not here this morning. Herod frantically searched for him, but he was nowhere to be found. He questioned the guards to no avail, and so ordered them to be executed.[16] Once more Herod's violent hands drip with blood. After executing the sentries, Luke informs the reader that Herod went from Judea to Caesarea and resided there.

13. Paul states that the risen Jesus "appeared to Cephas, then to the Twelve. Then he appeared to more than five hundred brethren at one time, most of whom are still alive, though some have fallen asleep. Then he appeared to James, then to all of the apostles" (1 Cor 15:4–7). That Paul distinguishes James from apostles means that this James was not one of the two apostles called James.

14. To what "place" did Peter go? This question does not have a precise answer. Luke informs us that Peter was back in Jerusalem for the council (see Acts 15:7). Paul relates that he was in Antioch where he had to rebuke Peter concerning the necessity of circumcision (see Gal 2:11). The early Christian tradition holds that Peter went to Rome and was martyred there in the early to mid-60s.

15. Unless otherwise noted, all Scripture passages in this section are taken from Acts 12:18–19.

16. Scholars note that guards who let a condemned person escape are subject to the same sentence as the prisoner.

## The Death of Herod (Acts 12:20-23)

> Now Herod was angry with the people of Tyre and Sidon; and they came to him in a body and having persuaded Blastus, the king's chamberlain, they asked for peace, because their country depended on the king's country for food. On an appointed day Herod put on his royal robes, took his seat upon the throne, and made an oration to them. And the people shouted, "The voice of a god, and not of man!" Immediately an angel of the Lord struck him, because he did not give God the glory; and he was eaten by worms and died.[17]

Herod did not go to the port city of Caesarea for vacation.[18] He went because he was infuriated with those who lived in Tyre and Sidon, two Phoenician port cities north of Caesarea. The citizens, as a body, came there begging Blastus, the king's administrator, for peace. Their concern was that they were dependent upon food from Herod's kingdom. This endeavor was successful, for Herod, on a specified day, regaled himself in his royal attire and sat upon his throne. Upon that throne, Herod gave an address to the people of Tyre and Sidon. Luke does not provide the content of that speech, but it must have been extremely pleasing to the people, for they proclaimed Herod a god and not a mere human being. This unmitigated approval not only testifies that the people were delighted by what Herod said, but also that they wanted to ingratiate themselves to him—they were, after all, dependent upon him for their continued sustenance. However, because he arrogantly accepted the people's designation of him as a god, an angel of the Lord, simultaneous to this very declaration, struck him, for assuming such glory to himself and not giving glory to God—who alone who deserves such divine praise and glory. The effect of the angel striking Herod was that he was immediately consumed by worms and died.[19] Thus, Herod underwent a death that was more hideously gruesome than any he inflicted on others—such was the judgment of God.[20]

17. Unless otherwise noted, all Scripture passages in this section are taken from Acts 12:20-23.

18. Caesarea is the same city to which Peter went and proclaimed the gospel to the Gentile Cornelius and his household.

19. Once again, we see a spiritual angel physically striking a bodily human being.

20. In the second book of Maccabees, King Antiochus Epiphanes was said to have been punished by God for his threats against Jerusalem. His death was like that of Herod's. "And so the ungodly man's body swarmed with worms, and while he was still living in anguish and pain, his flesh rotted away, and because of his stench the whole army felt revulsion at his decay" (2 Mc 9:9).

## Luke's Conclusion (Acts 12:24–25)

Chapter twelve concludes with Luke providing an overarching comment, and the whereabouts of Barnabas and Saul.

> But the word of God grew and multiplied. And Barnabas and Saul returned from [to?] Jerusalem when they had fulfilled their mission, bringing with them John whose other name was Mark.[21]

By stating that "the word of God grew and multiplied," Luke cannot mean that the gospel itself grew and multiplied, for it is one complete whole from its apostolic origin. Rather, he is once more relating that additional people were coming to believe in Jesus, and so the ranks of the Christian brethren were ever increasing.

Luke also speaks of Barnabas and Saul. Here the text in Acts is conflicted. Some ancient texts read that they "returned from Jerusalem," while others read that they "returned to Jerusalem." Previously, in Acts, chapter eleven, Luke speaks of prophets from Jerusalem coming to Antioch. There Agabus foretold a coming famine, whereupon the disciples coordinated a relief collection which would be delivered to the elders in Jerusalem by the hands of Barnabas and Saul. If such is the case, then Barnabas and Saul have now *returned to* Antioch having completed their mission in Jerusalem.[22] Moreover, Luke also states that Barnabas and Saul brought with them "John whose other name is Mark." As the reader knows, John Mark's mother is Mary, and she owned a house in Jerusalem, the house to which Peter came after his escape from prison. This text does not state that John Mark was residing at his mother's home when Peter arrived. Thus, if he came back to Jerusalem with Barnabus and Saul, he must have been living in Antioch. The above may not be of any theological significance, but it is, nonetheless, critical to keep straight Luke's ongoing historical narrative, for the importance of John Mark's relationship with Barnabas and Saul will become evident in what will later ensue.

## Conclusion

Although the risen Jesus is not physically present in any of the events contained within chapter twelve of the Acts of the Apostles, yet he continues to be Jesus being Jesus—YHWH-Saves. He is the Lord who sent the angel to

21. Unless otherwise noted, all Scripture passages in this section are taken from Acts 12:24–25.

22. See Acts 11:27–30.

rescue Peter from prison. He is the one who answered the prayers of those gathered at Mary's house. He is the one who finds safe refuge for Peter within that house, while Herod was in search of him. Moreover, Jesus is, again, the one who sends the angel to strike Herod whereby he dies a gruesome death—the just punishment for all his unjust, brutal acts that proceed from his violent blood-stained hands. Lastly, the risen Jesus is responsible for the unceasing growth of his body the church, for he is the one who continues to pour out his Holy Spirit upon all those who come to believe in him as their Savior and Lord. As Jesus, he is the ever-acting savior, and he will be so until the end of time.

## *Chapter 13*

# PAUL'S FIRST MISSIONARY JOURNEY

### Paul and Barnabas Return to Antioch (Acts 13:1-3)

Chapter twelve of the Acts of the Apostles concluded with Paul and Barnabas returning from Jerusalem to Antioch. Luke introduces chapter thirteen by narrating what first transpired upon their return.

> Now in the Church at Antioch there were prophets and teachers, Barnabas, Symeon who was call Niger, Lucius of Cyrene, Manaen a member of the court of Herod the tetrarch, and Saul. While they were worshiping the Lord and fasting, the Holy Spirit said, "Set apart for me Barnabas and Saul for the work to which I have called them." Then after fasting and praying they laid hands on them and sent them off.[1]

Luke first informs the reader that among the ecclesial community at Antioch "there were prophets and teachers." In First Corinthians, Paul states that "God has appointed in the Church first apostles, second prophets, third teachers, then workers of miracles, then helpers, administrators, speakers in various tongues" (1 Cor 12:28). There appears to be a hierarchy of ministries. That of "apostles" obviously takes pride of place, for they are the first to profess the apostolic faith, the faith that defines the church. In second place are the prophets, for they speak under the inspiration of the Holy Spirit.[2] Teachers are third in rank, for they continue to instruct and foster the apostolic faith. Those who work miracles both testify to the truth of the faith by which

1. Unless otherwise noted, all Scripture passages in this section are taken from Acts 13:1-3.

2. Spirit-inspired prophets foretell the future as was seen in Agabus who prophesied the future famine (see Acts 11:27-28). He will also later foretell Paul's arrest by the Jewish leaders and their handing him over to the Gentiles (see Acts 21:10-11). Moreover, prophets also exhort and embolden the Christian community (see Acts 15:32 and 1 Cor 14:3).

nonbelievers come to conversion as well as strengthen the faith of those who already believe. Helpers and administrators ensure good order within the apostolic community. Lastly, speakers in various tongues "speak not to men but to God; for no one understands him, but he utters mysteries in the Spirit."[3] The risen Jesus established these Spirit-anointed offices "to equip saints for the work of ministry, for the building up the body of Christ" (Eph 4:11–12). Luke presently enumerates only "prophets and teachers," for Barnabas and Saul, by means of a prophecy, were to be appointed to the ministry of teaching, that is, they will be sent forth to evangelize.

Thus, Luke names those who are prophets and teachers—"Barnabas, Symeon who was called Niger, Lucious of Cyrene, Manaen a member of the court of Herod the tetrarch, and Saul." All of these prophets and teachers spoke Greek. Such linguistic ability would be necessary, for they would be sent to preach the gospel among the Greek-speaking Gentiles. The reader already knows that Barnabas was from Cyprus and Saul was from Tarsus, and so Luke only identifies the remainder. Symeon must be from Africa, for he is also called "Niger," which is the Latin word for "black." Lucius is from Cyrene, which is in north Africa (present day Libya).[4] Manaen is identified as a member of Herod the tetrarch's court. This Herod would have been the tetrarch of Galilee, and so the ruler at the time when John the Baptist began his ministry.[5] Lastly, Luke names Saul. Thus, all those named are bracketed by Barnabas and Saul, for this twosome will now be assigned a specific ministry.

Now, while the church at Antioch "were worshiping the Lord and fasting," the Holy Spirit spoke to them. Luke employs the Greek word *leitourgeō*. This word was originally employed to describe public or civic worship of a deity. Within the Old Testament, it was applied to the temple worship that was performed by Aaronic priests and their Levite deputies.[6] Thus, following the biblical usage, Luke here employs the Greek word to specify that the Antiochian church was engaged in a liturgy, and more than likely it was the Eucharistic liturgy. This Eucharistic assembly was also fasting. The purpose of this fasting is unspecified; though, given what follows, it can be surmised that the Antiochian community desired to know the Lord's will. What did the risen Jesus want them to do? Their fast would both purge their thoughts from extraneous

3. 1 Cor 14:3. Paul notes that there are those who possess the gift of interpreting what is spoken in tongues "so that the Church may be edified" (1 Cor 14:5).

4. Earlier Luke spoke of Greek-speaking Jews coming to Antioch from Cyprus and Cyrene (see Acts 11:20). Lucius of Cyrene would probably have been one of them.

5. See Lk 3:1–2.

6. See Ex 28:43, Nm 18:2, and Sir 45:15. See also Heb 10:11.

distractions and focus their attention on what the Spirit might reveal.[7] Their prayer and fasting bore fruit. The Holy Spirit spoke to them.

The Spirit declared, "Set apart for me Barnabas and Saul for the work to which I have called them." The Spirit tells the Antiochians to set apart Barnabas and Saul "for me." It is for the sake of the Holy Spirit that this twosome is to be requisitioned apart from the others so that they might commence the work he has assigned to them. The Antiochian Christians once again prayed and fasted that they might be empowered to fulfill the Spirit's command. Having strengthened them by their prayer and fasting, "they laid their hands on them and sent them off." This laying on of hands was a calling down of the Holy Spirit upon Barnabas and Saul so that he might commission them, and so empower them, to undertake the task that he had given them. With the Spirit's blessing and empowerment, they "sent them off," and off they went.

## Paul and Barnabas Evangelize Cyprus (Acts 13:4-12)

> So being sent out by the Holy Spirit, they went down to Seleucia and from there they sailed to Cyprus. When they arrived at Salamis, they proclaimed the word of God in the synagogues of the Jews. And they had John to assist them.[8]

As instructed by the Holy Spirit, Saul and Barnabas began their first rather lengthy missionary journey. It would have been from AD 46 to 49. They first went to Seleucia, a port city south of Antioch, and then embarked on a boat to the island of Cyprus.[9] Their journey would take them from Cyprus north through much of southern Galatia, which today is part of Turkey. When they came to Salamis in Cyprus, they first went to the Jewish synagogues and "proclaimed the word of God," that is, the good news of Jesus Christ. That Barnabas and Saul initially evangelized the Jews is theologically significant. By going to the synagogues, they would find a significant Jewish congregation. More importantly, Saul was convinced that it was only right and proper for

7. In Luke's Gospel, aged Anna "did not depart from the temple, worshiping with fasting and prayer night and day. And coming up to that very hour, she gave thanks to God and spoke of him [Jesus] to all who were looking for the redemption of Jerusalem" (Lk 2:36-38). Anna's prayer and fasting enabled her to recognize the Savior and to tell of his coming.

8. Unless otherwise noted, all Scripture passages in this section are taken from Acts 13:4-12. However, because of the length of this present narrative, it would be of no benefit to provide the entire text at the onset. Further texts will be incorporated in due course.

9. Cyprus, as noted previously, was the home of Barnabas. Barnabas may have thought that because he as a native of Cyprus the populous would more easily come to believe in Jesus upon hearing his and Saul's proclamation of the gospel.

the Jews, as God's chosen people to whom the Messiah had been promised, to hear first the good news that the promise had now been fulfilled.[10] Luke also informs the reader that John Mark, Barnabas's cousin, was with them as an assistant to aid them in their evangelistic efforts.[11]

Luke next tells what transpires as they journey through Cyprus.

> When they had gone through the whole island as far as Paphos, they came upon a certain magician, a Jewish false prophet, named Bar-Jesus. He was with the proconsul, Sergius Paulus, a man of intelligence, who summoned Barnabas and Saul and sought to hear the word of God. But Elymas the magician (for that is the meaning of his name) withstood them, seeking to turn away the proconsul from the faith.

In the course of their evangelistic travels, Barnabas and Saul happened upon a Jewish magician named Bar-Jesus, who was a false prophet.[12] Bar-Jesus was with the proconsul, Sergius Paulus, and Luke emphasizes that he is an intelligent man, and thus not one to be easily hoodwinked. Since Sergius was perceptive, he, as proconsul, summoned Barnabas and Saul to appear before him, for he desired to hear the good news of the gospel that they were proclaiming. However, Elymas, which means "magician" or, ironically, "corruptor," opposed Barnabas and Saul in the hope of deterring the proconsul from believing in Jesus as his Lord and Savior. However, Saul possessed a power that exceeded that of Elymas—the Holy Spirit.

But Saul, who is also called Paul, filled with the Holy Spirit, looked intently at him and said, "You son of the devil, you enemy of all righteousness, full of deceit and villainy, will you not stop making crooked the straight paths of the Lord?"

Saul, who now, for the first time, is also referred to as Paul, could hardly be more condemnatory of Elymas, the false prophet.[13] Filled with the Holy Spirit, Paul keenly fixes his eyes on him. He condemns him as a "son of the devil,"

10. Throughout Acts, whenever Paul arrives in a new location, he consistently goes to the Jewish synagogue first (see, for example, Acts 13:14; 14:1; 17:1, 10, and 17; 18:4 and 19).

11. See Col 4:10.

12. Ironically, the magician's name is "Bar-Jesus," that is "Son of Jesus," though he, as a false prophet, will attempt to dissuade the proconsul from believing in Jesus. Bar-Jesus is definitely not a son of Jesus. Elymas is the second magician to be denounced by an apostle. Earlier, Simon the magician was reprimanded by Peter for wanting to purchase from him the power Simon saw that Peter and John possessed when they laid hands upon the Samaritans and the Holy Spirit fell upon them (see Acts 8:9–24).

13. As noted previously, "Saul" is the Semitic equivalent of the Roman "Paul." In the remainder of Acts and in the rest of the New Testament he will be called Paul. This is likely because he is traveling within a Roman-Greek environment, beginning with Cyprus. However, in his recounting of his conversion, he speaks of God calling him "Saul" (see Acts 22:7 and 26:14).

and, therefore he is filled with deceit and wickedness, for Satan and his cohorts are the source of all lies and the consummate perpetrators of all evil. Being consumed by villainy, Elymas possesses no righteousness, that is, he is devoid of holiness before God. His entire goal is to make devious the upright paths that lead to faith in the Lord Jesus Christ.[14] Paul has defined Elymas as the human personification of Satan and all that he embodies. Because of the evil that Elymas attempts to enact, Paul declares what presently will come upon him.

> "And now, behold, the hand of the Lord is upon you, and you shall be blind and unable to see the sun for a time." Immediately mist and darkness fell upon him, and he went about seeking people to lead him by the hand. Then the proconsul believed, when he saw what had occurred, for he was astonished at the teaching of the Lord.

What Elymas was to behold was that the hand of the Lord Jesus, the one whom he wished to disparage, was upon him. Because the condemnatory hand of the Lord was upon him, Elymas would be blind, and he would not be able to see the sun for a period of time, for a misty darkness came over him. Interestingly, although the Lord punished Elymas, the penalty enacted is transitory and not permanent. He would again see the light of day at some indeterminate point. It appears that the punishment imposed would hopefully lead Elmas to repentance and to the light of faith in Jesus. Until he regained his sight, however, Elymas would be forced to find people to lead him by the hand.[15] One gets the impression that finding such leading hands was difficult. Who would want to befriend such a scurrilous person? In observing all that took place, the proconsul was led to believe in Jesus, for he was astonished not only by what had happened to Elymas, but also by Barnabas's and Paul's preaching of the Lord's good news. Thus, he who wanted to obstruct others from believing in Jesus, leads others, such as the proconsul, to Jesus.

## Paul and Barnabas in Antioch of Pisidia (Acts 13:13-41)

> Now Paul and his company set sail from Paphos and came to Perga in Pamphylia. And John left them and returned to Jerusalem; but they passed on to Perga and came to Antioch of Pisidia. And on the sabbath day they went into the synagogue and sat down. After the reading of the law and the prophets,

14. Unlike John the Baptist, who made straight the way for the Lord (see Mt 3:1-3, Mk 1:3-4, Lk 3:2-4, and Jn 1:19-23), Bar-Jesus is determined to make crooked the path by which others may be hindered in coming to faith in Jesus.

15. Recall that after his conversion experience, Paul was blinded and so was led by the hand as he continued his journey to Damascus (see Acts 9:8-9).

> the rulers of the synagogue sent to them, saying, "Brethren, if you have any word of exhortation for the people, say it."[16]

From Paphos, Paul, and those who accompanied him, traveled by boat to Perga in Pamphylia.[17] Luke does not apprise the reader as to who "those" were who journeyed with Paul, though they must have been Christian brethren from Cyprus. For certain Barnabas would have been one of them. Luke informs the reader that it was here that John Mark left Paul and Barnabas's company and returned home to Jerusalem.[18] Nonetheless, Paul and his companions continued to Perga and then to Antioch of Pisidia.[19]

When in Antioch of Pisidia, Paul, and those with him, went to the synagogue on the sabbath. Upon entering, they sat down among those who were present. After the customary reading from the Scriptures, passages from the law and the prophets, the rulers of the synagogue inquired of their visitors if they had any words of exhortation for those present. Paul accepts the invitation.

> So, Paul stood up, and motioning with his hand said: "Men of Israel, and you that fear God, listen. The God of this people Israel chose our fathers and made the people great during their stay in the land of Egypt, and with uplifted arm he led them out of it. And for forty years he bore with them in the wilderness. And when he had destroyed seven nations in the land of Canaan, he gave them their land as an inheritance, for about four hundred and fifty years. And after that he gave them judges until Samuel the prophet. Then they asked for a king; and God gave them Saul the son of Kish, a man of the tribe of Benjamin, for forty years. And when he removed him, he raised up David to be their king, of whom he testified and said, 'I have found in David, the son of Jesse, a man after my heart, who will do all my will.'"[20]

16. Unless otherwise noted, all Scripture passages in this section are taken from Acts 13:13-41. Since this section includes Paul's lengthy discourse to the Jewish community assembled in the synagogue, further texts will be incorporated in due course.

17. Perga was twelve miles inland from the coast of Pamphylia, which is in present day Turkey. It was a province governed by Rome.

18. John Mark must have been quite young at this point, he could have become homesick and so returned to his mother, Mary, who lived in Jerusalem (see Acts 12:12). As will be seen later, when Barnabas wants John Mark to join them on their second missionary journey, Paul refuses this request, for John Mark abandoned them in Pamphylia, and therefore, does not deserve to rejoin them now since he failed to work with them previously. This disagreement resulted in Barnabas leaving Paul and his returning with John Mark to Cyprus (see Acts 15:36-39). Paul will later be reconciled with Barnabas and Mark (see Col 4:10).

19. Antioch of Pisidia is to be distinguished from Antioch in Syria. In Antioch of Pisidia there resided a large Jewish community, and, being aware of this, Paul came in order to evangelize his Jewish brethren there.

20. Although Paul's discourse, as with earlier discourses, such as Stephen's and Peter's, cannot be taken as a verbatim account, it is historically accurate in content and execution.

Although present with his companions, of which Barnabas would have been one, it is Paul who now stood up to preach to those in the synagogue. From this point on in Luke's narrative, Paul is no longer under the care and supervision of Barnabas, and so subordinate to him. By standing up, Paul has become his own man, and in so doing, he assumes the status of the principal evangelist.[21] In the act of standing up, Paul motioned with his hand to all present, that is, with his hand he was signaling that what he is about to say is for all those present. They are to hear with attentive ears.[22] He then specified who they are—the men of Israel and those who fear God. That these men are Israelites is of the utmost theological importance, as Paul will immediately substantiate. Moreover, Paul acknowledged the presence of those who fear God, that is, those Gentiles, though uncircumcised, who obey the law and affirm the prophets. Thus, Paul not only recognized that both Jews and Gentiles were present in the synagogue, but also that what he was about to proclaim pertained to them all—the good news of Jesus Christ is for all to hear and for all to accept in faith.

Paul proceeded to provide a summary history of all the marvelous deeds that God had done for Israel and, therefore, what he had wonderfully done for those Israelites present.[23] First and foremost, God chose their fathers, and, while they resided in Egypt, he made them a great people, not only in number but also in holiness as well. As his chosen people, with the might and power of his hand, God freed them from their Egyptian slavery.[24] For forty years God guided them through the wilderness, as if he bore them on his own back.[25] Moreover, when the Israelites came to the promised land, God annihilated seven nations in Canaan.[26] In so doing, God gave to the Israelites the land

21. Paul's standing up to address those in the synagogue is reminiscent of Jesus standing up in the synagogue at Nazareth to read from the Scriptures on the sabbath and then commenting on them (see Lk 4:16–22).

22. Scholars note that, in the ancient world, to quiet the audience, the common gesture of a public speaker was to raise his right hand with his thumb and little finger bent together and with the other three extended. See Acts 19:33, 21:40, and 26:1.

23. Paul's discourse is in a format similar to Peter's Pentecost sermon and Stephen's discourse before his martyrdom, that is, a summary history of God's previous actions as a prelude to what God has now done through his incarnate Son, Jesus Christ (see Acts 1:14–36 and Acts 7).

24. God told Moses what he will do to Pharaoh with his "strong hand" (Ex 6:1, see also 6:6).

25. Some ancient texts read that God "cared for" them. In the book of Deuteronomy, Moses reminded the people that in the wilderness "God bore you, as a man bears his son" (Dt 1:31).

26. The book of Deuteronomy enumerates these seven nations—the Hittites, the Girgashites, the Amorites, the Canaanites, the Perizzites, the Hivites, and the Jebusites, all of whom were mightier than the Israelites (see Dt 7:1).

as their perpetual inheritance.[27] Following their entrance into the promised land, God gave the Israelites judges until the time of Samuel, who was the first prophet.[28] Upon the Israelites' request for a king, "God gave them Saul the son of Kish, a man of the tribe of Benjamin, for forty years."[29] However, because he disobeyed God, God took from him his kingship (1 Sm 13:8–14). Having dethroned Saul, God "raised up David to be the king" of the Israelites. God himself testified, "I have found in David, the son of Jesse, a man after my own heart, who will do all my will."[30] For Paul, David is not only the greatest of Israel's kings, but he is also the progenitor of Jesus, who was of David's royal line. "Of this man's posterity God has brought to Israel a Savior, Jesus, as he promised." Jesus is thus the savior who will not only redeem Israel, but he is also the king over God's everlasting kingdom.[31] In Jesus, the Father's Spirit-anointed Son, God's promise to David has now been fulfilled.

Moreover, for Paul, the ministry of John the Baptist confirms the coming of the Messiah. "Before his coming John had preached a baptism of repentance to all the people of Israel. And as John was finishing his course, he said, 'What do you suppose that I am? I am not he. No, but after me one is coming, the sandals of whose feet I am not worthy to untie.'" Paul here is paraphrasing what is recorded in the Gospels. All the Gospels speak of John preaching a baptism of repentance in preparation for the coming of the Messiah, and declaring that he is not worthy to untie his sandal strap.[32] However, only in John's Gospel does the Baptist deny that he is the Christ, though some may judge him to be.[33] By preaching a baptism of repentance and by denying that

27. Because the manuscript tradition is obscure, scholars are unsure whether the reference to "four hundred and fifty years" applies to the years when God gave the Israelites judges, or to the number of years that the Israelites lived in Egypt. From a theological perspective, neither option is important.

28. Samuel is considered to be the last judge and the first prophet (see 1 Sm 7:15–17 and Acts 3:24).

29. Interestingly, King Saul and the apostle Saul/Paul not only have the same name but are also of the same tribe of Benjamin. See Rom 11:1 and Phil 3:5.

30. Paul is referencing Ps 89:20, though he has not quoted it verbatim. In the psalm, God declares, "I have found David, my servant; / with my holy oil I have anointed him."

31. The angel Gabriel appeared to the virgin Mary, who was "betrothed to a man whose name was Joseph, of the house of David" (Lk 1:26–27). Not only was Jesus's foster father from the royal line of David, but also Gabriel declared to Mary that the son to be born of her "will be great, and will be called the Son of the Most High; and the Lord God will give to him the throne of his father David, and he will reign over the house of Jacob forever; and of his kingdom there will be no end" (Lk 1:32–33).

32. See Mt 3:11, Mk 1:7, Lk 3:15–16, and Jn 1:27.

33. See Jn 1:19. In John's Gospel, John the Baptist also denies that he is the prophet Elijah (see Jn 1:20).

he is the Christ, John accentuated that the Messiah was coming; and, for Paul, he has now arrived—Jesus is the foretold Messiah.[34]

Having summarized the prophetic history of the coming of the Messiah, Paul narrates what transpired in Jerusalem concerning Jesus, he whom God sent as Israel's savior.

> Brethren, sons of the family of Abraham, and those among you that fear God, to us has been sent the message of this salvation. For those who live in Jerusalem and their rulers, because they did not recognize him nor understand the utterances of the prophets which are read every sabbath, fulfilled these by condemning him. Though they could charge him with nothing deserving death, yet they asked Pilate to have him killed. And when they fulfilled all that was written of him, they took him down from the tree and laid him in a tomb.

At the onset of his discourse, Paul addressed those present in the synagogue as "Men of Israel." Here, he addresses them more affectionately as "brethren," for they are all "sons of the family of Abraham," including those "that fear God."[35] Abraham is the father of faith, for he believed what God had revealed to him. Therefore, as Paul declared in his Letter to the Galatians, "So you see that it is men of faith who are sons of Abraham." Because it is by faith that one becomes Abraham's son, even the Gentiles, by believing in Jesus, are his sons. Thus, "all men of faith," and not just the Jews, "are blessed with Abraham who had faith," thereby fulfilling what God had promised.[36] To Jews and Gentiles, all of Abraham's sons, God has "sent the message of his salvation."[37] Jesus, as YHWH-Saves, the Son of God incarnate, is God's sent message of salvation.[38]

34. Though Paul did state that the Baptist declared that he was not the Messiah, he did not say that John further declared that the Spirit-filled Messiah would baptize with the Holy Spirit. See Mt 3:11, Mk 1:9 and 3:16, and Jn 1:29-34. In John's Gospel, John the Baptist declares that the Messiah, upon whom the Spirit rested, is the Son of God. It is precisely because Jesus is the Spirit-filled Messiah that he is empowered to baptize those who believe in him with the Holy Spirit.

35. By noting those who fear God, Paul is again referring to those uncircumcised Gentiles who believe in Israel's God and who keep the law.

36. Gal 3:6-9. See also Rom 4:3. See also Gn 15:6, 12:3, and 18:18.

37. Paul is here alluding to Ps 107:20. "He sent forth his word and healed them, / and delivered them from destruction."

38. John's Gospel declares, "For God so loved the world that he gave his only Son, that whoever believes in him should not perish but have eternal life. For God sent the Son into the world, not to condemn the world, but that the world might be saved through him" (Jn 3:16-17). Moreover, he who does not believe in the Son, "is condemned already, because he has not believed in the name of the only-begotten Son of God" (Jn 3:18). Paul, presently, is attempting to foster faith in Jesus as the Father's Son, lest they be condemned in their disbelief.

However, Paul reminds his Jewish brethren that those who resided in Jerusalem and the rulers, "because they did not recognize him nor understand the utterances of the prophets which are read every sabbath, fulfilled these by condemning him."[39] The Jews of Jerusalem and their leaders did not comprehend that Jesus was God's "message of salvation," and the reason for this misapprehension was that they did not understand what the prophets foretold—even though, as was done on this very day, they were read every sabbath.[40] The supreme irony is that, in not comprehending the utterances of the prophets, they fulfilled what the prophets foretold.[41] What prophesies would Paul have thought that the Jewish rulers unwittingly had fulfilled? Given the context, it seems that he primarily had in mind Isaiah's four Suffering Servant Songs. Isaiah speaks of God's servant who will take upon himself the suffering due to the sins of the people, and so he appears to be abandoned and bereft of God. Yet, he will make intercession on their behalf and so save them from their iniquities and make them holy. Because of his righteous suffering, God will exalt him and lift him up. God will prosper him and prolong his days.[42] Nonetheless, even though they could not level a charge against Jesus that was deserving of death, they convinced Pilate that he should be killed.[43]

Next, Paul again speaks of the Jewish leaders fulfilling what was written concerning Jesus. These passages, as noted above, would have been those passages from the prophet Isaiah pertaining to God's suffering servant.[44] Having

39. Paul is making a generalization. Not all the Jews in Jerusalem condemned Jesus. The Jewish leaders were primarily responsible.

40. What Paul states here is in keeping with the prologue to John's Gospel. The Word "came to his own home, and his own people received him not" (Jn 1:10). Israel was the Word's "home," for God spoke his word to his chosen people, the Jews, and it was in the temple in Jerusalem that God dwelt—thus making it particularly his own home.

41. Paul tells the Corinthians that God had imparted a secret and hidden wisdom, "which God decreed before the ages for our glorification. None of the rulers of this age understood this; for if they had, they would not have crucified the Lord of glory" (1 Cor 2:7–8). The Jewish and Roman leaders (Pilate) were guilty of their crimes. Nonetheless, from all eternity, God predestined that all would be saved by means of Jesus's sacrificial death on the cross. Because the leaders of this world did not know God's plan, they unknowingly fulfilled it.

42. See Is 42:1–4, 49:1–6, 50:4–9, and 52:13–53:12.

43. See Mt 27:15–23, Mk 15:6–15, Lk 23:1–5 and 13–25, and Jn 19:4–6 and 15. In all these Scripture passages, Jesus was never condemned for any crime. It was the sheer insistent will of the Jewish leaders that forced Pilate to hand him over to be crucified.

44. In Luke's Gospel, the risen Jesus tells the men on the road to Emmaus, "O foolish men, and slow of heart to believe all that the prophets have spoken! Was it not necessary that the Christ should suffer these things and enter into his glory?" Thereupon, "beginning with Moses and all of the prophets, he interpreted to them in all the scriptures the things concerning him" (Lk 24:23–27). Similarly, when Jesus appeared to his disciples, he reminded them, "These are

crucified Jesus, "they took him down from the tree, and laid him in a tomb."[45] Although the Jewish leaders may have thought that they had done away with him, "God raised him from the dead; and for many days he appeared to those who came up with him from Galilee to Jerusalem, who are now his witnesses to the people." By raising Jesus gloriously from the tomb, God confirmed that his death on the cross did indeed free humankind from its sins, and, in so doing, that he merited his resurrection, thus obtaining eternal life for all who believed in him. The verification of Jesus's risen state is found in that he appeared to those who came up with him from Galilee to celebrate the Passover in Jerusalem. All these people are presently bearing testimony to Jesus's resurrection, to everyone.[46] In light of Jesus's resurrection, Paul declared to the members of the synagogue, "And we bring you the good news that what God promised to the fathers, this he fulfilled to us their children by raising Jesus."

---

my words which I spoke to you, while I was still with you, that everything written about me in the law of Moses and the prophets and the psalms must be fulfilled," that is, "that the Christ should suffer and on the third day rise from dead, and that repentance and forgiveness of sins should be preached in his name to all nations, beginning from Jerusalem" (Lk 24:44–46).

Peter, in his First Letter, also writes a comparable passage. "The prophets who prophesied of the grace that was to be yours searched and inquired about this salvation; they inquired what person or time was indicated by the Spirit of Christ within them when predicting the suffering of Christ and the subsequent glory" (1 Pt 1:10–11).

45. This is the third time in the Acts of the Apostles that the cross is referred to as a "tree." See also 5:30 and 10:39–40. In all these instances, including the above, the term "tree" is employed when stating that the Jews hung Jesus on a cross. The irony is that, while the Jewish leaders may have condemned Jesus and thought him to be accursed, God raised him glorious from the dead. That God exalted him is also declared in all three passages.

Peter, in his First Letter, declares, "He [Jesus] himself bore our sins in his body on the tree, that we might die to sin and live to righteousness. By his wounds you have been healed" (1 Pt 2:24). Belonging to the sinful race of Adam, Jesus put that sinful body to death on the tree so that all who believe in him might be made holy before God. By quoting Isaiah 53:3, Peter sees Jesus as God's suffering servant, who, by taking upon himself our transgressions, has healed humankind of sin and made it new through his death and resurrection.

Moreover, as was noted previously, the term "tree" alludes to what is declared in the book of Deuteronomy: "And if a man has committed a crime punishable by death and he is put to death, and you hang him on a tree, his body shall not remain all night upon the tree, but you shall bury him the same day, for a hanged man is accursed by God; you shall not defile your land which the Lord your God gives you for an inheritance" (Dt 21:22–23).

46. Just as the Gospels enumerated some of Jesus's risen appearances, so does Paul for the Corinthians. "For I delivered to you as of first importance what I also received, that Christ died for our sins in accordance with the Scriptures, that he was buried, that he was raised on the third day in accordance with the Scriptures, and that he appeared to Cephas, then to the Twelve. Then he appeared to more than five hundred brethren at one time, most of whom are still alive, though some have fallen asleep. Then he appeared to James, then to all the apostles. Last of all, as to one untimely born, he appeared to me" (1 Cor 15:3–8).

Paul and his companions declared the gospel to those assembled, that is, that what God had promised to their fathers, those venerable ancestors of the past, has now been accomplished by God raising Jesus from the dead. This accomplishment was for the benefit of the fathers' present children—the very men to whom Paul is now speaking. Paul's desire is that his Jewish brethren be cognizant of the privileged position in which they now stand.[47]

To bolster his argument pertaining to Jesus's resurrection, Paul quotes three passages from Scripture, two from the book of Psalms and one from the book of Isaiah. The first passage is from the second psalm: "You are my Son, / today I have begotten you" (Ps 2:7). Psalm 2 speaks of God's anointing the king. While the kings of the earth rise up and plot against God's anointed king, yet God mocks them, for he has himself set his king upon his holy throne. In so doing, God has proclaimed that the king is his son, the one on that "today" he has begotten. For the apostolic church, this psalm is messianic, for it is fulfilled not by an earthly king, who rules in an earthly manner, but it finds it completion in Jesus. In raising him from the dead, the Father, on that day, begot his Son as Savior and Lord; and he seated him on a heavenly throne, whereupon he rules over an everlasting kingdom.[48] As Psalm 2, verse 8, further declares, "Ask of me, and I will make the nations your heritage, / and the ends of the earth your possession."[49]

47. The author of the Letter to the Hebrews declared, "These all [Jews from ages past] died in faith, not having received what was promised, but having seen it and greeted it from afar, and having acknowledged that they were strangers and exiles on the earth. For people who speak thus make it clear that they are seeking a homeland. If they had been thinking of that land from which they had gone out, they would have had the opportunity to return. But as it is, they desire a better country, that is, a heavenly one" (Heb 11:13-16).

While their faithful ancestors were seeking, from afar, a heavenly homeland, the present Jews, to whom Paul is now speaking, do not realize that the longed-for homeland of their fathers is now in their midst. All they need to do to enter it is to believe in Jesus as their Lord and Savior. He is the heavenly homeland.

48. By professing that Jesus is the Father's only begotten Son, the Christian theological tradition also holds that this passage declares that the Father eternally begot his Son such that the Son is divine as the Father is divine. That it took place "today" speaks of "the one everlasting day" of the Trinity's eternity. Earlier in Acts, when Peter and John were released from prison and returned to their brethren, those gathered joyfully prayed. Their prayer included verses one and two from Psalm 2. "Sovereign Lord, who made the heaven and the earth and the sea and everything in them, who by the mouth of our father David, your servant, said by the Holy Spirit, 'Why did the Gentiles rage, / and the peoples imagine vain things? / The kings of the earth set themselves in array, / and the rulers were gathered together, / against the Lord and against his Anointed'" (Acts 4:24-25). In declaring that Jesus's divine sonship is far superior to the angels, the Letter to the Hebrew states, "For to what angel did God ever say, 'You are my Son, today I have begotten you'?" (Heb 1:5).

49. Ps 2:8. In 2 Samuel, God also declared to David, "When your days are fulfilled and

The second scriptural passage that Paul quotes is from Isaiah. Paul applies God's words in Isaiah to Jesus's resurrection, by which God freed him from death and corruption forever: "I will give you the holy and sure blessings of David."[50] Through Isaiah the prophet, God assures the Israelites that he will give to them all the blessings that he promised to David, that is, an everlasting and blessed kingdom. Such a kingdom is now found in the risen, incorruptible Jesus, a kingdom that far exceeds anything that could have been imagined, for it is a kingdom of eternal life. In this light, Paul declares, "Therefore he [God] says also in another psalm, 'You will not let your Holy One see corruption.' For David, after he had served the council of God in his own generation, fell asleep, and was laid with his fathers, and saw corruption; but he whom God raised up saw no corruption."[51] Even though he served as God's anointed king for his time and prayed that God would not let him see corruption, David did die and was buried with his forebears, and so he did see corruption. Conversely, Jesus, whom God raised from the dead, did not see corruption.[52] He is gloriously alive. Having offered the Jewish assembly all his Davidic, scripturally founded arguments concerning Jesus's resurrection, Paul now sets forth his dramatic conclusion.

> Let it be known to you therefore brethren, that through this man forgiveness of sins is proclaimed to you, and by him every one that believes is freed from everything from which you could not be freed by the law of Moses. Beware, therefore, lest there come upon you what is said in the prophets: "Behold,

---

you lie down with your fathers, I will raise up your offspring after you, who shall come forth from your body, and I will establish his kingdom. He shall build a house for my name, and I will establish his kingdom forever. I will be his father, and he shall be my son" (2 Sm 7:12–14). As noted earlier, Jesus, as the Father's incarnate Son, is the new and everlasting Davidic king. See Lk 1:32–33.

50. Is 55:3. Paul here is paraphrasing this passage. It reads, "I will make you an everlasting covenant, my steadfast, sure love for David."

51. Paul is quoting verse ten of Psalm 16. The Hebrew of this text reads, "For you do not give me up to Sheol, / or let your godly one see the Pit." However, Paul is quoting the Greek Septuagint, which translated the Hebrew verb *shahath*, meaning pit, as "to be corrupt." Similarly, Peter, in his Pentecost sermon, quotes Psalm 16 and applies it to the risen Jesus. "For you (God) will not abandon my soul to Hades, nor let your Holy One see corruption" (Acts 2:27).

52. At the onset of his Letter to the Romans, Paul, who is a servant of Jesus Christ, and called to be an apostle, declares that he preaches "the gospel concerning his [God's] Son, who was descended from David according to the flesh and designated Son of God in power according to the Spirit of holiness by his resurrection from the dead, Jesus Christ our Lord" (Rom 1:1–4). In becoming man, the Son of God was born of the ancestry of David and, therefore, of his kingly line. Moreover, by being raised gloriously from the dead through the power of the Holy Spirit, Jesus Christ became Lord. Thus, as the risen Lord, Jesus's Davidic kingdom will last forever.

you scoffers, and wonder, and perish; for I do a deed in your days, a deed you will never believe, if one declares it to you."

Paul wants his fellow Jews to know that only through the man Jesus does one obtain the forgiveness of sins, and that this is what he has been proclaiming to them. Moreover, in believing that this man Jesus is their Savior and Lord and putting their faith in him, they "will be freed from everything." Here the English translates the Greek verb *dikaiothevai* as "be freed." However, a better translation would render it as "be justified." Thus, those who believe in Jesus, are "justified from everything." Moreover, they are "justified" from all that cannot be "justified" (*dikaioutai*) by the law of Moses. Thus, for Paul, the law of Moses is incapable of justifying, that is, making one righteous or holy before God. One is only justified through faith in Jesus Christ, and thus is set free from all sin—everything.[53]

Since one is only justified by faith in Jesus Christ and not by the law, Paul tells his fellow Jews that they need to be aware of what might befall them, for if they are not, they will suffer the consequences foretold by the prophets. Although he speaks of prophets in the plural, Paul only quotes Habakkuk, "Look among the nations and see; wonder and be astounded. For I am doing a work in your day that you would not believe if told" (Hab 1:5). Significantly, Paul intensifies what Habakkuk declares. Paul refers to "scoffers." It is scoffers who must behold, and, by implication, "scoffers" could very well be the Jewish brethren to whom he is speaking. They are the ones who refuse to believe the divine deed God has done in their day in sending them Jesus as the promised Messiah, their Savior and Lord. If they do not believe in Jesus, what God forewarned the unbelieving Israelites though Habakkuk "could come upon" them—God's judgment and chastisement.

53. Paul, in his Letter to the Romans, accentuates that it is only by faith in Jesus that one is justified and not by the law. "For no human being will be justified in his [God's] sight by works of the law, since through the law comes knowledge of sin. But now the righteousness of God has been manifested apart from the law, although the law and the prophets bear witness to it, the righteousness of God through faith in Jesus Christ for all who believe" (Rom 3:20–21). Moreover, "Therefore, since we are justified by faith, we have peace with God through our Lord Jesus Christ" (Rom 5:1). Likewise, Paul tells the Ephesians, "For by grace you have been saved through faith; and this not your own doing, it is a gift from God—not because of works, lest any man should boast. For we are his workmanship, created in Christ Jesus for good works, which God has prepared beforehand, that we should walk in them" (Eph 2:8–10).

## The Aftermath of Paul's Discourse (Acts 13:42–52)

With the close of Paul's evangelistic address, Luke narrates what transpires over the course of the following weeks.

> As they went out, the people begged that these things might be told them again next sabbath. And when the meeting of the sabbath broke up, many Jews and devout converts to Judaism followed Paul and Barnabas, who spoke to them and urged them to continue in the grace of God.[54]

Even though some of the Jews refused to believe what Paul had spoken concerning Jesus, others, upon leaving the synagogue, ardently requested that what was proclaimed to them presently would again be declared to them on the following sabbath. Moreover, as the sabbath assembly was disbanding, "many Jews and devout converts to Judaism," that is, the God-fearing Gentiles, "followed Paul and Barnabas." Paul and Barnabas exhorted them to be steadfast in God's grace, that is, the Spirit-filled faith that God had given them. However, Paul's and Barnabas's success fomented dissension.

> The next sabbath almost the whole city gathered together to hear the word of God. But when the Jews saw the multitudes, they were filled with jealousy, and contradicted what was spoken by Paul, and reviled him. And Paul and Barnabas spoke out boldly, saying, "It was necessary that the word of God should be spoken first to you. Since you thrust it from you, and judge yourselves unworthy of eternal life, behold, we turn to the Gentiles. For so the Lord commanded us, saying, 'I have set you to be the light for the Gentiles, that you may bring salvation to the uttermost parts of the earth.'" And when the Gentiles heard this, they were glad and glorified the word of God; and as many were ordained to eternal life. And the word of the Lord spread throughout all the region.

On the following sabbath almost the entire city of Antioch amassed to hear Paul and Barnabas once more proclaim the good news of Jesus Christ as Savior and Lord. The Jewish leaders having reckoned themselves underserving of eternal life, Paul and Barnabas will turn to the Gentiles and proclaim to them God's saving word. When the Jewish leaders saw the multitudes converting, they became furious with jealousy.[55] This resentment provoked them to

54. Unless otherwise noted, all Scripture passages in this section are taken from Acts 13:42–52. However, because of the length of this present narrative, it would be of no benefit to provide the entire text at the onset. Further texts will be incorporated in due course.

55. The jealousy of the present Jewish leaders replicates the jealousy that motivated the Jews to hand Jesus over to Pilate. Matthew states that Pilate "knew that it was out of envy that

contradict Paul and to revile him.[56] Such disparagement did not hinder Paul and Barnabas, for they continued to speak out boldly. Not only did they continue to preach the gospel, but they also spoke directly to the Jewish leaders. They declared that it was only proper and right that the Jews were the first to hear the word of God. However, since they cast away the good news, and so judged themselves "unworthy of eternal life," they must now "behold" the consequences of their refusal. Having reckoned themselves undeserving of eternal life, Paul and Barnabas will now turn to the Gentiles and proclaim to them God's saving word. This turning to the Gentiles, for Paul, is, then, directly due to the decided rejection of the Jews. Of theological importance, although Paul thought he was obliged to preach to the Jews first, yet it was Jews, and not Paul, who judged themselves unworthy of the salvation given to them through Jesus Christ. Moreover, the reason for their rejection is that they were jealous that the Gentiles were so eager to accept it. If the Gentiles were going to accept Jesus as their Savior and Lord, the Jewish leaders, in turn, were going to do the opposite and refuse to believe in Jesus, and so reject him. But by refusing to believe in Jesus, they were not simply discarding Jesus, but they were rejecting eternal life itself.[57]

To confirm his decision that he will now turn to the Gentiles, Paul provides a Scripture passage that verifies his judgment—a command that the Lord had given to him and Barnabas. Paul quotes Isaiah 49:6. The entire verse reads, "It is too light a thing that you should be my servant to raise up the tribes of Jacob and to restore the preserved of Israel; / I will give you as a light to the nations, that my salvation may reach to the end of the earth."[58] As given, this verse is

---

they delivered him up" (Mt 27:18; see also Mk 15:10). The Jewish leaders in both instances could be the same.

56. Luke does not specify what the Jewish leaders said by way of contradiction. Moreover, similar to what was noted above, as the Jews "reviled" Paul, so they reviled the crucified Jesus. See Mt 27:39–44, Mk 15:29–32, Lk 23:35–37.

57. As noted previously, Paul more fully addressed this issue of the Gentiles' acceptance and the Jews' rejection in his Letter to the Romans. Interestingly and of theological importance, Paul states that the rejection of Jesus by the Jews made it possible for salvation to come to the Gentiles. Moreover, that salvation came to the Gentiles will make the Jews jealous, so that, out of jealousy, they will be provoked to believe. See Rom 11:11. Ironically, as jealousy first motivated the Jews to reject Jesus, so it will be jealousy that will persuade them, in the end, to believe in Jesus.

58. When Joseph and Mary presented Jesus in the temple forty days after his birth, Simeon, inspired by the Holy Spirit and taking him in his arms, declared, "Let now your servant depart in peace, according to your word, for my eyes have seen your salvation which you have prepared in the presence of all peoples, a light for revelation to the Gentiles, and for glory to your people Israel" (Lk 2:29–32). In seeing the child Jesus, Simeon beheld the light of salvation

addressed to the Suffering Servant. He would be the one who would raise up and restore Israel. However, since he was worthy of even more honor, God will make him a light to all peoples so that salvation will encompass the entire world. Paul now applies this passage to himself and Barnabas, and by implication, to all the apostles. They are now God's servants who proclaim the gospel not only to the Jews but also to the Gentiles, and thus to the utmost bounds of the earth. They would do so often amid great suffering and persecution.

Although the unbelieving Jews were disgruntled by Paul's words, the Gentiles, when they heard them, "were glad and glorified the word of God; and as many were ordained to eternal life believed." The Gentiles rejoiced that they were beneficiaries of Jesus's saving work, and so they applauded the word of God that Paul had proclaimed to them. In response to Paul's proclamation, those who were "ordained" and so predestined to eternal life came to believe in Jesus as their Savior and Lord.[59] Luke then, by way of summary,

---

which God had prepared for the Gentiles, and this light of Jesus would be Israel's glory. Israel's grandeur is intrinsically conjoined to the salvation of the Gentiles. They would be salvation's light to all nations. By refusing to believe in Jesus, the present Jews have rejected Israel's glory, that is, they refuse to be the saving light to the Gentiles. In other words, they have failed to fulfill Isaiah's prophecy. God declared that it was not sufficient for Israel merely to be restored as a nation, but that its true greatness would by manifested by becoming the saving light for all. Nonetheless, Paul and the apostolic church, which will be composed almost entirely of Gentiles, will assume the Lord's command and become the light of salvation to all nations.

59. What Luke states concerning what is eternally "ordained" is in keeping with what Jesus declared in his Gospel. The seventy whom Jesus had sent out to preach should not rejoice that they saw Satan fall like lightning from heaven, but rather they are to rejoice that "their names are written in heaven" (Lk 10:17–20).

Paul himself would declare that for those who love God everything would be carried out according to his divine purpose. "For those whom he foreknew he predestined to be conformed to the image of his Son, in order that he might be the firstborn among many brethren. And those whom he predestined he also called; and those whom he called he also justified; and those whom he justified he also glorified" (Rom 8:28–30). Paul also encourages his fellow workers in Philippi to labor together, for their "names are in the book of life" (Phil 4:2–3). The author of the Letter to the Hebrews reminds his readers that they have been "enrolled in heaven" (Heb 12:23). The book of Revelation has four references to the book of life. "He who conquers shall be clad thus in white garments, and I will not blot his name out of the book of life" (Rv 3:5). Moreover, many will worship the beast; "everyone whose name has not been written before the foundation of the world in the book of life" (Rv 13:8). Similarly, in a vision John saw books being opened, one which was "the book of life" (Rv 20:12). Lastly, no abomination or falsehood will be allowed into heaven, "but only those who are written in the Lamb's book of life" (Rv 21:27). See also Acts 2:39.

The Old Testament also contains passages concerning what God has irrevocably written. Because the people have sinned, Moses asks God to forgive them, and not to blot them out the book he has written. However, God responds, "Whoever has sinned against me, him will I blot out of my book" (Ex 32:32–33). In Psalm 69, God declares, "Let them be blotted out of the book

observed that "the word of the Lord spread throughout all the region." This proclamation of the gospel throughout the region of Antioch of Pisidia would have been undertaken not only by Paul and Barnabas, but also by those who were newly converted—in their joy at knowing Jesus Christ, they were compelled to spread the good news to others.

However, the unbelieving Jews did not sit idly by as faith in Jesus advanced. "But the Jews incited the devout women of high standing and the leading men of the city, and stirred up persecution against Paul and Barnabas, and drove them out of their district." Interestingly, it was not devout men that the Jews provoked but devout women. Earnest women are more likely to gain sympathy among the public for a cause they deem desirable and necessary—especially for a religious cause where the integrity of one's faith is in jeopardy. Moreover, the Jews not only incited the religiously devout women, but they also marshalled the secular arm of the city—the leading men who, unlike the devout women, possessed administrative authority.

This combination of religious and civic interests motivated the ensuing persecution of Paul and Barnabas, a hounding whereby they were not only driven out of the city but also out of the entire region. Luke tells us how Paul and Barnabas departed—they enacted Jesus's command. "But they shook the dust from their feet against them and went to Iconium." In Matthew's Gospel, Jesus instructs his disciples, saying: "If anyone will not receive you or listen to your words, shake off the dust from your feet as you leave that house or town. Truly, I say to you, it shall be more tolerable on the day of judgment for the land of Sodom and Gomorrah than for that town."[60] Luke's rendering is equally severe. "But whenever you enter a town and they do not receive you, go into the streets and say, 'Even the dust of your town that clings to our feet, we wipe off against you; nevertheless, know that the kingdom of God has been near.' I tell you, it shall be more tolerable on that day for Sodom than for that town."[61]

The theological significance of Jesus's command is found in a Palestinian Jewish tradition. When Jews returned to Palestine after visiting a Gentile

of the living; / let them not be enrolled among the righteous" (Ps 69:28). God tells Daniel that at the coming of Michael, the angel, there will be much trouble as never before seen, "but at that time your people shall be delivered, everyone whose name shall be found written in the book" (Dn 12:1).

60. Mt 10:14–15. In Mark's Gospel, Jesus declares, "Whatever place does not welcome you or listen to you, leave there and shake the dust off your feet in testimony against them" (Mk 6:13).

61. Lk 10:10–12. In Lk 9:5, Jesus states, "And wherever they do not receive you, when you leave that town shake off the dust from your feet as a testimony against them."

country, they shook the dust off their feet as a condemnatory sign against the uncleanness of the pagan Gentiles. Jesus reinterprets that derogatory sign. Those who refuse to believe in the gospel are the ones who are unclean, and, therefore, the dust from their homes and towns are unclean. Thus, one must shake the dust off one's feet as a sign of judgment against them. Only by believing in Jesus is one cleansed by the Holy Spirit whereby one is made holy. Moreover, on the day of judgment, the refusal to believe in Jesus will be more deserving of condemnation than the sins committed by Sodom and Gomorrah.

In this context, when Paul and Barnabas shook the dust off their feet as they left Antioch of Pisidia and set off for Iconium, they were both shaking off the dust of unbelief as well as a sign which bore testimony to the condemnation of the Jews who refused to believe in Jesus.[62] This condemnatory sign "against them" manifested that their sin of unbelief was greater than the sins committed by Sodom and Gomorrah. Despite the departure of Paul and Barnabas, Luke closes chapter twelve by stating that "the disciples were filled with joy and with the Holy Spirit." Their rejoicing in the Holy Spirit was doubtless due to their coming to know Jesus.

## Conclusion

Chapter thirteen of the Acts of the Apostles is lengthy, being composed of various parts. First, through the prophetic words of the Holy Spirit, Paul and Barnabas were commissioned to set out on their first missionary journey. Second, while proclaiming the Gospel in Cyprus, they met a false, Jewish prophet, Bar-Jesus. He was a deceitful son of the devil and so attempted to disrupt their preaching and to deter others from believing. By way of punishment, he became blind for a period of time. From Cyprus, Paul and Barnabas came to Antioch of Pisidia. Here, in his first extensive evangelistic discourse, Paul assumes his role as a consummate preacher of the gospel. At the local synagogue on the sabbath, Paul addresses the Jewish congregation. He begins by noting all that God had done for his chosen people beginning with Moses to the day when they entered the Promised Land. He reminds them that God had promised David that a king would arise from his posterity and possess an everlasting kingdom. Moreover, John the Baptist prepared his way. However, when the foretold Messiah appeared, the Jews in Jerusalem rejected him and had him put to death on a tree. Nonetheless, God raised him gloriously from the

62. Iconium was a city in southern Galatia (now part of Turkey) near the Taurus mountains about 80 miles southeast of Antioch of Pisidia.

dead. It is this proclamation that Paul is proclaiming to them—the risen Jesus is their Savior and Lord. Thus, for Paul, one is not justified and made holy by the Mosaic law, but through faith in Jesus Christ. Because the Jews have now rejected him, Paul is compelled to turn to the Gentiles, who joyfully received the saving word of God.

Within the entirety of this chapter, we perceive Jesus being Jesus in that he was constantly speaking and acting primarily through the Spirit-filled words and actions of Paul. What Jesus did while on earth, Paul continues to do presently, and what Jesus salvifically achieved through his death and resurrection, Paul now proclaims—the forgiveness of sins and the obtaining of life eternal. As the Jewish leaders rejected Jesus, so now they continue to do so to their own detriment and self-condemnation. However, the Gentiles now rejoice in that they were preordained to faith and so to glory everlasting.

Paul and Barnabas next set off to Iconium, and Luke's narrative will continue to tell of their travels, not only to Iconium, but also to Lystra and Derbe, and so we will now proceed to journey with them.

# *Chapter 14*

# PAUL'S FURTHER MISSIONARY ACTIVITY

Chapter thirteen of the Acts of the Apostles began with the prophetic words of the Holy Spirit, whereby Paul and Barnabas were commissioned to set out on their first missionary journey. This journey first took them to Cyprus and then to Antioch in Pisidia. In Antioch, Paul gave his first extensive evangelistic discourse, and he did so in the local Jewish synagogue on the sabbath. Although many of the Gentile converts to Judaism came to believe in Jesus as their Lord and Savior, the Jews refused to believe, and, in their disbelief, they persecuted Paul and Barnabas. Ultimately, Paul and Barnabas were driven out of town, and, having cast the dust from their feet, they went to Iconium.

In chapter fourteen, Luke narrates Paul's and Barnabas's evangelistic endeavors in Iconium, and their subsequent journeys to Lystra and Derbe, from whence they return to Antioch. Within this concluding portion of Paul's first missionary journey, Luke tells of the gospel's successes and challenges among the Jews and Gentiles, and of the ongoing lack of faith among many of the Jews. This refusal to believe gives rise to further Jewish persecutions of Paul and Barnabas as they continue to proclaim the gospel throughout the region.

## Paul and Barnabas in Iconium (Acts 14:1-7)

Now at Iconium they entered together into the Jewish synagogue, and so spoke that a great company believed, both of Jews and of Gentiles. But the unbelieving Jews stirred up the Gentiles and poisoned their minds against the brethren. So, they remained for a long time, speaking boldly of the Lord, who bore witness to the word of his grace, granting signs and wonders to be done by their hands. But the people of the city were divided; some sided with the

> Jews, and some with the apostles. When an attempt was made by both Gentiles and Jews, with their rulers, to molest them and stone them, they learned of it and fled to Lystra and Derbe, cities of Lycaonia, and to the surrounding country; and there they preached the gospel.[1]

As they did earlier when they reached Antioch of Pisidia, Paul and Barnabas, having arrived at Iconium, first went to the Jewish synagogue.[2] Their preaching of the gospel was so powerful and anointed that many came to believe in Jesus—both Jews and Gentiles. However, because of the many converts, those Jews who refused to believe in Jesus incited the unbelieving Gentiles against the new Jewish and Gentile Christians by poisoning their minds. Luke's use of the word "poison" implies that the unbelieving Jews not only spread adverse rumors against the converts, but that they also did so in a noxious or deadly manner, that is, in a manner that would make it impossible for the Gentiles to view the faithful in an impartial and tolerant way. Luke is here making the reader aware of a developing pattern, one that is becoming ever more evident and one that is ever intensifying. The Jews who refuse to believe in Jesus are not simply settled in their disbelief, but their hardened disbelief becomes the inflammatory spark that ignites their ensuing persecution of those who do believe.[3] Belief in Jesus as the messianic, Spirit-filled Savior and Lord must be eradicated.

Nonetheless, it appears, ironically, that the persecution was itself the incentive for Paul and Barnabas to remain in Iconium. "So, they remained for a long time, speaking boldly." Moreover, the reason for their long-term stay was that the Lord "bore witness to the word of his grace, granting signs and wonders to be done by their hands." Paul's and Barnabas's forthright proclamation of the gospel was accompanied by Jesus's own confirming witness, for "the word of his grace," that is, the salvific effect that he himself embodies, was manifested by the signs and wonders that he empowered them to perform by their own hands. Luke does not specify what the "signs and wonders" were, but since they were enacted by the laying on of Paul's and Barnabas's hands, one can presume that healings and exorcisms were performed. The accompanying working of such signs and wonders that accompanied the proclamation

1. Unless otherwise noted, all Scripture passages in this section are taken from Acts 14:1–7.

2. Iconium is approximately 80 miles southwest of Pisidian Antioch in present-day Turkey.

3. This pattern of disbelief followed by persecution begins with the arrest of Peter and John in Acts 4:1–22, followed by the later arrest of the apostles and imprisonment of Peter in Acts 5:17–39, the subsequent arrest and stoning of Stephen in Acts 6:8–15 and 7:54–60, followed by Paul's persecution in Acts 8:1–3. Later James is killed, and Peter is once again imprisoned in Acts 12:1–5. As will be seen, this same pattern continues throughout the whole of Acts.

of the gospel is in accord with Jesus's own earthly ministry. His miracle-signs bore witness to the truth of what he proclaimed—that he was the Father's Spirit-filled, incarnate Son, and so the long-expected messiah. What we perceive here is the risen Jesus being Jesus—YHWH-Saves. Jesus is acting through Paul and Barnabas. The signs and wonders enacted by Paul and Barnabas replicate and so continue Jesus's own saving ministry, a ministry wherein his signs and wonders testified that salvation is obtained through him alone. The crucified and risen Jesus is the source of forgiveness and the guarantee of eternal life. This proclamation is "the word of his grace" which Paul and Barnabas profess, and to which the signs and wonders bear testimony.

Nonetheless, in the midst of Paul's and Barnabas's proclamation of the gospel with its accompanying signs and wonders, "the people of the city were divided; some sided with the Jews, and some with the apostles." Although some people sided with the unbelieving Jews, those whose minds had been poisoned, others believed the word of grace that Paul and Barnabas proclaimed. Significantly, Luke refers to them as "apostles," thus giving them equal status with the original Twelve.[4] In so doing, Luke judges that what they profess is in accordance with the apostolic tradition that flows directly from what Jesus had revealed about himself as the Father's incarnate Son and the saving work that he has accomplished through his death and resurrection.

Although the populace of Iconium was divided concerning Paul and Barnabas, it appears that those who opposed them gained the upper hand. "When an attempt was made by both Gentiles and Jews, with their rulers, to molest them and to stone them, they learned of it and fled to Lystra and Derbe, cities in Lycaonia, and to the surrounding country." Along with the unbelieving Gentiles and Jews, Luke also mentions that "their rulers" sought to abuse and even to stone Paul and Barnabas. Since "rulers" refers to the Gentiles and the Jews alike, they must be the civil authorities that govern Iconium. Thus, the civil authorities must have been exasperated by all the turmoil that the presence of Paul and Barnabas caused within their city. However, having gotten wind of the plots against them, Paul and Barnabas quickly fled first to Lystra and then to Derbe.[5] Nonetheless, in these Lycaonian cities and throughout the countryside, Paul and Barnabas continued to proclaim the gospel, thus making the best of a bad situation. For Paul and Barnabas, nothing can stop

4. As was noted earlier, Paul is adamant that he is an apostle of equal standing with the Twelve. See 1 Cor 15:8–10.

5. In southern Galatia, Lystra was a Roman colony of former retired army veterans about 100 miles from Pisidia Antioch. Derbe was a little further south and east of Lystra.

the advancement of the gospel, for it is founded upon him who is unstoppable—the risen Jesus Christ. Jesus will always be Jesus—YHWH-Saves.

## Paul and Barnabas in Lystra and Derbe (Acts 14:8-23)

Luke continues his narrative by stating,

> Now at Lystra there was a man sitting, who could not use his feet; he was a cripple from birth, who had never walked. He listened to Paul speaking; and Paul, looking intently at him and seeing that he had faith to be made well, said in a loud voice, "Stand upright on your feet." And he sprang up and walked. And when the crowds saw what Paul had done, they lifted up their voices, saying in Lycaonian, "The gods have come down to us in the likeness of men!"[6]

This healing by Paul parallels Peter's earlier healing of the lame man at the temple's Beautiful Gate. In both instances the healers, earlier Peter and now Paul, gaze or look attentively at the one to be healed; they proceed to heal the man; whereupon the healed man springs to his feet and walks to the amazement of the onlooking crowds.[7] For Luke, this intentional parallelism testifies, as also noted above, that Paul has apostolic status equal to that of Peter.

Interestingly, Luke accentuates the man's immobility. He "could not use his feet." He "was a cripple from birth." He "never walked." Such emphasis, in turn, heightens the significance of the miracle both as to Paul's ability to heal the man and to the man's unwavering faith that he could be healed. Here, again, one perceives another parallel. In the Synoptic Gospels, Jesus frequently acknowledges the faith of those whom he heals. For example, the woman with the hemorrhage believed that if she could only touch the fringe of Jesus's garment she would be healed. She did touch it, and Jesus immediately became aware that healing power came forth from him. When the healed woman acknowledged that she was the one who touched him, Jesus replied, "Daughter, your faith has made you well; go in peace."[8] Here in Acts, the cripple listens to Paul proclaiming the Gospel, and he does so in faith. Paul, in intently looking

6. Unless otherwise noted, all Scripture passages in this section are taken from Acts 14:8-23. Because this section contains many verses, I will provide the remainder of them in due course.

7. See Acts 3:1-10.

8. Lk 8:43-48. See also Mt 9:18-26 and Mk 5:21-34. A similar case is found in the blind man who kept crying out to Jesus to have mercy on him. When Jesus asked what he wanted, he replied that he wanted to see. In turn Jesus declared, "receive your sight; your faith has made you well" (Lk 18:35-43). See also Mt 20:29-34 and Mk 10:46-52.

at him, and in seeing that he possesses the faith wherein he can be healed, loudly declared, "Stand upright on your feet." At Paul's command, the sitting cripple "sprang up and walked." The immediacy and vibrancy with which the man leapt up and walked testifies to the man's unwavering faith—even though he had never "used his feet," was "a cripple from birth," and "never walked."

Now the response of the crowd to the healing of the cripple was not what Paul and Barnabas would have expected. They presumed that the crowd would be amazed, and thus they would have hoped that the people would come to faith in Jesus, for it was by his power that the miracle was performed. Instead, as Paul had commanded the cripple, "in a loud voice," to stand up, so the crowd now "lifted up their voices, saying in Lycaonian, 'The gods have come down to us in the likeness of men!'" Moreover, Luke informs the reader that they called Barnabas Zeus, and Paul, "because he was the chief speaker, they called Hermes." Within the Greek pagan religion, Zeus was the foremost of the Olympian gods, and was recognized as the father of all the other gods and of humankind. Hermes was a son of Zeus and was the herald or messenger of the gods. Not surprisingly then, Paul was designated Hermes, given that he, as is evident throughout Acts, is the chief herald of the gospel. Barnabas, in contrast, plays the role of his willing silent and supportive sidekick. Nonetheless, Barnabas, remarkably, is called Zeus, and thus the preeminent god, who would then be the father of Hermes, who is Paul. Such a designation would also be appropriate since Barnabas (Zeus) would have been older than Paul (Hermes), and thus thought to be Paul's father.

Not only was the crowd convinced that the gods had come down to them, but also "the priest of Zeus, whose temple was in the front of the city, brought oxen and garlands to the gates and wanted to offer sacrifice with the people." The scene must have been bursting with electric, frenzied, religious zealotry.[9] Although the temple to Zeus would have been prominent just outside the city gates, it is not every day that Zeus descends from the celestial realm and personally appears among his devotees. The only fitting response to such an unexpected divine appearance would be that of sacrificing garland-clad oxen in his honor. Not only was the crowd consumed with religious fervor, but Paul and Barnabas were also overwhelmed by what was taking place, though in a manner not to their liking.

9. I use the adjective "electric" with a bit of humor. Zeus, according to Greek mythology, was given a lightning bolt by his father Cronus. The lightning bolt was a symbol of his power and authority over the other gods. If the gods did not obey him, they would be zapped. Here the crowd is electrified in the belief that Zeus stands in their midst.

> But when the apostles Barnabas and Paul heard of it, they tore their garments and rushed out among the multitude crying, "Men, why are you doing this? We also are men, of like nature with you, and bring you good news, that you should turn from these vain things to the living God who made heaven and earth and the sea and all that is in them. In past generations he allowed all the nations to walk in their own ways; yet he did not leave himself without witness, for he did good and gave you from heaven rains and fruitful seasons, satisfying your hearts with food and gladness." With these words they scarcely restrained the people from sacrificing to them.

That Barnabas and Paul were distressed is first seen in the tearing of their garments, for within the biblical tradition to rend one's garments manifested one's displeasure, disapproval, and anger at what had taken place.[10] Moreover, the apostles rushed into the midst of the frenzied crowd, crying out in a loud voice so that they might be heard above the din.[11]

They initially cried out a rhetorical question, "Men, why are you doing this?" Barnabas and Paul already knew why they were "doing this." They were doing it because they thought that Barnabas and Paul were gods. However, that rhetorical question also contains the implication that what they were doing was nonsense. Why their actions were absurd, Barnabas and Paul immediately declare. "We also are men, of the same nature with you." They do not possess some divine nature that has now appeared in human form. Rather, they are simply men like themselves. However, and more importantly, they do have a divine message—"the good news, that you should turn from these vain things to a living God who made the heaven and the earth and the sea and all that is in them." The futile things that the Lycaonians must abandon are their beliefs in nonexistent gods, such as Zeus and Hermes, and instead believe in "a living God." That this God is living is manifested in the fact that he made heaven and earth and the sea, that is, the entire cosmos. Likewise, as the living God, he created all that inhabits the heaven and the earth and the sea—all existing and living things. Moreover, "in past generations he [God] allowed all the nations to walk in their own ways; yet he did not leave himself without witnesses, for he did good and gave you from heaven rains and fruitful seasons, satisfying your hearts with food and gladness." Throughout the

10. See for example, Nm 14:6, Jdt 14:16, Mt 26:65, and Mk 14:6.

11. Interestingly, in this passage Luke names Barnabas prior to naming Paul. There is probably no significance to this unusual reversal of names. Note also, that Luke, once again, refers to them as "apostles." Likewise, Luke's account gives the impression that both Barnabas and Paul addressed the crowd, since both cried out. Historically, this could very likely be the case, since both were upset at what was taking place. However, for the sake of literary clarity, Luke summarizes what they said as if only one were speaking.

centuries, God gave all peoples and nations the freedom to live according to their own laws and customs. Yet, there were "witnesses" to God's existence. In his goodness, he provided fruitful rain which brought forth food that gladdened their hearts. It is to this living and lifegiving God that they must turn in faith. In the above, Barnabas and Paul are alluding to the first creation story in the book of Genesis wherein, over a six-day period, all that God has created is enumerated. They would also have been echoing Exodus 20:11. God, in giving the Ten Commandments, reminds Moses that "the Lord made heaven and earth, the sea, and all that is in them." Similarly, Psalm 146:6 also exclaims that God "made heaven and earth, the sea, and all that is in them."

The question, nonetheless, arises, why did Barnabas and Paul not speak of Jesus Christ as Lord and Savior? Why did he, instead, focus on God as the creator of all and of his continuous providential care of humankind? Since this was their first encounter with a totally Gentile audience, Barnabas and Paul were attempting to meet them at their philosophical, theological, and cultural level. Thus, unlike the nonexistent gods, such as Zeus and Hermes, Barnabas and Paul proclaimed the living and true God who is the creator of all and the benevolent guardian of all of humankind. It is difficult to know how successful they were with this evangelistic approach since Luke concludes by stating, "With these words they scarcely restrained the people from offering sacrifice to them." Luke, here, seems to be more concerned about the issue of the Lycaonians' false belief that Barnabas and Paul were gods, than in their coming to believe in the one true and living creator God. However, since Luke did not note that many came to believe, which he normally does when such evangelistic efforts are successful, one might assume that few, if any, Lycaonians came to believe.[12]

12. In his Letter to the Romans, Paul condemns past generations for their ungodliness and for suppressing the truth.

> For what can be known about God is plain to them, because God has shown it to them. Ever since the creation of the world his invisible nature, namely his eternal power and deity, has been clearly perceived in the things that have been made. So, they are without excuse; for although they knew God, they did not honor him as God or give thanks to him, but they became futile in their thinking and their senseless minds were darkened. Claiming to be wise, they became fools, and exchanged the glory of the immortal god for images resembling mortal man or birds or animals or reptiles. (Rom 1:19-23)

The Lycaonians are perfect examples. Instead of worshiping the living God who is manifested in his visible works, they worshiped images resembling men, such as Zeus and Hermes.

In light of the question as to how successful Barnabas and Paul were in their evangelistic efforts, it is interesting that later in Acts, at the Areopagus in Athens, Paul employs the same

Having narrated Barnabas's and Paul's evangelistic efforts among Lycaonians at Lystra, Luke immediately informs the reader of the ensuing persecution. "But Jews came there from Antioch and Iconium and having persuaded the people, they stoned Paul and dragged him out of the city, supposing that he was dead." The fact that the unbelieving Jews from Antioch and Iconium so easily turned the minds of the Lycaonians against Barnabas and Paul testifies to the utter lack of success in evangelizing them. Their dislike and loathing for them was so great that they stoned Paul and dragged his supposedly dead body out of the city.[13] The irony here is that because of the healing of the cripple, the Lycaonians initially believed that Barnabas and Paul were gods who had come to them in the likeness of men, but in the end they attempted to kill Paul—such was the fickleness of the crowd.

"However, when the disciples gathered around him, he rose up and entered the city; and on the next day he went with Barnabas to Derbe." The "gathering" of the disciples around Paul had to be more than simply his disciples

---

evangelistic template as he did at Lystra. Noting the altar "to the unknown god," Paul proclaims to those present that he knows this unknown god.

> The God who made the world and everything in it, being Lord of heaven and earth, does not live in shrines made by man, nor is he served by human hands, as though he needed anything, since he himself gives to all men life and breath and everything. And he made from one every nation of men to live on all the face of the earth, having determined allotted periods and the boundaries of their habitation, that they should seek God, in the hope that they might feel after him and find him. Yet he is not far from each one of us, for "In him we live and move and have our being"; as even some of your poets have said, "For we are indeed his offspring." Being then God's offspring, we ought not to think that the Deity is like gold, or silver, or stone, a representation by the art and imagination of man. (Acts 17:24–29)

Here, as with the Lycaonians, it is unclear what the response of the men of Athens was. However, when Paul speaks of the risen Jesus, they mock him and refuse to believe—"except for Dionysius the Areopagite and a woman named Damaris and others with them" (Acts 17:34). Because of his lack of success, when Paul proceeded to Corinth, he changed his entire evangelistic approach. As he reminded the Corinthians, "When I came to you, brethren, I did not come to you proclaiming the testimony of God in lofty words or wisdom. For I decided to know nothing among you except Jesus Christ and him crucified" (1 Cor 2:1–2). Paul learned that philosophical arguments or human wisdom do not bring about conversion, whether in Lystra or Corinth, but rather the proclamation of the crucified and risen Lord Jesus Christ.

13. Unlike the Jewish practice where the blasphemous person was taken outside of the city and stoned, such as found in the case of Stephen, the pagan Lycaonians stoned Paul within the city walls and then dumped his body outside the city. For the Jews, the stoning took place beyond the city lest the blasphemy contaminate the city itself.

In his First Letter to the Corinthians, Paul enumerates all the dangers that he has endured in the course of preaching the gospel. He states, "Once I was stoned" (1 Cor 11:25). Obviously, he is recalling what happened to him in Lystra.

mourning his supposed death. Rather, it must have been a prayer-filled gathering wherein, they were interceding on Paul's behalf—that Jesus would heal him and raise him back to life. Paul was immediately healed for he not only "rose up," presumably without a scratch or bruise, and even "entered the city." That Paul went back into the city is rather surprising, since that would be the last place one would think that he would want to go. By returning to the city, Paul was making a statement. "I am alive." Luke does not inform the reader as to the reaction to Paul's reappearance, but it could have been one of fear—the divine Hermes has come back to life, intent on seeking revenge! Nonetheless, Luke tells the reader that on the following day Paul went with Barnabas to Derbe. It is difficult to know, but the text gives the impression that Barnabas had decided that it was best to move on to Derbe for Paul's safety, and so Paul consented and went with him. If such was the case, once again, one finds Barnabas being the brotherly guardian of Paul.

Luke's continues his narrative:

> When they preached the gospel to that city and had made many disciples, they returned to Lystra and to Iconium and to Antioch, strengthening the souls of the disciples, exhorting them to continue in the faith, and saying that through many tribulations we must enter the kingdom of God.

Unlike in Lystra, Barnabas's and Paul's evangelistic endeavors in Derbe were very successful, for many came to believe in Jesus and so became his disciples.[14] From Derbe, they retraced their steps through Lystra and Iconium back to Antioch of Pisidia. In the course of their return, they encouraged the disciples to remain steadfast in the faith, noting that they would undergo many trials and persecutions, for only in enduring these tribulations does one enter the kingdom of God and fully abide in the risen Lord Jesus forever.[15]

Rather unexpectedly, Luke next states that "when they appointed elders for them in every church, with prayer and fasting, they committed them to the Lord in whom they believed." This is the first instance within the Acts of the Apostles where the appointment of leaders within local ecclesial assemblies is mentioned. As rendered here, having prayed and fasted, Paul and Barnabas, committing them to the Lord Jesus in whom they believed, appointed elders in every church. The Greek for "appointed" (*xeiprotonesantes*) is literally translated as "to stretch forth hands," and the Greek for "elders" is *presbuterous* from which the English word "presbyter" is derived. Thus, what is

14. Derbe is approximately 60 miles southeast of Lystra in the province of Galatia.

15. Luke speaks of "we" in relation to entering the kingdom of heaven. This "we" is a remnant of Paul's actual words of exhortation.

narrated here is the liturgical rite of priestly ordination. With the laying on of their hands, Paul and Barnabas ensured that the apostolic priesthood would be established among the local churches, and they assured that the apostolic succession of the priesthood would continue through the subsequent history of the church.[16]

## The Return to Antioch in Syria (Acts 14:24–28)

At the close of chapter fourteen of Acts, Luke speaks of Paul and Barnabas returning to Antioch in Syria and of the marvelous works that God had done during their missionary journey.

> Then they passed through Pisidia, and came to Pamphylia. And when they had spoken the word in Perga, they went down to Attalia; and from there they sailed to Antioch, where they had been commended to the grace of God for the work which they had fulfilled. And when they arrived, they gathered the Church together and declared all that God had done with them, and how he had opened a door of faith to the Gentiles. And they remained no little time with the disciples.[17]

16. Within the Catholic theological tradition, the apostles, including Paul and Barnabas, are recognized as bishops (*episkopoi*), and thus sharers in the fullness of Jesus's own priesthood. Peter, in his first letter, refers to Jesus as "shepherd and bishop" (*episkapon*). The apostles, by sharing in Jesus's episcopal priesthood were, in turn, empowered, through the laying on of hands, to ordain other bishops and priests. Bishops and priests, through their sacramental ordination, later were seen as acting *in persona Christi* (in the person of Christ), and so in a manner that differed in kind from the baptismal priesthood of the laity.

Later in Acts, Paul, at Miletus, called together "the elders" (*presbuterous*). He exhorted them to "take heed of yourselves and to all the flock, in which the Holy Spirit has made you guardians [*episkopous*—bishops], to feed the church of the Lord which he obtained by his blood" (Acts 20:17 and 28). Here we perceive that to be a priest is the pastoral equivalent of being a bishop—a shepherd and guardian.

In his Letter to the Philippians, Paul and Timothy address their letter to "the bishops [*episkopois*] and deacons" (Phil 1:1). Again, it appears that to be a bishop is comparable to being a priest. In his First Letter to Timothy, Paul states that "a bishop [*episkopon*] must be above reproach" (1 Tm 3:2). Here, the bishop seems to possess a hierarchical authority above that of a priest. However, later Paul reminds Timothy not to neglect the gift that was given him when "the elders" (*prsebuteriou*) laid hands upon him (1 Tm 4:4). Thus, the priests who laid hands on Timothy could be bishops. In his Letter to Titus, Paul reminds Titus that he is to appoint "elders" (*presbuterous*) in each of the cities in Crete (Ti 1:5). In all the above there is a fluidity of terminology. There may be an ecclesial difference between a presbyter or priest and an episcopal bishop, but such terms could also be interchanged. Only later would the sacramental difference between a priest and a bishop become clearly defined, but such a history cannot be narrated here.

17. Unless otherwise noted, all Scripture passages in this section are taken from Acts 14:24–28.

So, from Derbe, Paul and Barnabas, making their way south, passed through the provinces of Pisidia and Pamphylia. At the coastal city of Perga, they preached the gospel, before they proceeded to Attalia, which was also a coastal city. From there, they sailed to Antioch in Syria. Luke, now, reminds the reader that it was here that Paul and Barnabas were first commissioned by the prophetic word of the Holy Spirit to undertake their missionary journey, a journey that they have now successfully completed.[18] Upon their arrival, Paul and Barnabas "gathered the Church" and told of all the wondrous works God had done through them. Significantly, Luke specifies that God "opened the door of faith to the Gentiles," something that may have surprised their hearers.[19] The crucified and risen Lord Jesus is not only the Savior of the Jews but also of the Gentiles. Chapter fourteen concludes with Luke saying that Paul and Barnabas "remained no little time with the disciples." It would appear that they needed to rest after their lengthy evangelistic journey, and that there was no better way of doing so than to abide with the faithful brethren.

## Conclusion

Luke, in chapter fourteen, continues to narrate Paul's first missionary journey, a journey which began in chapter thirteen when, through the prophetic inspiration of the Holy Spirit, he and Barnabas were set apart to do the work that the Spirit had given them to do. So, Paul and Barnabas set off from Antioch in Syria. They first preached the gospel in Cyprus and proceeded to Antioch in Pisidia. There they initially proclaimed the word of God in the synagogue on the sabbath whereupon many Jews came to believe in Jesus. However, the unbelieving Jews spoke out against Paul and Barnabas, so they proceeded to evangelize the Gentiles. In the end, they were forced out of the district. At this point, chapter fourteen begins with Paul and Barnabas arriving at Iconium.

Again, they first preached in the Jewish synagogue where many Jews and Gentiles came to believe. The people of the city became divided—some sided with the unbelieving Jews and some with the apostles. It was noted that Luke,

18. See Acts 13:1–3.

19. Paul speaks of God opening "doors" on other occasions. He informs the Corinthians that, while he will visit them, he will, for the present, stay in Ephesus, "for a wide door for effective work has opened to me" (1 Cor 16:9). In his Second Letter to the Corinthians, Paul tells them that in Troas "a door was opened to me in the Lord; but my mind could not be at rest because I did not find my brother Titus there. So, I took leave of them and went to Macedonia" (2 Cor 2:12–13). Paul asks the Colossians to pray for him "that God may open to us a door for the word, to declare the mystery of Christ, on account of which I am in prison, that I may make it clear, as I ought to speak" (Col 4:3–4).

in referring to Paul and Barnabas as apostles, implicitly gave them the same authority as the original Twelve. Some of the Jews and Gentiles in the city attempted to stone Paul and Barnabas, but, becoming aware of this, they fled to Lystra and Derbe.

Largely, chapter fourteen tells of what transpires in Lystra. Paul heals a man crippled from birth. Upon witnessing this miracle, the pagan Lycaonians concluded that the gods had come down to them in the form of men. They called Barnabas, Zeus, and Paul, Hermes, since he was the chief speaker. Moreover, the priest of the temple of Zeus brought oxen to sacrifice to Barnabas/Zeus and Paul/Hermes. However, in consternation, Paul and Barnabas cried out that they were not gods and exhorted the crowd to believe in the living God who created heaven and earth and the sea, and all that is contained within them. Unlike the nonexistent and dead gods Zeus and Hermes, the living God providentially watches over all, providing food to satisfy human hearts with gladness.

What is apparent throughout the whole of Luke's narrative is that Jesus is being Jesus. Jesus may not have been visible, yet through the preaching of Paul and Barnabas and through the signs and wonders that they work, the risen Jesus is ever present, pouring out his Spirit upon those who come to believe in him as their Lord and Savior—Jews and Gentiles alike. As gloriously risen, Jesus is enacting his name—YHWH-Saves. Jesus, too, is the living and saving God. Precisely because Jesus is acting in communion with Paul and Barnabas, the unbelieving Jews continually stir up opposition against them. The preaching of the gospel cannot be tolerated lest more and more Jews and Gentiles come to believe in him. So much is this to be feared that in Lystra the unbelieving Jews stoned Paul and dragged his supposedly dead body out of the city. However, because Jesus is indeed risen, he hears the prayers of his disciples, and Paul is raised up.

After going to Derbe, Paul and Barnabas begin to retrace their steps back to Lystra and Iconium, and then to Pisidia and Pamphylia, and finally arrive where they began, at Antioch in Syria. In the course of their return journey, Paul and Barnabas appoint elders within all of the churches, that is, they sacramentally ordain priests/bishops, thus establishing and ensuring continual ecclesial apostolic succession. Here one perceives the ecclesiastical means by which and through which Jesus continues to be Jesus—YHWH-Saves. Through the ordained ministry, Jesus continues to act sacramentally within the church throughout all ages. In so doing, the saving benefits of his sacrificial death and glorious resurrection are made present, for all who partake of

Jesus's sacramental presence come to abide in him—he who embodies all that is good.

With the conversion of the Gentiles, the issue of whether or not converted Gentile men need to be circumcised raises it head. So intense is this issue and so passionately is it debated that a council had to be called in Jerusalem. The holding of this council with its results is the topic of chapter fifteen of the Acts of the Apostles.

# CONCLUSION

With chapter fourteen, the Acts of the Apostles has reached the midpoint of Luke's historical narrative. Moreover, the present theological interpretation of Acts has also reached the conclusion of its first volume. The second volume will interpret theologically chapters 15-28. At this juncture, then, it would be beneficial to offer a summary of what was divinely revealed and theologically ascertained in these fourteen chapters, as well as a sketch of the progression and development of the various theological themes.

Jesus being Jesus has been the major premise upon which this study has been founded. All that takes place within the nascent church as a whole and all that is enacted by the apostles is done through the power of the Holy Spirit—the Spirit that the risen Jesus has poured out upon the church and the apostles. Thus, through the apostolic church, Jesus continues to be Jesus—YHWH-Saves. The conclusion of this volume will, hopefully, provide a theological synopsis of what Jesus has thus far salvifically done in, with, and through his Spirit-filled, apostolic church.

## Chapter One: The Ascension of Jesus

Chapter one of Acts is Luke's summary portrayal of salvation history. God's actions, as narrated throughout the whole of the Old Testament, lead to and find their culmination in his incarnate Son, Jesus Christ. In Jerusalem, Jesus enacts his saving deeds—his death, resurrection, and ascension. From Jerusalem, the gospel will spread throughout the whole earth until the end of time, and so the world's history will be the history of the world's salvation. Until the end of this age, Jesus will enact his name. He will always be Jesus, YHWH-Saves. Again, when Jesus descends upon the clouds and all the faithful rise and ascend into heaven with him, Jesus will then have enacted his name fully, for all will have obtained the fullness of his risen glory. For Luke, all God's saving deeds prior to Jesus led to Jerusalem where Jesus, YHWH-Saves, enacted his Father's definitive saving deeds—his sin-destroying death on the cross and his lifegiving resurrection. From Jerusalem, this apostolic gospel will then go forth until it finds its completion in the new Jerusalem that comes down out of heaven. The trajectory of salvation history leads to Jerusalem, is definitively enacted in Jerusalem, and finds its terminus in the heavenly Jerusalem, which comes down from heaven, and into which all the faithful will ascend, and so abide in the risen Jesus as the Father's Spirit-filled children. There will then be a new heaven and a new earth.

Chapter one sets the stage for the next era within the history of salvation—the outpouring of the Holy Spirit upon the apostles and the birth and growth of the church. Pentecost will initiate the remainder of Acts—the preaching of the gospel and the bearing witness to Jesus to the ends of the earth.

## Chapter Two: Pentecost, the Birth of the Church

In chapter two of the Acts of the Apostles, Luke narrates the Pentecostal event, followed by Peter's Pentecostal discourse, with the subsequent baptism of those who came to believe. In this sequence, the reader easily perceives the risen Jesus being Jesus—YHWH-Saves. Jesus baptized with the Holy Spirit those gathered in the upper room, and Peter, who now represents the apostolic church, in turn baptized in the Holy Spirit those who came to believe through the ministry of his preaching. Jesus will continue being Jesus, YHWH-Saves, through the agency of the apostolic church—through the evangelistic preaching of the apostles and the faithful, and through the sacramental actions of baptism and the Eucharist. In both instances Jesus is acting through the church, and through the actions of the church, Jesus continues to be present in and with the church. The apostolic church, then, is the living sacramental expression of Jesus being Jesus within the world for the salvation of the world.

## Chapter Three: The Healing of the Lame Man

Peter's healing of the lame beggar in the name of Jesus Christ of Nazareth once more confirms that Jesus continues to be Jesus—YHWH-Saves. The healing is but a sign of the deeper healing that comes through the crucified and risen Jesus—forgiveness of sins and new life in the Spirit. As healer and sanctifier,

Jesus, he who is YHWH-Saves, is the prophet promised from of old, the author of everlasting life, the one who blesses all nations.

## Chapter Four: The Arrest of Peter and John

As Peter and John were addressing the people, trouble was brewing. Priests, the temple captain, and the Sadducees were annoyed that they were proclaiming that through the risen Jesus the dead could be raised. Because of this maddening proclamation, Peter and John were arrested. The members of the Sanhedrin demanded to know by what power and in whose name they healed the lame beggar. Peter responds that it should be known that it was in the name of Jesus Christ of Nazareth. Thus, in no other name than that of Jesus is salvation to be obtained. Peter is proclaiming that Jesus is indeed YHWH-Saves, and that the healing of the beggar signifies that salvation is found in his name alone. As risen, Jesus continues to be the lifegiving Jesus. Moreover, Luke describes the communal life of the apostolic community. This shared life also gives testimony that Jesus, YHWH-Saves, was active among them and making them one.

## Chapter Five: Tribulations and Successes

Not everything is idyllic, however, within the Christian community, for the church continued to experience tribulation. The Satanic-instigated deception of Ananias and Sapphira was thwarted by Peter only because he lived in the truth of Jesus Christ. As God's risen Word incarnate, Jesus defeated Satan's kingdom of lies. Thus, this event was a contest between Satan and Jesus. That Ananias and Sapphira fell dead testifies to the truth that the risen Jesus continues to be Jesus. As YHWH-Saves, he has vanquished Satan, and so he does not tolerate deceit within or among his followers. To do so would corrupt the truth through which he has set his people free from the deceitful wiles of Satan. Furthermore, Luke's noting that the apostles continue to work signs alerts the reader of Acts again to the reality of Jesus being Jesus, for the apostles replicate the miraculous wonders he did during his earthly ministry. The signs themselves testify to Jesus continuing to be Jesus, YHWH-Saves.

Because of the signs and wonders worked by the apostles in Jesus's name, the Sadducees arrest them, having warned them on several occasions to cease filling Jerusalem with their testimony. However, this persecution allows the apostles to further bear witness to the risen Jesus. No amount of harassment can keep the apostles from professing that God raised Jesus from the dead. Through such proclamation, Jesus is the ever-acting Jesus—for many came to believe in him through the faith-giving light of the Holy Spirit.

## Chapter Six: The Hellenists and Stephen's Arrest

Luke next narrates a problem that had arisen in the nascent church. The Hellenists, that is, Greek-speaking Jews, complained to the Hebrew Jews, that is, those who spoke Aramaic, that their widows were neglected in the daily distribution. A solution was found by choosing seven deacons upon whom the apostles laid their hands.

One of the deacons was Stephen, who having worked many signs and wonders, debated with the members of the synagogue of Freedmen, that is, Hellenistic Jews. Stephen is a means through whom Jesus continues to be Jesus, YHWH-Saves. Because the Freedmen were not able to refute Stephen's Spirit-filled proclamation that Jesus is risen, they procured false witnesses against Stephen, whereupon they seized him and brought him before the council.

## Chapter Seven: Stephen's Discourse and Stoning

Chapter seven of Acts contains Stephen's lengthy discourse before the council. He accentuates that the history of the Jews is a history of their rejection of God's revelation, and their present refusal to believe in Jesus as the promised Messiah is the ultimate culminating act of their defiance. What they rebuff is the truth that Jesus is YHWH-Saves, and as the risen Lord, he continues to be Jesus and their Savior.

## Chapter Eight: The Preaching of Philip

As noted previously, immediately prior to his ascension, Jesus informs the apostles that they will bear witness to him in Judea and Samaria, and to the ends of the earth. Peter, John, and Stephen have done so in Jerusalem and Judea. In chapter eight, Luke tells of Philip going to Samaria where he worked many signs and proclaimed to the people that Jesus is the risen Christ. Many Samaritans believed in Jesus and upon being baptized were filled with the Holy Spirit. Philip also proclaimed the gospel to the Ethiopian eunuch, who believed and was baptized. Into the narrative Luke also weaves the story of Simon the magician who wants to purchase Peter's and John's ability to baptize in the Holy Spirit. Peter severely reprimands him, saying that his heart is not right before God.

In all the above, we find Jesus being Jesus. Through the ministry of Jesus's apostolic church, specifically through the apostolic preaching and sacramental actions of Philip, Peter, and John, Jesus's work of salvation continues to flourish—now in regions outside of Jerusalem among the Samaritans and the Gentiles. Moreover, through the power of the Holy Spirit, the risen Jesus triumphs over all forms of superstition and magic, specifically as found in Simon the magician.

## Chapter Nine: Paul's Conversion and Peter's Healings

In chapter nine, we find Saul continuing his raging against the Christian community. He is not satisfied with persecuting the church in Jerusalem, and he zealously wishes to harass the Christians in other cities as well. However, God had other plans for Saul. In all his glory, the risen Jesus appears to Saul, and so we easily perceive Jesus being Jesus. Paul comes to believe that Jesus is the risen Lord. Moreover, he learns that to persecute Jesus's followers is to persecute Jesus himself. Both points are doctrinally important. They will be the basis for the apostle Paul's later teaching that Christ, the risen Lord Jesus, is the head of his body, the church. Paul subsequently preaches the gospel both in Damascus and in Jerusalem. As an apostle, Paul has become the voice of Jesus being Jesus, for many come to believe in Jesus as their Savior.

Similarly, we observe Jesus being Jesus through Peter's healing of Aeneas in Lydda, and particularly in his raising Dorcas from the dead in Joppa. Although Peter is the efficacious instrument, it is Jesus, as YHWH-Saves, who is the healer and the restorer of life. All of which is a prefigurement of the ultimate healing and restoration in Christ. In the abiding of the saints in the heavenly resurrection, Jesus will have fully enacted his name, YHWH-Saves, for all will have been totally transformed into his risen likeness.

## Chapter Ten: Peter and the Conversion of the Gentiles

After focusing on Paul, Luke, in chapter ten, turns again to the apostolic ministry of Peter. In Caesarea, Cornelius has a vision of an angel. He is to send men to Joppa to bring back a man by the name of Simon. In Joppa, Peter also has a vision. He saw the heavens opened and a sheet was let down with all kinds of animals, reptiles, and birds. He was told to kill them and eat. Peter protested, for he had never eaten anything common or unclean. He was told that what God has made clean he must not call common.

With the arrival of Cornelius's men, Peter goes with them to Caesarea. Upon arriving, Peter asks why they sent for him. Cornelius responds by recounting his vision and asks to hear what Peter has to say to all who have assembled. Peter tells all that Jesus did and that he was crucified, but that God raised him from the dead. While Peter was still speaking, the Holy Spirit fell upon all who heard the word. The Jews who were present were amazed that the Spirit had been poured out even upon the uncircumcised Gentiles, for they were speaking in tongues and glorifying God. Peter declares that there is no reason why the Gentiles should be refused water baptism, and so he commands that they be baptized in the name of Jesus Christ.

In this chapter we see both a historical and a doctrinal development within the nascent apostolic church. By enacting his name, Jesus reveals that he is not only the Savior of the Jews but also of the Gentiles, for the Holy Spirit can also fall upon them. Thus, Jesus has set in place the foundational doctrine of the apostolic church—Jesus is the universal Savior and the definitive Lord.

## Chapter Eleven: Peter's Defense of His Actions and the Church in Antioch

Chapter eleven begins with Luke informing the reader that the apostles and brethren in Judea heard that the Gentiles came to faith in Jesus. However, when Peter arrived in Jerusalem, the circumcision party faulted him for socializing with uncircumcised men. In response, Peter relates the entire story of how the Holy Spirit came to fall upon the Gentiles just as he had come down upon them on Pentecost. Peter reminded his Jewish listeners that the Lord Jesus told them that, although John baptized with water, they would baptize with the Holy Spirit. Upon hearing this, they were silenced, and many glorified God that the Gentiles have been granted repentance unto life.

Within Peter's retelling of all that had taken place concerning the Gentiles, we do not find Jesus being Jesus, YHWH-Saves, in that he does not perform any new saving actions. However, what we do find is Peter defending the radically new revelatory action that Jesus did enact—that of sending the Holy Spirit upon Cornelius and the Gentiles. As noted, this salvific action doctrinally revolutionized the nascent apostolic church—both Jews and Gentiles were now equal members of the Spirit-filled ecclesial community.

Luke, next, abruptly moves the reader's attention to Antioch. Following upon the persecution in Jerusalem and the martyrdom of Stephen, many of the brethren were scattered and traveled to Phoenicia, Cyprus, and Antioch. Some evangelized only Jews, but others from Cyprus and Cyrene spoke of the Lord Jesus to the Gentiles. The result was that many turned to the Lord. Again, it is noteworthy that both Jews and Greeks came to faith in Jesus, and that this took place outside of Jerusalem and Judea, thus manifesting the ever-growing outreach of the now-recognized Christian church. Although the catalyst for this expansion was persecution, yet Jesus, being Jesus, YHWH-Saves, used it as a means of furthering the salvation that only he can bring.

Chapter eleven concludes with prophets coming from Jerusalem to Antioch. Inspired by the Holy Spirit, Agabus foretells a famine that would grip the whole world. The brethren in Antioch took up a collection to help support the brethren in Judea. Barnabas and Saul were appointed to fulfill this task. In this event, a further characteristic of Jesus being Jesus is observed. Although individuals are saved through faith in the risen Jesus, yet that faith makes all believers one in him; and in this oneness all members are to care for one another. Thus, inherent within the Antiochian disciples' care for the brethren in Jerusalem, there resides the reality of Jesus being Jesus—the making of distinct ecclesial assemblies into the one apostolic church in him.

## Chapter Twelve: Peter's Imprisonment and the Death of Herod

In chapter twelve of Acts, Luke returns to narrating the continuing persecution of the church in Jerusalem. King Herod killed the apostle James, the brother of John. Because this pleased the Jews, he arrested Peter and put him in prison. However, during the night, with the help of an angel, Peter escaped and returned to the brethren, who were interceding on his behalf. At dawn, the soldiers were dismayed, for Peter could not be found. They informed Herod of Peter's disappearance, whereupon he had the soldiers executed.

Although the risen Jesus is not physically present in the events surrounding Peter's miraculous escape, yet Jesus continues to be Jesus—YHWH-Saves. He is the Lord who sent the angel to rescue Peter. He is the one who answered the prayers of those who had gathered. He is the one who found Peter a safe place while Herod was in search of him. Amid persecution, Jesus's saving hand continues to direct, guard, and protect his disciples. Chapter twelve concludes with Luke noting that, amid Herod's persecution, God's word bore the fruit of many conversions. Thus, Jesus is responsible for the ever-increasing growth of his body the church, for he is the one who continues to pour out his Holy Spirit upon all who come to believe in him as their Savior and Lord. As Jesus, he is the ever-acting Savior.

## Chapter Thirteen: Paul's First Missionary Journey

Chapter thirteen of the Acts of the Apostles is lengthy, being composed of various parts. First, there were prophets and teachers in the church at Antioch, including Barnabas and Saul. While they were praying and fasting, the Holy Spirit directed them to set aside Barnabas and Saul for the ministry that he had assigned to them. In obedience, they laid their hands on them and so commissioned them to commence their first missionary journey.

Second, while proclaiming the Gospel in Cyprus, Barnabas and Saul met a false Jewish prophet named Bar-Jesus or Elymas who attempted to deter others from believing. Saul rebuked him, whereupon he became blind. Upon seeing what had happened, the proconsul believed in Jesus.

Third, from Cyprus, Paul and Barnabas came to Antioch of Pisidia. On a sabbath day, they entered a synagogue. The members invited Saul to give a word of encouragement to the congregation. Beginning with Moses, he tells them all that God has done for them throughout their history. He reminds them that God had promised David that a king would arise from his posterity and possess an everlasting kingdom. That promised Savior of Israel is Jesus. However, the rulers of Jerusalem did not recognize him, and so they hung him upon a tree and laid him in a tomb. But God raised him from the dead, for he would not let his begotten Son see corruption. It is this risen Jesus that Paul proclaims and in whom there is forgiveness of sins. Luke says that many Jews and devout converts to Judaism followed Paul and Barnabas, who encouraged them to remain faithful to God's grace.

In the fourth segment Luke narrates what took place on the following sabbath. Almost the entire city gathered to hear God's word. However, the Jews, being jealous, mocked Paul. Since the Jews judged themselves to be unworthy of eternal life, Paul and Barnabas would turn to the Gentiles. Upon hearing this, the Gentiles joyfully glorified God, and many came to believe.

Jesus being Jesus, YHWH-Saves, is first seen in the commissioning of Barnabas and Saul. Moreover, in laying their hands upon Barnabas and Saul, the faithful would have, in the name of Jesus, called down the Holy Spirit upon them—the commissioning Spirit that would send them off on their evangelistic journey. Likewise, in Paphos, Paul, in the Spirit of the risen Jesus, thwarted the diabolical designs of the false Jewish prophet, Bar-Jesus, and, in so doing, brought about many conversions. Similarly, Paul's entire discourse to the Jews at Antioch of Pisidia was anointed by the Holy Spirit, who inspired both Jews and Gentiles to believe in Jesus. Thus, these converts experienced the risen Jesus being Jesus—YHWH-Saves.

## Chapter Fourteen: Paul's Further Missionary Activity

Luke, in chapter fourteen, continues to narrate Paul's and Barnabas's first missionary journey. Arriving at Iconium, they, again, first preached in the Jewish synagogue where many Jews and Gentiles came to believe. Because some of the Jews and Gentiles in the city attempted to stone Paul and Barnabas, they too fled Lystra and Derbe.

In Lystra, Paul heals a man crippled from birth. The pagan Lycaonians, upon witnessing this miracle, conclude that the gods had come down to them in the form of men, whereupon they called Barnabas, Zeus, and Paul, Hermes. Moreover, the priest of the temple of Zeus brought oxen to sacrifice to Barnabas/Zeus and Paul/Hermes. However, in dismay, Paul and Barnabas cried out that they were not gods and exhorted the crowd to believe in the living God who created all that exists.

Once again, though Jesus may not have been visible, yet through the preaching of Paul and Barnabas and through the signs and wonders that they work, the risen Jesus is ever present, pouring out his Spirit upon those who come to believe in him as their Lord and Savior—Jews and Gentiles alike. As gloriously risen, Jesus is enacting his name—YHWH-Saves. Jesus, too, is the living and saving God.

After going to Derbe, Paul and Barnabas begin to make their way back to Antioch in Syria. During their return journey, Paul and Barnabas appoint elders within all the churches where they had previously taught. Such appointments imply that they sacramentally ordained priests/bishops. Such ordinations, in turn, establish and ensure continual, ecclesial apostolic succession. Significantly, the ordination of priests/bishops is the ecclesiastical means by which and through which Jesus continues to be Jesus—YHWH-Saves. Through the ordained ministry, Jesus continues to act sacramentally within the church. In his so doing, the saving benefits of his sacrificial death and glorious resurrection are made present, for all who partake of Jesus's sacramental presence come to abide in him—who embodies the fullness of salvation.

Hopefully, having provided a helpful summary of our theological interpretation of the first fourteen chapters of Luke's Acts of the Apostles, we can now turn to the remaining fourteen chapters. These chapters will be interpreted theologically in volume two of *Jesus Being Jesus: A Theological Interpretation of the Acts of the Apostles*.

# INDEX